A Way with Words

Toni Brougher

A Way with Words

How to Improve Your Relationships Through Better Communications

Nelson-Hall *nh* Chicago

LIBRARY OF CONGRESS CATALOGING IN PUBLICATION DATA

Brougher, Tonette.
  A way with words:

  Bibliography: p.
  Includes index.
  1. Interpersonal communication.   2. Interpersonal
relations.   I. Title.
HM132.B75   302.2   81-18841
ISBN 0-88229-645-0 (cloth)   AACR2
ISBN 0-88229-810-0 (paper)

Copyright © 1982 by Tonette Brougher

All rights reserved. No part of this book may be reproduced in any form without permission in writing from the publisher, except by a reviewer who wishes to quote brief passages in connection with a review written for broadcast or for inclusion in a magazine or newspaper. For information address Nelson-Hall Inc., Publishers, 111 North Canal Street, Chicago, Illinois 60606.

Manufactured in the United States of America

10   9   8   7   6   5   4   3   2   1

The paper in this book is pH neutral (acid-free).

Contents

Preface vii

Introduction ix

1. Directness, Honesty, and Responsibility 1
- Learning about Purposes
- Stating Your Intentions and Motives
- Expressing Yourself Directly and Responsibly
- Helping Others to Be Direct, Honest, and Responsible

2. Using Nonverbal Cues Effectively 95
- Learning about Nonverbal Cues: Why They Are Important
- Observing Nonverbal Cues in Others
- Your Nonverbal Cues
- Matching Nonverbal Cues to Your Purpose

3. Appropriateness 133
- Learning about Appropriateness: Discussion and Examples
- Checking Social Limits and Customs
- Choosing the Appropriate Time and Place
- Matching What You Say to the Person and the Relationship

4. Acknowledging Others 159
- Learning about Acknowledgment: Why It Is Important
- Paying Attention to Others
- Showing Interest in Others
- Being Considerate: Avoiding Presumptions

- Acknowledging Others Even When You Disagree
- Incorrect Acknowledgments: What They Are and How to Avoid Them

5. Providing Relevant, Descriptive, and Precise Information   211
- Providing Relevant Information
- Being Descriptive
- Learning How Language Affects Thinking: Being Precise and Avoiding Exaggeration
- Checking How You Come Across
- Asking for Specific and Descriptive Information

6. Communication as Interaction   259
- Relationships: Basic Elements and Decisions to Be Made
- Impact
- Decisions to Be Made When Conflict Occurs
- A Final Comment

Appendix A: Answers to Practice Exercises   321

Preface

THIS BOOK IS A COMPILATION of my ideas about people and relationships, developed over the years. The ideas have been enhanced by my clinical practice as a psychologist and refined by the development of a communication training program for patients at the Danville Veterans' Administration Medical Center.

It is written for the general reader and is intended as a self-help guide for people who are interested in improving the quality of their communication and their relationships.

I especially want to thank my husband, Jim, and Dr. Jack Griffiths for their encouragement and enthusiasm throughout this project. Most of all, I want to thank Karen Ashley for her patient and conscientious typing of all the rough drafts and revisions. Without her, there would have been no book.

My very special thanks go to Fred Kanfer, John Hilmo, and Connie Daye. Their comments helped to refine my thinking, and their suggestions and support were very important to me.

Al Sheva, Bob Canetta, Ann Beck, and Don Parker gave of their time and talents to produce the photographs, and I appreciate that very much. John Deck, Jim Linden, and Mary vanReken contributed in various ways. To all of them, my thanks.

Introduction

THIS BOOK IS ABOUT COMMUNICATION and relationships. Its purposes are (1) to present communication as an important part of relationships, (2) to show how communication affects relationships, (3) to define effective communication and show how to achieve it, (4) to illustrate how effective communication can increase the chances for satisfaction in relationships that are important, and (5) to help you identify aspects of your communication that you might want to change.

In this book, communication is defined as what we say and do: our words and actions, our expressions and gestures, our silences, responses, and our failures to respond. It is what we use to let others know how we are reacting, what we are thinking, or what we are trying to do. Our communication—our words, expressions, and actions—contribute to the atmosphere between the people in a relationship. Communication conveys what one person thinks and intends to the other. It is the process by which people come to know each other, it is the way people have of shaping a picture of what each means to the other, and it is the means whereby they hold a relationship together or fail to do so.

Developing and maintaining relationships and communicating with people require some effort, but this need not seem complicated. In order to simplify the processes of communication and maintaining relationships, I have developed some general rules and principles about human interaction. This book is a compilation of my ideas, and it presents some guidelines for understanding and relating to people. It points out some principles to use when explaining your thoughts to others and some rules to follow when you are trying to understand other people's ideas. In this book, I offer my definition of effective communication and present some ways to achieve this goal. The book shows how this way of communicating can be of benefit to you, other people, and to your relationships. It illustrates how you can apply these principles and guidelines in order to increase your personal and interpersonal satisfaction.

WHAT IS EFFECTIVE COMMUNICATION?

Communication can be considered effective when it increases understanding between people. Effective communication has these qualities:

1. It is an interaction with another person.
2. It acknowledges the other person; one is attentive and responsive to the other.
3. It is appropriate. Time, place, situation, social customs, and relationships are taken into account.
4. It includes nonverbal communication (tone of voice, facial expressions, gestures, body posture, etc.) that matches or enhances what you say.
5. It is honest, responsible, and direct.
6. It provides relevant, descriptive and accurate information.

General principles about communication and relationships can be used to achieve these goals, and this book sets them out for you in a step-by-step fashion.

FORMAT

Each chapter of this book discusses one of these six qualities of effective communication and presents general principles or "skills" needed to achieve the goals described. The skills are discussed in the following way:

1. Description and examples of the skill
2. Discussion of how, when, and why you might use the skill
3. Explanation of how you and your relationships might benefit
4. Examples from everyday conversations
5. Exercises involving common situations and occurrences in relationships.

At the end of each chapter, the skills are summarized and more exercises are provided.

Introduction xi

The basic aspects of communication are covered in the first chapters. In this way, you can build upon the skills discussed in these chapters in order to achieve the more complicated skills presented in the later sections. The final chapter presents you with specific information on how to apply skills to increase satisfaction in important and ongoing relationships. You may find it worthwhile to glance at this last section before beginning the first chapter.

HOW TO USE THIS BOOK

This book can be used in at least two ways, so you must decide what you want from it in order to use it effectively. The two approaches are as follows:

1. If you want some interesting ideas about people and communication, read the book casually and omit the practice exercises.
2. On the other hand, if you want to make some significant changes in your communication and in your relationships, the book provides a structured step-by-step approach for you to follow. If you choose this method, here are some further suggestions:
   a. Imagine that you are studying for a course. Set up some times to read the material and try to eliminate as many distractions as possible. Have paper and pencil handy to take notes.
   b. Work on small sections. Do not try to do a chapter in one sitting. Learn one principle or skill at a time.
   c. If possible, get a partner—your spouse, friend, neighbor. Explain to your partner what you are trying to accomplish. Work on the book together. Discuss each skill that you learn.
   d. Practice the principles. When you learn a skill, make a point of using it at least once a day.
   e. Review what you have learned. Check your progress.

If, after following this approach, you continue to feel disappointed with your relationships, you might consider asking for some help from a professional therapist.

This book can also be a way of learning about yourself and how you come across to others. As you look at the examples, notice if any of them sound like things that you would say. Ask for feedback from people who will be honest with you.

CHAPTER ONE

Directness, Honesty, and Responsibility

THE PURPOSE OF THIS chapter is to point out the value of directness, honesty, and responsibility in speaking and to describe some ways to achieve these qualities. The four skills described in this chapter are:

1. Learning about purposes.
2. Stating your intentions and motives in communicating.
3. Expressing yourself directly and responsibly.
4. Helping others to be honest, direct, and responsible.

SKILL 1: LEARNING ABOUT PURPOSES

In order to tell someone what you are thinking in a way that will be understood, you must first become aware of yourself. You must have a clear understanding of yourself (your thoughts, feelings, reactions) and a clear idea of what you are trying to do or say. This awareness of yourself and your intentions helps to make your communication clear and, in turn, increases your chances for being understood.

When you speak with another person, you often have one or more purposes in mind. Some of these are momentary purposes while others are long-range goals. Before you can achieve any of these goals, you must be aware of them.

To help you become aware of your goals, this section presents three skills:

1a. Increasing self-awareness — deciding on your purpose.
1b. Noticing and eliminating "mixed messages" (this is what happens when you try to accomplish more than one purpose at a time).

1c. Checking the consequences of your purpose, statement, or action.

These skills are designed to help you become aware of your reactions and what you are trying to say or do. Although these skills cannot produce complete self-understanding, they can encourage you to consider your thoughts, reactions, and what you are trying to say or do.

Skill 1a: Increasing Self-Awareness: Deciding on Your Purpose

The skill of deciding on your purpose involves the following steps:

1. Ask yourself what things you hope to accomplish by speaking or interacting with the other person. For example, do you want to:

   - Show interest?
   - Thank someone?
   - Explain your ideas?
   - Get someone to like you?
   - Complain?
   - Seek sympathy?
   - Act angrily?
   - Show off?
   - Give information?
   - State a preference?
   - Seek reassurance?
   - Criticize?
   - Put someone in his or her place?
   - Persuade someone to agree with you or to do what you want?
   - Reach a mutual understanding?
   - End a relationship?
   - Improve a relationship?

   This list presents some questions to ask yourself; of course, there are other purposes you might have. In any event, be honest in your decision.

2. From this list above, decide what you want to accomplish most. For example, you found out that your friends had a barbeque and you were not invited. You are surprised and hurt. What do you want to accomplish in general? Tell them that you are upset? Get back at them; act angrily? Find out why you weren't invited? Criticize them? Of these, what is the main thing that you want to accomplish?

Instead of using this approach, people often speak or act with only a vague notion of what they are feeling, thinking, or trying to accomplish. They do not stop to consider if they are pleased, sad, angry, or hurt. Because of their limited self-awareness, they do not know what effect they are having or what they are trying to do. This helps to create

THINGS TO DO TODAY

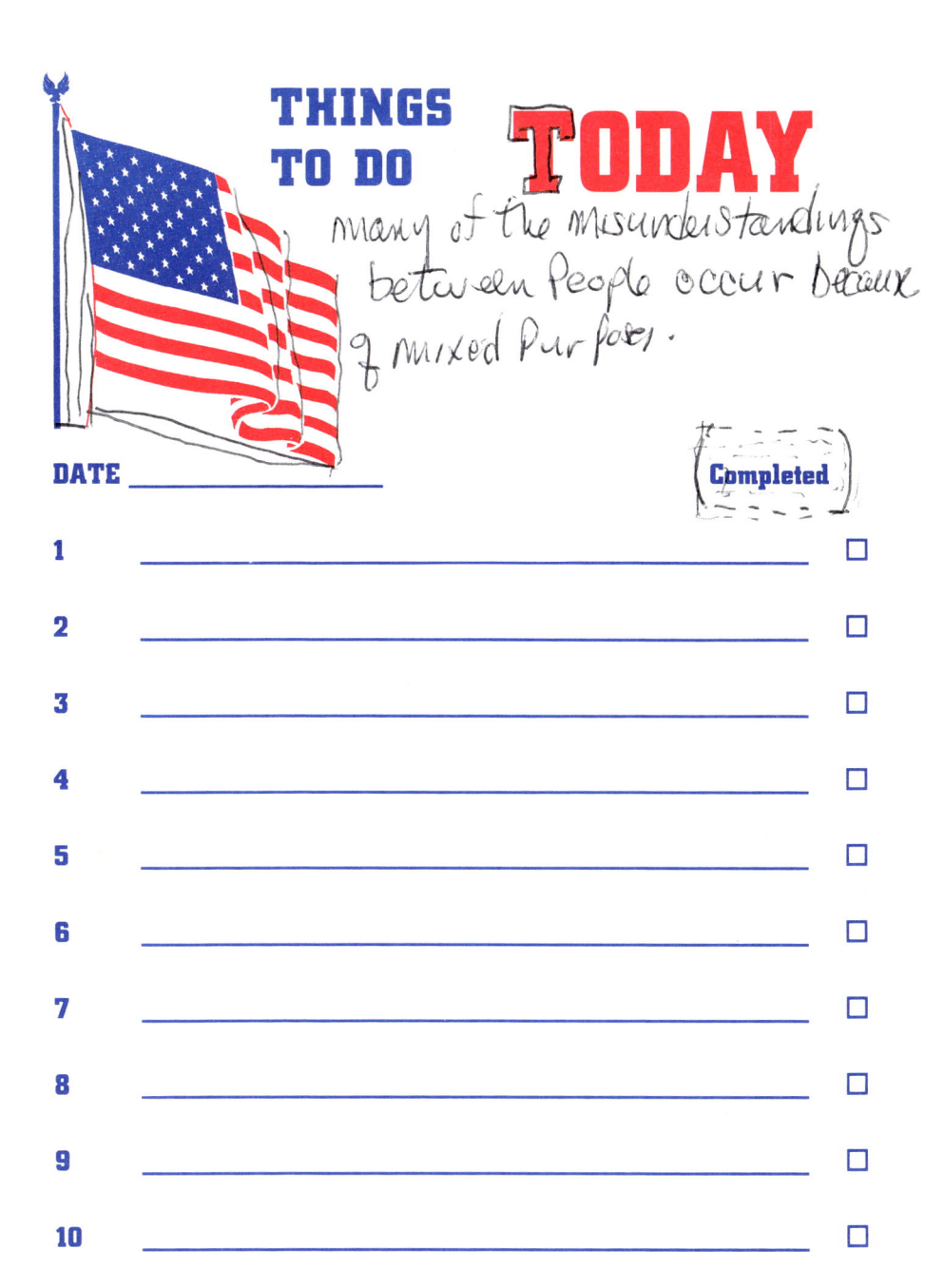

Many of the misunderstandings between people occur because of mixed purposes.

DATE _____   **Completed**

1 _____ ☐

2 _____ ☐

3 _____ ☐

4 _____ ☐

5 _____ ☐

6 _____ ☐

7 _____ ☐

8 _____ ☐

9 _____ ☐

10 _____ ☐

COMPLIMENTS OF
State Representative
Nick Micozzie
6 South Springfield Rd., Clifton Heights, PA 19018
(610) 259-2820

complexities and misunderstandings in relationships. If people do not know how they are feeling or what they are trying to say, it is nearly impossible for another person to guess what is happening. Further, people usually do not stop to decide on their main purpose and, instead, attempt to communicate all their purposes and reactions at the same time.

Many of the misunderstandings between people occur because of mixed purposes. Often, these purposes compete with one another. It is difficult, for example, to come to some resolution of a problem while you also are hurt and angry, putting other people down, and wanting revenge. The "mixed message" that this gives is complicated and confusing to other people. As a result, they are more likely to misinterpret your actions and statements. Misunderstanding on both sides will likely follow, and the chances of communicating effectively are markedly decreased.

This skill of deciding on your main purpose works for the following reasons:

1. It increases your self-awareness by encouraging you to think about your goals and to decide which of these you most want to accomplish.
2. Because your self-awareness is heightened, there is a greater possibility that you can tell the other person what you mean.
3. It is easier for you, the speaker, to explain and try to accomplish one purpose.
4. It is easier for the listener to understand one purpose instead of multiple, sometimes competing, purposes.

The following examples demonstrate the difference between deciding on your purpose and not doing so:

Situation: Mary visited her friend Sharon. When she arrived, Sharon was entertaining guests for dinner. Mary felt that Sharon was cool and unfriendly to her. She felt hurt. The next day Sharon phoned.

Not Deciding on Your Purpose	*Deciding on Your Purpose*
SHARON: I wanted to let you know that I was very rushed last night when you came over. That's why I didn't say very much.	SHARON: I wanted to let you know that I was very rushed last night when you came over. That's why I didn't say very much.

MARY: Oh, don't use that excuse on me. (*coldly*) I know when I'm not wanted.
SHARON: What are you talking about?
MARY: Look, I don't have to put up with that. When I got there, you didn't act friendly or glad to see me. If your manners are that bad, it's your problem!
SHARON: Now, just a minute . . . I'm getting angry. If you didn't come barging in unannounced all the time, maybe I'd be friendlier. You never call before you come over and that's rude, if you ask me.

MARY: *(before speaking she stops to consider her purposes:*
- *I want to criticize her*
- *I want to act angrily*
- *I want to let her know that I feel hurt*
- *I want to keep the friendship*

Mary decides that, most of all, she wants Sharon to know that she feels hurt.) Sharon, I want you to know that my feelings are really hurt. When I came over last night, I thought you seemed very cool and unfriendly.
SHARON: I didn't want you to feel that way. I was just preoccupied with cooking.

Discussion: In the example on the left, Mary does not consider what she wants to accomplish. Instead, she says the first thing that comes into her head. She blames Sharon and accuses her of being "unfriendly" and "bad-mannered." Sharon feels hurt and angry, as most people would. To defend herself, she counterattacks and implies that Mary is to blame by dropping in and by being "rude." The situation escalates into name calling, and each person tries to accuse the other of worse traits and characteristics. If Mary had wanted to achieve some degree of resolution, she has achieved the opposite.

In contrast, in the example on the right, Mary stops to decide what she wants to accomplish. Although she would like to act angrily and criticize Sharon, Mary decides that she most wants to express how hurt she is. As a result of her focus on this one purpose, she is better able to communicate it clearly. Sharon, in turn, understands, and some resolution is reached.

Situation: The boss has assigned an assistant to Ron, who has repeatedly complained to the boss about the mistakes and the negative attitudes of this assistant. In fact, Ron has recommended that the young man be fired. The boss has reassured him that there would be some improvement. So far, there has been none.

Directness, Honesty, and Responsibility 5

Yesterday, the assistant made a substantial error that affected several employees. Ron goes to speak to his boss.

Not Deciding on Your Purpose

RON: (*angrily*) Look, I've had it with that guy, and I've about had it with you, too.
BOSS: Wait a minute. What are you talking about?
RON: You know what I'm talking about! My marvelous assistant . . . (*sarcastically*) you know, the one you wouldn't fire, the one you kept telling me to be patient with! You should see the mistake he made this time. And, really, it's your fault, too . . . for keeping him on!
BOSS: (*condescendingly*) Now, cool off, Ron. What are you so mad about? (*sarcastically*) I never knew you got so upset and irrational. I'm surprised at you.

Deciding on Your Purpose

RON: (*before speaking, he stops to consider what he wants to accomplish; he decides that he wants to:*
• *tell the boss that he wants something done about the assistant*
• *complain*
• *express his frustration*
• *blame the boss*
• *keep his "cool" and persuade the boss that his judgment is good*
• *persuade the boss to fire the assistant*
Ron would like to accomplish all of these, but, most of all, he wants something done about the assistant) I want to tell you what my assistant did yesterday. I am very frustrated with this situation and I want something done about it.
BOSS: OK, what happened?

Discussion: In the example on the left, Ron is trying to accomplish many things at once: complaining, expressing frustration, blaming the boss, and trying to get the assistant fired. As a result, he does not accomplish any one purpose. The boss is distracted by Ron's criticism and accusations. He becomes defensive and uses a condescending and sarcastic statement to put Ron down.

In contrast, on the right, Ron decides on his main purpose. Because he is focusing on only one purpose at a time, it is easier for him to express himself clearly and it is easier for the boss to comprehend.

In general, in the examples on the left, the speakers tried to accomplish several things at once. This was confusing and distracting to their listeners. Expressing and understanding multiple, competing purposes is very complicated. As a result, it lessens the chances for effective communication and understanding.

In contrast, in the examples on the right, the speakers decided on *one* main purpose. The simplicity made it easier for their listeners to comprehend. As a result, the speakers were more likely to achieve their purposes, and the chances for effective communication were increased.

Note: Different purposes have different effects on people and situations. Deciding to work out a problem with a friend has a different effect than deciding to end the relationship because you are angry. In the same way, deciding to get back at your spouse for being late will have different consequences than asking him or her to be on time. This important skill of judging consequences is presented in section 1c of this chapter.

Practice

Each of the examples below describes a situation, several purposes, and possible responses. Imagine that you are in each situation; decide on your purpose and what you would say.

A. You and a friend planned an outing, but, when the weekend came, your friend cancelled. You are disappointed and upset.
   1. Do you want to end the friendship? ("I've had it! I can never count on you to do anything! As far as I'm concerned, you're no friend!")
   2. Do you want to criticize? ("You are irresponsible and undependable. No wonder you have no friends!")
   3. Do you want to express disappointment? ("I was really disappointed that we had to cancel our plans.")
B. Your spouse frequently leaves newspapers scattered on the floor. You find this annoying.
   1. Do you want to complain? ("You always leave papers scattered around!")
   2. Do you want to criticize? ("You are so sloppy — you never pick up the papers!")
   3. Do you want to make your spouse feel guilty or bad? ("You always leave these papers around and I have to pick them up.")
   4. Do you want to ask if he or she would be willing to pick up the papers? ("I'd like it if you didn't leave the papers scattered on the floor. Will you pick them up?")

In summary, remember to ask yourself what you want to accomplish. Of the several purposes that you think of, decide what you want

Directness, Honesty, and Responsibility 7

to accomplish most. Remember that different purposes have different effects on other people and on situations.

Skill 1b: Noticing and Eliminating Mixed Messages

A "mixed message" is a statement or action that attempts to accomplish several conflicting purposes at once. It is important to know when you are expressing more than one purpose. This can be a cue for you to check your main purpose, eliminate the confusion in yourself, and replace your mixed message with more effective communication. This section will help familiarize you with mixed messages and will give you practice in substituting clearer speaking for these confusing statements.

There are several common types of mixed messages.

1. Saying two different things at the same time. For example, "Of course, I love you, but don't touch me." "I want us to get along. But if you wouldn't be so obnoxious, we would."
2. Saying one thing with words and another with actions or expressions. For example, (*in a tight voice*) "No, I'm not angry. I'm not angry at all." (*walks off and slams door*)
3. Mixing compliments and criticisms. For example, "You can be such a wonderful person when you're not immature and demanding." "You really are nice looking. It's too bad you're overweight."
4. Disguising an assumption, accusation, or blaming statement as a question. For example, "Why are you so selfish?" "Why can't you learn to be more responsible?"
5. A disagreement statement disguised as an agreement. For example, "What you said may be true, but I still think it's dumb for you to say that."

These mixed messages confuse other people. They wonder what part of the message is true and what you really mean. Mixed messages most often occur in the following situations.

1. When you are emotionally involved. When your feelings are strong, pay particular attention to your purposes and to the messages that you give. If you feel angry, excited, upset, or hurt, let that be a cue to use this skill. Remember that you often express emotions by your nonverbal communication (e.g., facial expres-

sions, posture, and tone of voice). Be certain to check the message that you are giving nonverbally as well as verbally.
2. When you are, for some reason, hiding a motive or purpose from yourself or others. For example, you want to be polite to some friends who have stopped by your office unannounced. They interrupted you at a bad time, but you do not say so. Instead, you give a mixed message by saying, "Oh, no, you're not bothering me." All the time that they are there, you fidget, look at the clock, and rearrange the papers on your desk.

Besides letting these situations serve as cues to you, learn to notice the reactions of other people. If they seem confused or defensive, begin checking for a mixed message that you may be giving. You can do this by following these steps.

1. Ask yourself:
    a. What message am I giving the other person? (Am I saying that I'm happy/sad/upset/angry? Am I telling him or her that I want to get along/fight/make up/resolve our differences?)
    b. Am I giving more than one message with my words?
    c. Am I giving the same message with my nonverbal expressions and with my actions?
2. If you remain unclear, ask the other person, "What did it seem I said (or did)?"
3. When you notice yourself giving more than one message at a time, use the first skill described in this chapter. Decide on your purpose and then decide what one thing you want to accomplish most.

For example, you notice that you feel a bit annoyed with your spouse and you say in a critical tone of voice, "I know you're a hard worker on the job, but I wish you had some of the same characteristics around here at home." Your spouse seems taken aback and says, "Now just what is that supposed to mean?"

If you follow the steps outlined above:

1. You ask yourself:
    a. What message am I giving my spouse? You are giving a compliment on one hand and a criticism on the other — something like: "You're a hard worker there but lazy here."
    b. What is my spouse's reaction? He or she seems defensive.

Directness, Honesty, and Responsibility

2. Since you notice that you are giving more than one message, you check your purpose. What are you trying to accomplish?
   a. You want to persuade your spouse to share half the household chores.
   b. You want to work out a solution to the situation. Since you are giving a mixed message, ask yourself if you have a purpose that you are hiding from yourself and the other person.
   c. Yes, I don't like the way things are and I want them to change.
3. You decide to say, "I want to work out another way to handle the chores. I don't like it the way it is now." This makes your intention clear. It does not guarantee that your spouse will do what you want, but it does eliminate the confusion of the mixed message.

People frequently do not notice their mixed messages, nor do they try to replace them with clear, direct speaking. When you give a mixed message, you risk confusing your listeners. They are likely to become frustrated and defensive, particularly if you combine compliments and criticisms.

This skill of noticing mixed messages and replacing them with clear communication works for the following reasons.

1. It increases your self-awareness by focusing on multiple or hidden purposes that you may have.
2. It gives you the opportunity to decide the main thing that you want to accomplish.
3. Because you are clear about your main purpose, you can eliminate competing purposes and can express what you want more clearly to your listener.
4. Further, deciding on one purpose can be a self-control technique. It helps you to set your limits on what you can accomplish. By explaining your purpose, you structure the situation for your listeners. This decreases confusion and increases the chances that they will understand what you are trying to say or do.
5. In a mixed message, listeners must hear and respond to conflicting demands. As a result, they are likely to become frustrated and defensive. Eliminating mixed messages lessens the possibility of eliciting confusion, defensiveness, and frustration and increases the chances for clear communication and mutual understanding.

Some examples will help you to become more familiar with mixed messages. The following show the difference between giving more than one message and giving one clear and consistent message.

Mixed Messages	*Clear, Consistent Message*
SUE: You're my best friend . . . except, after what you did and said, I feel very unfriendly. DONNA: Now just a minute. I will not accept all the blame for our disagreement.	SUE: I feel pretty hurt because of the disagreement we had. I still want us to be friends, but I'm very hurt right now. DONNA: I guess I can understand that. SUE: OK, I hope there's some way that we can work this out. DONNA: I do, too. And I'm sorry. I didn't want you to feel hurt.

Discussion: On the left, Sue says two different things: "You are my friend" and "I feel very unfriendly." This is confusing to Donna. She, in turn, jumps to her own conclusions about what is going on. This does nothing to resolve the problem or restore the relationship. In fact, it makes matters worse. In contrast, in the example on the right, Sue gives a clear and consistent message.

Mixed Message	*Clear, Consistent Message*
HUSBAND: Do you want to hear what happened with the boss today? WIFE: Of course, I'm always interested in hearing about your work, dear. (*busies herself around the kitchen, reads cookbooks while husband is talking; he gives up and stops trying to talk to her*)	HUSBAND: Do you want to hear what happened with the boss today? WIFE: (*sounding interested and enthusiastic*) I want to hear it. But, first let me finish reading this. Then I can listen and I won't be distracted.

Discussion: In the example on the left, the wife says one thing with her words and gives a different message with her actions. The husband chooses to believe her actions. In contrast, on the right, the wife gives one clear message.

Mixed Message	*Clear, Consistent Message*
WIFE: You're really a fantastic person—except for when you get in one of these childish, pouting moods.	WIFE: When you seem unhappy, I feel frustrated and I don't know what to do to cheer you up. I want you to be happy, like you usually are.

HUSBAND: (*angrily*) What do you mean? I am not pouting! I may be unhappy, but I'm just being quiet and keeping to myself. You're the one who pouts and is childish.

HUSBAND: There's nothing you can do. I'm just disgusted with my job and I'll get over it.

Discussion: In the example on the left, the wife mixes a compliment with a criticism, probably hoping to soften the negative words and persuade the husband to change his behavior. This does not work. The compliment is contaminated and made ineffective by the criticism. The interaction is unpleasant and, in fact, may become a sensitive point or "sore spot" in the relationship.

In contrast, in the example on the right, the wife expresses her intention and feelings clearly, directly, and responsibly. The two people exchange reactions and a greater degree of acceptance and understanding is reached.

Mixed Message

HUSBAND: (*impatiently*) The checking account is off again. Can't you ever do anything right?
WIFE: Yes, I can do things just fine if you'd leave me alone! Besides, it's only off by a few cents and you're making a big deal of that.
HUSBAND: It is a big deal. I'm just trying to get you to do things right. It's for your own good.
WIFE: My own good! All you ever do is criticize me! (*begins to cry, walks out of room, refuses to talk the rest of the evening*)

Clear, Consistent Message

HUSBAND: I want you to be more careful with the checking account. It's a few cents off. I like it to be exact and I get frustrated when it's off.
WIFE: Well, I don't. It's not like it's off by a lot.
HUSBAND: I know—but that bothers me.
WIFE: Well, since it bothers you and not me, what about separate accounts? You can have yours and I can have mine. If my balance is off, it's my problem.

Discussion: In the example on the left, the husband disguises an accusation ("You never do anything right") as a question. The wife responds to the "phony" question by trying to defend herself. The situation deteriorates, and, rather than leading to some degree of mutual understanding and satisfaction, it leads to unpleasantness and may become a sore spot in the relationship.

In contrast, in the example on the right, the husband gives one clear message and does it in a direct manner, stating his preference as his own and taking responsibility for his feelings. As a result, husband and wife achieve some degree of understanding. Although they are not in total agreement, they are beginning to work on some ways to resolve the issue.

In general, the speakers in the examples on the left have communicated mixed messages. The listeners in these illustrations are confused as to which is the "real" message. As a result, they are frustrated and suspect that the more negative or critical message is the one that was intended.

In contrast, the examples on the right show how one clear message, even a relatively negative one, can be expressed in a direct, responsible fashion. When this is done, other people are more likely to listen and to understand. The possibility of defensiveness and counterattack is lessened while the chances for achieving a greater degree of understanding and satisfaction are increased.

Practice

This section gives you the opportunity to practice the skill of noticing and eliminating mixed messages.

I. Below are listed various situations. Circle those in which you should tune in on yourself and look for mixed messages.

A. Your best friend has said something that sounds like a criticism of you. You feel hurt.
B. You are relaxing and watching TV.
C. You have several things that you want to tell your spouse. You're not sure where to begin.
D. You are making small talk with your neighbors.
E. You are working on a project and are really concentrating on what you're doing.
F. You are pretty angry at your mother-in-law for something she did to one of your children. She comes over to visit and you try to be polite and pretend that you are not angry.
G. You go to ask your boss for vacation time.
H. You are talking with your spouse and notice that he or she is looking at you in a puzzled way.

II. The examples below contain pairs of statements. One of these is a clear message that tries to accomplish one purpose; the other presents a mixed message.

Place a check next to the statement that is unclear.

A. *Situation:* Parents drop by, unannounced. You and your spouse are entertaining your neighbors.

Directness, Honesty, and Responsibility

1. ___YOU: Come on in; we're not doing anything. But you'll have to excuse me — I'm in the middle of making appetizers and setting the table. (*You act somewhat cool and distant, hoping they will get the message that they should call before they come to visit*)

2. ___YOU: (*you are polite while they are there; the next time that you have a chance to talk with them alone you say*): I don't want to sound critical, but I would prefer it if you called before you came over to visit. When we're not expecting you, we feel like we have to drop everything.

B. *Situation:* The boss often told Jane that she was to supervise the people in her section as she decides. Whenever she goes in to tell him of her plans or actions, he says, "You don't have to tell me! Use your own judgment." One day he calls Jane in.

1. ___BOSS: I hear that you reassigned Wilson and Thomas in your section. (*accusingly*) Why didn't you tell me what you were planning to do? I need to know about these matters and you have to tell me.

2. ___BOSS: I know that I've told you to use your own judgment and not to ask me about your plans. In this case, with Wilson and Thomas, it has to go before the board of directors. I need to know about that.

III. The following examples give you the opportunity to practice the skill of noticing and eliminating mixed messages.

A. *Situation:* You are planning to wallpaper your home over the weekend. On Friday, your spouse offers to help and you say, "No, I can handle it better alone. If you want to help, take care of the errands and the laundry and pull the weeds. Then do what you want — just keep the kids away." On Saturday, everything is going wrong with the wallpapering. You feel very frustrated and annoyed. You are aware that this is a time when it is easy to give mixed messages. Which of the following would be better to say to your spouse?

1. ___YOU: I have had it around here. Everything is going wrong — and you didn't even stay around to see if you could help me! The least you could do is offer to fix me some coffee or something. You don't even appreciate all the work I do.

2. ___YOU: I am really frustrated and angry. I know I told you that I didn't want you to help, but I've changed my mind. Would you fix me some coffee and then come in here and give me a hand?

B. *Situation:* You have had a frustrating day with a co-worker who is refusing to do his share of the work. You telephone your boss to explain what has occurred. You say, in a frustrated, annoyed tone of voice, "Paul is refusing to carry his share of work around here and I've had it. You'd better realize what's going on here and figure out how you're going to solve this." Your boss reacts quickly and snaps back in an angry, exasperated tone, "What do you expect me to do?"

  1. Because your boss reacts in a defensive way, you wonder if you are giving a mixed message. You also realize that you are angry, and this is another cue to you that you may have multiple or hidden purposes. You realize that you are giving at least three messages:

    a. "I want you to know what happened."
    b. "I am very angry. . . . Maybe I'm angry at you."
    c. "I demand that you figure out how to solve this."

From this combination you realize that your boss may think that:

    a. You are blaming her.
    b. You are angry at her.
    c. You are demanding that she do something to solve the problem.

  2. You stop to check your purposes and realize that you are not angry at the boss but at Paul and at the situation. Your main purpose, you decide, is to tell your boss what happened and ask her to work out a solution.

  3. You decide to clear up your message. Check the statement that sounds most clear.

a. ____YOU: (*in a matter-of-fact tone*) Paul is refusing to do his share of the work, and I am frustrated and angry. I want you to know what's going on, and I'd like you to work out some solution to this.	b. ____YOU: (*angrily*) Paul is refusing to do his share of the work. Maybe you have given him the wrong idea about what he can get away with.

Skill 1c: Checking the Consequences of Your Purpose

Deciding on your purpose is not sufficient to insure clear communication. Since different purposes have different effects on people and

relationships, you must also determine how your purpose will affect others. Check the consequences of your purpose to see if it will accomplish what you want. You can do this by following these steps.
1. Ask yourself what reaction you are likely to get if you follow your purpose. For example, you want to straighten out your financial situation with your spouse. You decide that you really are angry and that you want to criticize your spouse. You want to say, "I think that you are really stupid and irresponsible when it comes to money! You have made a mess of our budget, and you'd better sit down with me right now and straighten it out."
   a. Ask yourself, "How is the other person likely to think or react? How would I feel?" Attacked? Upset? Happy? Angry? Ready to listen?
   b. Ask yourself, "How is the other person likely to behave?" Will he be upset? Talk angrily to me? Listen? Go away?

In response to your threat ("You'd better sit down and straighten this out") and your accusation ("You are stupid and irresponsible"), your spouse probably will be hurt, angry, and resentful. Instead of listening to you, he or she is likely to become defensive, make accusations about you, say that you do not understand, or walk away. In this case, your purpose and statement probably will achieve the opposite of your original goal: straightening out your financial situation with your spouse.

2. If, in checking consequences, your purpose seems likely to have an effect that you do not want, let this be a cue to you to decide on another purpose. For example, you decide that it might be more effective to tell your spouse that the financial situation is important to both of you and that you need your spouse's help with it. You want to say, "I think that it is important to settle some financial issues. I really want to get our budget straightened out. Will you sit down and help me with it?"
   a. How is the other person likely to feel? How would you feel? Attacked? Upset? Happy? Ready to listen? Respected? Asked for help?
   b. How is the other person likely to behave? Answer back angrily? Be upset? Listen?

In this case, your spouse is more likely to listen. Because there is no criticism or attack, he or she is less likely to be defensive, annoyed, or upset. By asking for cooperation, your chances for being understood and achieving some sort of resolution are much greater. You decide that this purpose and statement are more likely to accomplish what you want.

People frequently do not stop to think about the consequences of their purposes. Instead, in a moment of frustration or anger, they often say or do the first thing that comes to mind. For example: Your friend Diane says that she feels very depressed. You want to cheer her up and you decide to tell her what she is doing wrong. You say, "Your problem is that you're acting like a big baby and feeling sorry for yourself. You're doing something wrong!" Despite your good intentions, this probably will not achieve what you wanted. Diane is likely to feel criticized, hurt, and more depressed than before.

In general, if you do not stop to consider the consequences of your purpose, you are less likely to realize how others may react and are less likely to achieve your goal. Taking time to consider the effects of your purpose increases the chances of accomplishing what you want.

The examples below will help to point out the differences between not considering the consequences of your purpose and doing so:

Situation: A wife is excitedly explaining a disagreement with the neighbors. As she speaks, her voice becomes louder and louder. Her husband finds this very annoying. He wants to hear her story but in a softer tone of voice.

Purpose Without Considering Consequences	*Consequences*	*Purpose Considering Consequences*
The husband decides to let her know that, at times, she really is a loudmouth and that he cannot stand to hear her talk. He figures that this criticism will get her to speak more softly.	Wife becomes upset and annoyed; she feels criticized and hurt, walks out of the room, and refuses to speak the rest of the evening.	The husband decides that it would be more effective to tell his wife that she is speaking excitedly and ask her if she would speak more quietly.

Situation: Steve is a close friend of yours. Recently, the two of you had an argument. You want to settle the issue and go back to being good friends.

Directness, Honesty, and Responsibility 17

Purpose Without Considering Consequences	Consequences	Purpose, Considering Consequences
You decide that you want to: (1) let him know that he never sees anything but his side of things and (2) tell him that he misunderstood the situation. You figure that telling him this will help him to understand what happened.	Steve becomes very angry. The two of you have another argument and exchange many angry words. You do not speak for weeks.	You decide that it is more effective to tell Steve that you want to settle the issue but that maintaining the friendship is more important to you.

Situation: You want your spouse to be more affectionate.

Purpose Without Considering Consequences	Consequences	Purpose, Considering Consequences
You decide that you want to criticize him or her for being "a cold fish." You want to prove how important affection is to you by threatening a divorce if he or she does not change.	Your spouse becomes upset and feels harassed; he or she says that you can get a divorce any time that you want. Both of you are upset.	You decide that it is more effective to tell your spouse that you would like it if he or she were more affectionate.

Situation: Mary is someone who is under your supervision at work. She often takes advantage of your good nature and teases you in front of others. In the past, you have ignored this, but you are becoming progressively annoyed with this behavior.

Purpose Without Considering Consequences	Consequences	Purpose, Considering Consequences
You decide that you want to be a "nice guy" and ignore it, hoping that she will change.	Mary continues the teasing behavior.	You decide that it is more effective to tell Mary that you want her to stop teasing you.

The purposes in the first column do not consider consequences. They are likely to have the undesirable effects that are listed in the middle, which are the opposite of what the person wanted to accomplish.

In contrast, the purposes on the right are honest, but, in addition, they also consider the possible effects on people and on relationships. When you consider consequences, you are better able to judge if a particular purpose will help you to accomplish what you want. If you think that your goal is likely to have a different effect than you intended, this is a cue to reconsider your purpose.

Practice

The following section provides practice in checking out consequences of purposes and deciding if they accomplish what you want.
I. The column on the left presents some things that you may want to accomplish. The column on the right contains descriptions of purposes and statements. Some of these would be effective in achieving the goal while others would not.

Match the goal to the purpose and statement most likely to achieve it.

What You Want to Accomplish

A. To persuade your children to come visit more often.

B. To let your spouse know that you appreciated the gift.

C. To express frustration with a situation and a desire to change it.

D. To get some encouragement and support.

Purpose and Statement

1. *Purpose:* To make your children feel guilty and obligated to come visit. ("Don't you ever think about your parents? What ungrateful children you are!")

2. *Purpose:* To remind your spouse to save money. ("You shouldn't have bought me such an expensive gift. You're wasting money.")

3. *Purpose:* To criticize your spouse. ("Why can't you ever give me a little praise and encouragement? Or are you too selfish?")

4. *Purpose:* To express appreciation. ("I really appreciated your thoughtfulness.")

5. *Purpose:* To express a desire for change. ("I am frustrated; I don't like the way things are now. I'd like to change them.")

6. *Purpose:* To express your desire

Directness, Honesty, and Responsibility

or preference. ("I'd like it if you came to visit more.")

7. *Purpose:* To ask for some support. ("I'd like some encouragement from you.")

8. *Purpose:* To blame your spouse for a situation. ("This is awful. How can you expect me to put up with this?")

II. Below are pairs of statements. One is more effective at achieving the stated purpose than the other. After considering the likely consequences of each, choose the one that is more effective.

A. *What you want to accomplish:* Let your spouse know your thinking or preferences on a matter.
   1. ____"You've been so busy blabbering that you never even think of what I want. Now I'm not going to tell you! If you're not smart enough to guess . . . that's too bad!"
   2. ____"I'd like to tell you my thinking on this."

B. *What you want to accomplish:* Let a friend know that you don't like it when he interrupts you.
   1. ____"You are really being rude and obnoxious."
   2. ____"I don't like it when you interrupt me. Please let me finish what I'm saying."

III. Each example describes a situation and what the person wants to accomplish. Some possible purposes together with statements and actions are listed below the description.

Check the purpose that is most likely to help the person with what he or she wants to accomplish.

A. *Situation:* Jack's wife is upset.
   What Jack wants to accomplish: He wants her to calm down.
   1. ____*Purpose:* To criticize her for being upset. ("Why are you so irrational? You're always exaggerating! There's nothing to be upset about!")
   2. ____*Purpose:* To express his feelings of frustration. ("I am so frustrated with you when you're like this.")

3. ____*Purpose:* To show that he is disgusted with her. (*walks away*)
4. ____*Purpose:* To find out what it would take for her to be less upset. ("I want you to be less upset, but I don't know what to do to help. Is there something that I can do or say?").

B. *Situation:* Bruce is a good worker but is not tactful.
What the boss wants to accomplish: To persuade Bruce to be more tactful.
1. ____*Purpose:* To complain. ("I'm tired of your inconsiderate and rude remarks.")
2. ____*Purpose:* To tell Bruce his preference ("You're a good worker, Bruce, but I would really like you to be tactful with the other employees.")

C. *Situation:* You come home from work and are very tired. You want to sit quietly and read the paper.
What you want to accomplish: To be left alone; at the same time, you do not want your spouse to be upset.
1. ____*Purpose:* To pick a fight. (Walk through the door and say to your spouse, "I don't want to hear one word from anyone!" Stomp off to your room.)
2. ____*Purpose:* To express your preference and ask your spouse's cooperation. ("I'm tired and would like to be quiet. Can you keep the kids away from me for an hour or so?")
3. ____*Purpose:* To expect your spouse to read your mind. (Say nothing. When your spouse speaks to you, say, "Can't you see how tired I am? Leave me alone.")

SKILL 2: STATING YOUR INTENTIONS AND MOTIVES

Deciding on your main purpose, judging the consequences, and knowing about mixed messages is not enough to insure clear communication. When you speak, other people still may be unclear about what you are thinking or trying to do. For this reason, once you have decided on your purpose, it is helpful to explain what you are trying to accomplish. This can be done by telling the other person your intention. For example, "I want to make a suggestion. I think your latest report is fine now, but it could be even more persuasive if you organized it a bit differently."

Since communication between people is so complicated, intentions

Directness, Honesty, and Responsibility

are easy to misread. The other person easily could jump to any one of a number of conclusions about what you are trying to do. By using this skill of stating your intentions, you have the following advantages.

1. You increase your self-awareness by deciding on your intention. Your thinking is clear about what you want to accomplish.
2. You clearly state your intentions, motives, and what you are trying to do.
3. You structure the situation for the listener and thus decrease the number of possible motives that the listener could attribute to you incorrectly.
4. In general, you keep the communication fairly clear and limit the chances for confusion. In this way, each of you has a better chance of understanding each other's ideas.

When intention is not stated, complications can occur. For example,

JOHN: Why don't you try reorganizing your latest report?

TOM: (*somewhat offended*) Why? Is there something wrong with the way it is now?

In this example, John's motives for speaking are unclear. Tom does not know if John is suggesting, criticizing, or hinting that there is something wrong with his report. For this reason, Tom does not understand the situation and may misinterpret John's remarks. This is more likely to lead to confusion, defensiveness, or hurt feelings; and it lessens the chances for clear and effective communication.

The following examples illustrate the differences between not expressing your intentions and doing so.

Does Not Express Intentions or Purpose	*Expresses Intentions or Purpose*
ANN: I'm just so sick and tired of everyone in the office. Everyone is obnoxious around here. CATHY: (*sarcastically*) Thanks a lot.	ANN: I'm having a hard time here at work, and I'd like you to give me some advice on how to handle it. CATHY: What are you having trouble with?

Discussion: In the example on the left, Cathy is given no instruction as to Ann's intention. Cathy may think that Ann is angry at her, and, of course, she does not know the reason. She decides that Ann includes her in the "obnoxious" group of people. Since Ann does not explain what she wants, it is very difficult to accomplish her purpose.

In contrast, in the example on the right, Ann tells Cathy her reason for speaking. As a result, the words that follow are more easily understood. Cathy is less likely to be misled; she is clearer about what it is that Ann is trying to say; she has an idea about how to respond. This leads to more effective communication.

Does Not Express Intentions or Purpose

HUSBAND: "Let me explain . . ."
WIFE: I don't want to hear any more explanations.
HUSBAND: Wait . . . you don't understand.
WIFE: I don't want to understand.

Expresses Intentions or Purpose

HUSBAND: (*calmly*) I don't want to fight. I want to settle this issue. I did not mean to sound critical. Let me explain what I meant and let's see if we can find some way to compromise.
WIFE: I don't want to fight, either.

Discussion: In the example on the left, the husband does not express his intentions or his perspective of the situation. As a result, the wife thinks that he is extending the argument and she does not want to listen.

In contrast, in the example on the right, the husband states clearly what he is trying to do. As a result, the wife has a better idea of his positive intentions and does not react defensively. There is a better chance for some discussion and resolution of the issue.

Situation: Boss calls a staff meeting.

Does Not Express Intentions or Purpose

BOSS: We have spent more than we should have, so no more workshops or conventions for anyone.
EMPLOYEE: (*angrily*) Why not? We need educational leave!
BOSS: Well, you can't have it. (*Employees are silent but feel angry and frustrated.*)

Expresses Intentions or Purpose

BOSS: I have had a frustrating meeting with the board of directors. I don't want to take out my frustrations on you, but I do want to tell you the problem. An audit has been done and we have a deficit. The first cut suggested is in travel and education. I do not like cutting this, but I must.
EMPLOYEE: We don't like it any more than you do.

Discussion: In the example on the left, the boss does not express intentions or purpose. Instead, he or she plunges into new policy. As a result, the employees do not understand and become argumentative and defensive.

Directness, Honesty, and Responsibility 23

On the other hand, in the example on the right, the boss explains intention, purpose, and what has occurred. This structures the situation, and, as a result, the employees are better able to listen and understand. Although the boss' news is not pleasant, the chances for effective communication and some degree of resolution are increased.

Situation: Husband urged wife to make plans for them to go out of town for Labor Day weekend. She planned and arranged for a holiday, including a dinner with old friends. Three days before the weekend, Ted tells Sue that he has too much work to do at the office and in the yard. He says that they cannot go to San Francisco for the weekend. She is upset and disappointed. On Saturday evening she says:

Does Not Express Intentions or Purpose

WIFE: (*sarcastically*) This is just a *great* weekend we're having. I never had so much fun. I'm just sitting here listening to the kids scream and hearing you complain while you mow the lawn. I guess this is why I got married. What fun!

HUSBAND: Oh, shut up. If you're in one of your angry, bitter moods, I don't want to hear about it! Leave me alone.

WIFE: Great. I can see exactly how you feel about our marriage. (*walks off, goes into bedroom, slams door*)

Expresses Intentions or Purpose

WIFE: I don't want to create an unpleasant scene, but I do want you to know that I am upset and disappointed. I really looked forward to this weekend in San Francisco away from the kids and by ourselves for a change.

HUSBAND: I didn't know you took that so seriously.

WIFE: I did. When you say, "Let's make reservations for Labor Day weekend," I believe you. I like us to spend some time alone, away from the kids and I want you to know that.

HUSBAND: I didn't realize that. I thought you understood that I wanted a weekend in San Francisco, but I didn't mean it definitely.

WIFE: When you said, "Call Rich and Joan and tell them we'll be there over Labor Day," I figured you were serious.

HUSBAND: I guess that sounded definite . . . but I meant to say that it depended on how much work I had to do.

Discussion: In the example on the left, the wife does not explain her intentions or purpose. As a result, her husband becomes defensive, communication is unclear, and confusion and misunderstanding increase. The chances for some degree of resolution and satisfaction are reduced dramatically.

In contrast, on the right, the wife precedes her statement with an explanation of her intention and purpose. As a result, the husband is better able to comprehend her feelings and her point of view. Instead of becoming defensive, he is better able to listen to her reactions. The chances for effective communication and mutual understanding are increased.

In general, in the left-hand examples, the speakers do not explain what they are trying to do. As a result, their words and actions are subject to many interpretations and the listeners become defensive. The situations are unpleasant, and the chances for effective communication and understanding are decreased.

In contrast, in the examples on the right, the speakers explain what they are trying to do and provide information about their intentions and motives. This gives their listeners a better idea of what is going on, and the chances for understanding and for some degree of satisfaction are increased.

How to Use This Skill in Conjunction with Others Learned So Far

This skill is to be used with those that you learned earlier in the chapter. Follow this sequence:
1. Decide on your purposes. What do you want to accomplish?
2. Most of us have more than one goal in mind at a time. Choose the one that you most want to accomplish.
3. Check the consequences of what you want to say or do.
4. If you are satisfied with the consequences of your purpose, tell your listener what you are trying to say or do.

Here is an example of how to use this sequence of skills:

Situation: A wife wants to go out to eat; she does not want to fix dinner.
1. She decides on her purposes.
   a. To complain about how hard she's worked and how bad the children have been.

Directness, Honesty, and Responsibility 25

   b. To make her husband feel guilty for not taking her out to dinner last week.
   c. To express her desire to go out to eat and ask her husband if he will take her.
2. After looking at her purposes, she decides that, most of all, she wants to express her desire to go out to eat.
3. She checks the consequences. She decides that, if she says that she wants to go out to eat, her husband will understand better than if she complains or tries to make him feel guilty.
4. Since she is satisfied with the consequences, she tells her spouse what she wants to do and asks him if he is willing to go along with it, "I want to go out to eat tonight. Are you willing to do that?"

You will be given further opportunity to review this sequence of skills in practice sections throughout the chapter.

Practice

The section below provides practice in recognizing and formulating statements of intention.

I. In each pair of statements, check the one that states intentions and motives more clearly.

A. 1. ____WIFE: I want to buy a house, I want to tell you why, and I'd like to persuade you to agree with me.
   2. ____WIFE: Well, you think we should not buy a house and I think we should. You just don't realize how much houses are going to go up! And, besides, you're stingy!

B. 1. ____BOSS: What do you know about our competitor's sales?
   2. ____BOSS: I want you to be aware of our competitor's sales techniques and how their sales compare to ours. So, if you don't know, find out.

C. 1. ____HUSBAND: Those Smiths sure are sensitive! You'd think I'd said something nasty to them. Don't you think they're sensitive?
   2. ____HUSBAND: I'm worried about how I came across. I'd like some reassurance that I didn't come across too angrily with the Smiths tonight.

D. 1. ____FRIEND: You didn't go over too well at that meeting.
   2. ____FRIEND: I want to prepare you for some of the reactions

you might get from people. Because of what you said, some people may be angry with you.

E. 1. BOSS: I am going to outline some new procedures. I want to be sure these are clear, so ask questions as I go along.
2. BOSS: The following new procedures will begin.

II. The following examples do not state intentions or motives. Rewrite each one so that it expresses the purpose indicated.

A. FRIEND: John had the nerve to call me a stuffed shirt! I'm not that overbearing. Besides, he's pretty overbearing himself.
Purpose: To get some honest information about how he comes across.
Rewrite:

B. WIFE: I just can't take this any more. I keep dieting and don't lose those five pounds.
Purpose: To ask for reassurance that she looks all right even if she hasn't lost weight.
Rewrite:

III. Write a statement of intention for each of the examples below.
A. To ask a friend's advice on a used car you want to buy.

B. To tell a new employee about your expectations of him.

C. To ask for a co-worker's cooperation in starting a new project.

SKILL 3: EXPRESSING YOURSELF DIRECTLY AND RESPONSIBLY

This chapter has suggested that you decide on your purpose, check the consequences of this decision, eliminate mixed messages, and state your intention. In order to communicate clearly, it is also important to express yourself directly and responsibly. This section explains how to achieve these qualities of directness and responsibility. It presents the following skills.

1. The ability to express thoughts directly and responsibly.
2. The ability to express desires and preferences directly and responsibly.

3. The ability to express feelings directly and responsibly.

Skill 3a: Expressing Thoughts or Ideas

You express your thinking directly and responsibly by letting others know that what you say represents your perceptions, impressions, ideas, or reactions. You can accomplish this by using "I," "me," and "my" in your statements. For example, "I think that you are being too strict with the children." "This is my opinion—your mother is easily upset." "In my experience, it is better if everyone works independently." "It seems to me that you handled that well." This skill helps you to say what you mean in a way that does not disguise your thinking and does not confuse the other person.

Frequently, people do not express their ideas, nor do they explain their thinking in a direct and responsible fashion. Instead, they hide their thoughts, feelings, and preferences from themselves and from others. This happens most often when people fear that others will reject them or will disapprove, disagree, or deprive them of what they want. In these instances of expected rejection, individuals often choose one of the following forms of indirect speaking.

1. Keeping their thoughts and preferences to themselves. This can be done by saying nothing, walking away, changing the subject, or saying, "I don't know." For example:
   a. HUSBAND: I think that we can afford a new car.
      WIFE: If you think so . . . (Instead of, "I don't agree. I'd rather wait for a few months.")
   b. WIFE: I want to move to a larger city. Would you do that?
      HUSBAND: I don't know, we'll see. (Instead of, "I don't think so. I may change my mind, but right now I prefer a small town.")
   c. HUSBAND: I want to work on the budget.
      WIFE: (*walks away to kitchen*) (Instead of, "I don't want to do that right now. I'll do it after supper. Is that OK?")
2. Disguising their thoughts or expressing them indirectly:
   a. Copping out to another person. For example:
      FATHER: Your mother will be very angry if you do that. (Instead of, "I don't want you to do that.")

SPOUSE: The kids really should have a dog. (Instead of, "I'd like to have a dog.")
  b. Copping out to authorities, using "experts" to express what they really want to say. For example, "Everyone says that Hawaii is the place to go." (Instead of, "I'd like to go to Hawaii.")
  "The doctor said that it is best for me not to get upset." (Instead of, "I'd rather not talk about this.")
  c. Criticizing or blaming others, fostering shame or guilt, trying to force agreement by stating opinions as facts. For example, "People who swear are despicable." (Instead of, "I don't like swearing.") "Anyone who's intelligent can see that this is the only way to go." (Instead of, "I think that this is the best solution.") "You are mixed up!" (Instead of, "I don't see things the same way that you do.") "What you need to do is . . ." (Instead of, "In my experience, I have found that this works.")

There are consequences to both of these forms of indirect speaking. If you refrain from expressing yourself, others do not have information about what you are thinking or trying to do. If you choose the option of expressing yourself indirectly, others remain unclear about your thinking and your intentions and are more likely to feel manipulated and uneasy. As a result of these complications, the chances for clear communication and understanding are dramatically reduced.

The skill of stating your ideas directly and responsibly works for the following reasons.

1. It helps to keep your thinking straight, direct, and responsible.
2. It lets others know that what follows is your thought. It provides information about your thinking.
3. It increases the chances for effective communication and mutual understanding. Your listeners are less likely to feel manipulated or defensive. As a result, they are better able to understand what you are trying to do or say.

The examples below help to show the difference between not expressing your thoughts and ideas directly and responsibly and doing so.

Directness, Honesty, and Responsibility

Indirect, Does Not Take Responsibility	*Direct, Takes Responsibility*
WIFE: Cooking is a terrible job. It is unfair that I get stuck with it. HUSBAND: Oh, come on, it's not that bad. Yard work is much worse.	WIFE: I don't like to cook. HUSBAND: I accept that. I don't like to cook either. So how can we work this out?
PAUL: This is the kind of music that anybody with good taste would like. JOHN: Well, I don't like it. And there's nothing wrong with my taste!	PAUL: I like this type of music. JOHN: Well, we're different in that.
WIFE: All the wives of successful men have fur coats. HUSBAND: (*angrily*) Thanks a lot. With you for a wife who needs enemies?	WIFE: I'd like to have a fur coat. HUSBAND: We can't afford it this year.
CO-WORKER A: That plan of yours is dumb. CO-WORKER B: Not half as dumb as yours.	CO-WORKER A: I don't agree with your plan. CO-WORKER B: OK, but I'm going ahead with it.

In the examples on the left, the speakers express themselves indirectly in a number of ways. They accuse others of being "unfair," "having bad taste," being "unsuccessful" or "dumb." The speakers try to induce guilt or put others down in order to get what they want. The result is self-defense, counterattack, or guilt inducement from the other person. Misunderstanding and unpleasantness are created, and the chances for effective communication and satisfaction are diminished.

On the other hand, in the examples on the right, ideas are expressed directly and responsibly. Clear information is provided. By taking responsibility for their ideas, the speakers eliminate guilt inducement, accusations, and other manipulations. As a result, the likelihood of eliciting resentment and defensiveness is reduced. When your ideas or thoughts are responsibly stated as belonging to you, others are more likely to hear, understand, and find it easier to respond. The chances of settling an issue and achieving some degree of mutual understanding and satisfaction are increased.

Direct and responsible speaking is an important aspect of effective communication. To increase your familiarity with this concept, more conversations and discussions are provided below. These examples help to illustrate the difference between statements that are indirect and do not take responsibility and those that are direct and responsible.

Situation: Two close friends are discussing children and careers.

Indirect, Does Not Take Responsibility

ANN: Anyone who is interested in the welfare of her children shouldn't work!
DOROTHY: Wait a minute! I'm interested in the welfare of my children. I also like to work . . . anyone who wants to stay home is lazy, untalented, or "cops out"! You're just way behind the times in your thinking!

Direct, Takes Responsibility

ANN: I stay at home with the children and it works out well for me.
DOROTHY: I'm glad that it works out for you, and I can understand some of your thinking. But it does not work for me. I'm much happier combining work and a family. So, for a woman who feels as I do, I think it is good to combine the two careers.

Discussion: In the example on the left, Ann states her opinions as facts. She expresses herself in a way that evaluates Dorothy and tells her what she should do (or else she is "not interested in her children.") Since Dorothy is accused of being a "bad mother," she feels misunderstood, annoyed, and angry. As a result, she decides to defend herself and respond with accusations and judgments of her own.

In contrast, in the example on the right, Ann expresses her ideas as her own and does not accuse Dorothy or try to make her feel guilty. In response, Dorothy states her thinking differently. Although they do not agree, their differences are accepted and the situation remains pleasant.

Indirect, Does Not Take Responsibility

MARGARET: (*in a critical tone*) You don't have your white wine chilled? You've ruined the flavor.
BILL: Since when are *you* a wine expert? If you don't like it, don't bother to drink it.

Direct, Takes Responsibility

MARGARET: I like white wine chilled.
BILL: I don't, but I can chill some for you, if you like.

Discussion: In the example on the left, Margaret disguises her opinion about white wine as a fact. It becomes a way to assert her superiority and criticize Bill for not complying with her opinion. As a result, Bill feels attacked and becomes defensive. In contrast, in the example on the right, Margaret states her preferences and opinion as her own. This makes it easier for Bill to understand and to react nondefensively.

Indirect, Does Not Take Responsibility	*Direct, Takes Responsibility*
TIM: Why don't you take more interest in neatness and organization? You'd be a lot more productive if you did.	TIM: I think that it's important to have things well organized and neat. Of course, that's just me and that's the way I work best.
KAY: I have more important things to be interested in than cleanliness and organization.	KAY: I can understand that, but, as you know, I'm different.

Discussion: The statement on the left implies that Kay is "bad" because she does not value organization and neatness as Tim does. Kay feels criticized and evaluated, and she reacts defensively by putting down Tim. In contrast, the statement on the right does not judge Kay. In it, Tim states his values as his own and it is easier for both Kay and Tim to hear and to understand each other's thinking.

In general, the examples on the left present thoughts, impressions, and ideas as statements of fact. When this happens, listeners are likely to feel disrespected, frustrated, judged, hurt, or annoyed. They are likely to respond by defensive reactions, and these, in turn, shut off communication and lead to more misunderstanding.

In contrast, in the examples on the right, the speakers take responsibility for their thoughts, opinions, impressions, and experiences. This way of speaking acknowledges that others may have different views. It encourages others to express their ideas, and, as a result, there is better exchange of ideas and the chances for effective communication and understanding are increased.

Note: As with most communication, nonverbal cues also are important. For example, saying "it is my opinion" with a scowl or in a harsh, angry tone of voice has quite a different effect than saying it pleasantly. How to express your ideas with appropriate nonverbal cues will be discussed in the chapter on nonverbal communication.

Practice

This section provides practice in stating your thoughts directly and responsibly.

I. Each of the examples below contains pairs of statements. One expresses thoughts or preferences directly; the other does not. Check the direct expression and underline the part that expresses thoughts or preferences.

A. 1. ____HUSBAND: I don't like it when you act so angrily toward me.

2. ____HUSBAND: What kind of a wife are you? If you're that angry, you need to see a psychologist and get yourself straightened out.

B. 1. ____BOSS: It's a disappointment to me that you didn't have the sense to ask me before you acted.

2. ____BOSS: I prefer that you ask my advice before taking a major step like that.

C. 1. ____WIFE: People who live in the city are generally brighter and more cultured. Not like your family and the people who live in the country.

2. ____WIFE: I miss the city. I'd like to move back there.

D. 1. ____HUSBAND: You're ridiculous! Those are the dumbest ideas I've ever heard of.

2. ____HUSBAND: I don't agree with your ideas. I think that I know more about finances than you do.

E. 1. ____BOSS: In my experience I've found that tactfulness works better than anger. I suggest that you use tact.

2. ____BOSS: That's obviously not the way to handle the situation. Getting angry, as you do, just leads to more trouble. But that's nothing new — you've always been a troublemaker!

II. The column on the left contains statements that are indirect and irresponsible. Pair each irresponsible, indirect statement to the more responsible one.

Irresponsible, Indirect

A. You are absolutely wrong! You misunderstood everything that was said.

B. You're a grown woman — you should know how to handle your boss. You shouldn't come whining to me.

Responsible, Direct

1. It seems to me that you are putting the blame on John for what happened. I don't see him as the cause of the incident. I certainly don't think that he intended for you to be hurt and upset.

Directness, Honesty, and Responsibility

C. You are blaming John for what happened, and that's unfair. You're really screwed up.

2. My understanding of what happened at the meeting is different from yours.

3. I think that you are capable of handling your boss on your own.

III. The examples below give you the opportunity to use most of the skills that you have learned so far.

A. A mother wants to persuade her son to help his father. She wants to say, "Your father is working so hard! You should help him before he collapses." Pretend that you are the mother in this situation. Use the sequence of skills outlined below:

Decide on your purpose. What is it that you want to accomplish?

- To make your son feel guilty?
- To criticize your son?
- To express a preference that your son help his father?

Of these, which do you want to accomplish most?

Check the consequences of your purpose to be certain that the effect is what you want.

Express your intention. Remember to explain your ideas directly and responsibly.

If you were the mother, what would you say? Check the statement that you think would be most effective.

1. ___"You are so lazy—you never help your father!"
2. ___"I'd like you to help your father."
3. ___"Your father is working so hard! Someday you'll feel sorry that you never helped him!"

B. A physician wants a patient to stop worrying about certain symptoms. The doctor wants to say, "Why are you so worried about these symptoms? You must be a very anxious person." Pretend that you are the physician in this statement. Use the sequence of skills outlined below.

Decide on your purpose. What is it that you most want to accomplish?

- To criticize the patient
- To put him down and persuade him to stop bothering you

- To reassure him
- To express understanding of the patient's upset and concerns

Of these, which do you want to accomplish most?

Check the consequences of your purpose to be certain that the effect is what you want.

Express your intention. Remember to explain your ideas directly and responsibly.

If you were the physician, what would you say? Check the statement that you think would be most effective.

1. ___"There's no need to worry."
2. ___"I understand how you could be upset."
3. ___"It is really silly for you to worry about these symptoms."
4. ___"Don't bother me with all your whining and complaining."

Skill 3b: Expressing Desires, Preferences, and Requests

In the preceding section, we talked about stating what you think in a direct and responsible fashion. It is also very important to use the same approach to tell the other person what you want or prefer. This skill involves taking responsibility for your preferences and stating them as directly as possible. For example, "I want . . ." "I prefer that . . ." "I like to . . ."

Sometimes, instead of saying what they want, people couch their desires in indirect terms. For example, a spouse may say, "Do we have any plans this weekend?" instead of, "I want to have a party." At other times, people try to get what they want by inducing guilt, blaming, making threats, using false flattery, or other manipulations. For example:

WIFE: You never call when you are going to be late. Why can't you be considerate like other husbands?

A more responsible and direct way of stating this would be, "I want you to call when you are going to be late."

When you do not express your preference directly, your listeners lack clear information and this increases the chances for confusion and misunderstanding. Furthermore, if you try to get what you want by means of flattery, guilt, blame, or other manipulations, you risk some negative consequences. When you use these methods to trick or to coerce people into doing what you want, you are likely to elicit feelings of defensiveness and resentment from them. Sooner or later, others realize your manipulations and feel controlled, used, and betrayed. These feelings interfere with effective communication and lessen the chances for satisfaction in a relationship. In fact, when people have a strong sense of betrayal or resentment, they can lose their motivation to continue a relationship. While manipulation may be useful in certain competitive situations, do not use it with people who matter to you.

In contrast, the skill of stating what you want directly and responsibly has the following advantages.

1. It keeps your thinking clear. You take responsibility for your desires or preferences and for expressing them directly.
2. It gives other people information about your likes, dislikes, desires, and preferences. As a result, they have a clearer idea about what you want, and they do not have to guess what you mean.
3. It is easier for others to listen, understand, and respond to your preferences when they are not distracted or tricked by dishonest questions, accusations, guilt inducements, threats, or "hidden" agendas. This increases the chances for effective communication and understanding.

Using this skill does not guarantee that others will comply with your wishes or preferences. People have the right to think and to react in a different way than you do, and they also have the right to want different things than you do. While it cannot guarantee that you will get what you want, the use of this skill does increase the chances for effective communication and mutual understanding in a relationship. It is meant to be used in situations and in relationships that are important to you. Do not use it to disclose your deepest wishes to people whom you do not trust. If someone is manipulative or is involved in a power relationship with you (for example, a boss, rival, or competitive co-worker), do not use this skill to disclose anything that can be used against you. This decision depends, of course, upon the individual, the nature of your relationship, and whether the person has demonstrated that he or she is worthy of your trust. When you do not trust the other person, use this skill only to state your preferences and your limits.

The following examples point out the differences between dishonest, indirect, irresponsible statements of desires and honest, direct, responsible statements of them.

Main Purpose	Dishonest, Indirect, Irresponsible Statement	Honest, Direct, Responsible Statement
To keep things the way that they are.	"Your idea doesn't make any sense at all! The boss will never buy it!"	"I like things the way that they are now, and I want them to stay the same."
To state a preference and to make a request.	"I'll catch a cold if I have to walk."	"I want to be dropped off as close as possible. Will you drive me to the door?"
To find out how to get a promotion.	"Don't you think the promotion policy here is old-fashioned?"	"I want a promotion as soon as possible. What do I have to do to get one?"
To tell your spouse that you'd like to buy a new car.	"How can I be a successful real estate salesman with that junky car that we have?"	"I want a new car. How's the budget — any chance for a new car soon?"
To persuade someone to play bridge.	"You'll never fit in around here if you don't play bridge."	"I'd like you to join our bridge club."

In the middle column, the speakers do not express their thinking, preferences, or requests directly. The statements are disguised and indirect; they are likely to elicit a feeling of obligation, guilt (for example, "I'll catch cold if you don't drive me to the door") or defensiveness ("Don't you think your promotion policies are old-fashioned?"). This confuses the issues and is likely to lead to misunderstanding.

In contrast, in the examples on the right, the speakers state their desires, preferences, and requests directly and responsibly. Their listeners need not guess at any hidden or secret meanings, wonder what the speaker wants, nor get sidetracked on other issues. This, of course, leads to clearer, more effective communication.

Directness and responsibility are essential aspects of effective communication, and it is important for you to be familiar with these qualities. In order to increase your familiarity with the concepts, further examples are provided below.

Directness, Honesty, and Responsibility

Indirect, Does Not Take Responsibility	*Direct, Takes Responsibility*
WIFE: Why don't you get a little culture and come to a concert with me? I can't understand how anyone would not want to learn about classical music! HUSBAND: I have plenty of culture! Most of you people who go to concerts are nothing but phonies anyway.	WIFE: I realize that not everyone enjoys classical music as I do, but I'd really like it if you came along with me to the concert. HUSBAND: Well, I'm not in the mood this week. Maybe sometime I'll come along, just to see what it's like.

Discussion: In the example on the left, the wife judges the husband and evaluates him negatively. By using "why don't you," she is asking him a dishonest question and trying to force him to agree with her ideas and preferences. Instead of stating her preference directly, she is accusing him of not being "cultured."

In contrast, on the right, the wife states her preference clearly, directly, and takes responsibility for it. She does not try to persuade her husband to comply by threatening him with the label of "uncultured." As a result, it is easier for the husband to respond and to state his own preference.

Indirect, Does Not Take Responsibility	*Direct, Takes Responsibility*
HUSBAND: (*sweetly*) Why don't you take care of the kids? You're so good with them and you have so much more patience with them than I do. WIFE: Forget it. I used to fall for those phony lines of yours, but I don't anymore. Do you really think I'm that stupid?	HUSBAND: I want to take a nap and it's my time to watch the kids. Would you be willing to watch them for awhile? Then I'll take care of them while you fix dinner. WIFE: OK. That's reasonable. Can you wait until I finish what I'm doing?

Discussion: The example on the left demonstrates "false praise," a compliment that is insincere and is intended only to get what you want. Flattery like this produces an atmosphere of dishonesty and exacts a price in relationships. When people "find out" that they have been misled, feelings of resentment and betrayal follow.

In contrast, on the right, the husband honestly explains what he wants. This gives his wife a clearer idea of his purpose, and she does not feel "tricked" or manipulated.

Indirect, Does Not Take Responsibility

HUSBAND: All the wives stay at home with their children! Why should you go back to work?
WIFE: All the wives that I know that stay home with their children are stale and boring!

Direct, Takes Responsibility

HUSBAND: I prefer that you stay at home with the children.
WIFE: I realize that this is your preference, but, I, too, have a preference. I want to work and to keep up in my career. Maybe there is some way that we can compromise on this.

Discussion: In the example on the left, the husband is trying to persuade his wife to agree with him. He does this by evaluating and comparing her to "other wives." If she does not comply with his wishes, he implies that she is "not like other wives" and, therefore, is "unfeminine" and "bad." No one likes being evaluated or compared negatively, and, as a result, the wife reacts defensively.

In contrast, on the right, the husband states his preference without trying to induce guilt or use comparisons. She, in turn, does not attack him for his preference, states her own, and suggests that they try to work out a compromise. This keeps the exchange of ideas open and is more likely to lead to a satisfactory solution.

Indirect, Does Not Take Responsibility

MOTHER: Why can't you be thoughtful like other daughters and come visit your parents once in awhile?

Direct, Takes Responsibility

MOTHER: I certainly enjoy it when you visit and I'd like to see you more often.

Discussion: In the example on the left, the mother does not take responsibility in stating her preference. Instead, she encourages her daughter to feel guilty and obligated to visit. The daughter may come to visit, but her feelings of guilt, obligation, and resentment will interfere with any genuine enjoyment. Getting someone to do something because of guilt or obligation only lessens the chances for a satisfying and comfortable relationship. In this case, the mother defeats her own purpose of trying to establish a closer relationship with her daughter.

In contrast, the example on the right is a straightforward statement of preference. The mother takes responsibility for what she wants.

Directness, Honesty, and Responsibility

This statement is more likely to lead to an open exchange of ideas and a more honest understanding of each other.

Indirect, Does Not Take Responsibility

WIFE: Why don't you want to save any money? You're just like the rest of your family—wasteful and self-indulgent.
HUSBAND: "I'd rather be like that than a bunch of misers like your family."

ED: We have been consistently late to work. Is there something we can do about getting there on time?

Direct, Takes Responsibility

WIFE: I want to trim our budget and save one hundred dollars more a month. You said that you don't want to do this. How can we work this out?
HUSBAND: Fifty dollars a month I'd agree to . . .

ED: I want to be at work on time and I do not want to be delayed. Often I have to wait for you for ten minutes. Either you find a different way to work or, if you come with me, be ready on time.

Discussion: These examples were chosen because they involve compromises. In the first example on the left, the wife is accusing and blaming. Because she does not express her desire to work out a compromise, the husband reacts with name calling; the situation easily could escalate into a bitter quarrel. In contrast, on the right, the wife expresses her desires directly and honestly and the couple is on the way to a solution of the difficulty.

The second example shows a situation where the speaker does not want to compromise. On the left, Ed is indirect and leads the other person on with false notions of compromise. In contrast, in the example on the right, he clearly lets his rider know that there is no compromise available. When you are not open to compromise, it is important to tell the other person that the matter is not negotiable.

Indirect, Does Not Take Responsibility

WIFE: Why can't we go on vacation in March? That's when everyone else is going.
HUSBAND: I don't care if everyone else is going in March. We're going in April, and that's final!

Direct, Takes Responsibility

WIFE: I want to go on vacation in March. I hear it's a good time to go, and, besides, I don't want to wait until April.
HUSBAND: Well, I can appreciate your preference, but leaving in April is more convenient for me at work.

Discussion: In the example on the left, the wife tries to persuade her husband to do what she wants to do by implying that, to be similar to "everyone else," they must vacation in March. The husband is annoyed, reacts angrily, and holds even more rigidly to his plans to vacation in April.

In contrast, on the right, the wife's direct and responsible statement of her preference is more effective. Because she is not indirect and manipulative, it is easier for her husband to respond. In general, a straightforward statement of preference is easier for the listener to understand and to acknowledge.

Indirect, Does Not Take Responsibility	*Direct, Takes Responsibility*
HUSBAND: Do you want to stay home tonight? WIFE: No, I don't want to; I'd like to go out somewhere. Maybe to dinner. HUSBAND: (*angrily*) You never think about me! Maybe I'm tired. I had a rough day at the office and I don't want to hear any noise. I just want to sit home quietly and watch television.	HUSBAND: I'd like to stay home tonight. I want some peace and quiet and relaxation. Will you go along with that? WIFE: Well, I had been looking forward to going out this weekend, but, I'd be willing to stay in tonight if we go out tomorrow.

Discussion: In the example on the left, the husband avoided saying that he wanted to stay home. Instead, he expected his wife to guess what he wanted, and, when she did not, he blamed her for not considering his feelings.

In contrast, on the right, the husband took responsibility for stating his preferences. Because he was direct, it was easier for the wife to understand and to respond with her own preferences.

Indirect, Does Not Take Responsibility	*Direct, Takes Responsibility*
WIFE: I can't see how you can put up with this tool shed. It is such a mess in here! HUSBAND: This is not a mess! And I can put up with it because I'm not a fuss-budget like you are. I have more important things to do than to be a fanatic about neatness.	WIFE: I prefer things neat. I wish you would clean up this tool shed. HUSBAND: No one sees this but me, and, I'd prefer to keep it this way. WIFE: OK, I guess you're right. I want to make a request: You can keep your tool shed whichever way you want, but will you try to keep

the books and magazines in the living room in a pile?
HUSBAND: Well, that seems fair enough. I'll try to be neat with the books and magazines if you remind me . . . and if you let me keep my tool shed whichever way I want.

Discussion: In the example on the left, the wife evaluates the husband and implies that he is "bad" and "messy." The husband reacts to the evaluation defensively, and the wife's communication does not accomplish its purpose. Neither person has a clear idea of what the other person is trying to say, and the husband is even more resistant to requests about being neat.

In contrast, on the right, each person states a preference. Although the preferences are different, there is no manipulation, evaluation, and very little defensiveness. A compromise is worked out, and each of them has a clear understanding of what the other person was saying.

In general, in the examples on the left, the speakers are indirect and do not take responsibility for their preferences. They make demands on other people in a dishonest fashion. They try to get what they want by false praise, criticism, guilt, or threats. Because of this, the other people involved feel annoyed, resentful, frustrated, and defensive, and they respond with counterattacks or resistance.

Indirect, irresponsible statements often defeat your purpose for the following reasons.

1. They do not provide information about your preferences, desires, or values.
2. They elicit defensiveness and upset on the part of your listener.
3. Since they try to persuade the other person to do what you want in indirect, dishonest ways, your listener is likely to feel "hustled" and resentful.

The total effect is to lessen the chances for a clear exchange of ideas.

In contrast, in the right-hand examples, preferences, desires, and requests are expressed directly and responsibly. One person does not have to guess what the other is trying to say or accomplish. Furthermore, the distractions of demands, threats, guilt inducements, or "hidden agendas" are eliminated. As a result, the people involved are better able to listen and to understand. The chances for clear communication and some degree of mutual understanding and satisfaction are increased.

Practice

This section gives you the opportunity to practice the skill of stating your requests, preferences, and desires directly and responsibly.

I. Below are pairs of statements. One contains direct, responsible statements; the other does not. Check the one that is direct and responsible.

A. 1. ____FRIEND: I don't like it when you expect me to wait for you.

2. ____FRIEND: You are rude and inconsiderate. Don't you have any sense of responsibility?

B. 1.____HUSBAND: I'd like some Chinese food. Will you fix some, please?

2. ____HUSBAND: I'm just in the mood for something different tonight.

C. 1.____MOTHER: I guess you've forgotten your mother. Children are all alike — you never remember what your parents have done for you.

2. ____MOTHER: I enjoy having you come to visit. I'd like you to come for dinner more often.

D. 1.____HUSBAND: I'd like to get out and play some golf. Will you come along?

2. ____HUSBAND: What a beautiful day to play golf.

E. 1. ____FRIEND: I don't want you to get hurt and I also don't like your confiding in Paul, because I don't want him interfering with our friendship.

2. ____FRIEND: Paul is not someone you should confide in. You should know better than to trust him.

F. 1. ____WIFE: You shouldn't get involved in so many clubs and things. You must be running away from something here at home. What's wrong with you?

2. ____WIFE: I prefer that you spend more time with me and the kids. I don't like it when you have meetings every night.

G. 1. ____HUSBAND: I'd like it if you called my mother once a week.

2. ____HUSBAND: It would really make my mother feel better if you called her once a week. Why don't you try being more considerate?

II. The following statements are indirect. Rewrite each one so that it expresses preferences or requests directly and responsibly.

A. "You should know better than to contradict what I said to the kids."
Rewrite: I prefer . . .

B. "If you really loved me, you wouldn't make me live in this awful town."
Rewrite: I want to . . .

Skill 3c: Expressing Your Feelings as Your Own

Another aspect of directness, honesty, and responsibility is that of describing your feelings as your own. Instead of viewing feelings as caused by other people's actions, think about and describe your feelings in the following way.

1. Begin your statements with "I." For example, "*I* feel happy." (Instead of, "*You make me* happy.") "I am disappointed." (Instead of, "*You* really disappointed me.")
2. Describe what you are reacting to in a specific way. For example, "I feel good when the house is clean." "I am annoyed when you are late for dinner and don't phone."

Using this skill reminds you that you are in charge of your own feelings. No one really can "hurt you" or "make you upset" if you do not want to be. When you think that another person is responsible for your feelings, you feel helpless, upset, and at the mercy of other people. Using this skill helps you to feel in control of your feelings and reactions and to express this sense of control to others.

Instead of taking responsibility for your feelings, people often describe situations and other persons as the cause of their emotions. For example, "You really hurt my feelings when you forgot my birthday." "That situation at work is driving me crazy." "You make me feel so good."

When you describe things in this fashion, you disown responsibility for your feelings. As a result, other people feel that they are the cause of your reactions or emotions. When your feelings are negative, the other person feels blamed and is likely to become defensive. When your feelings are positive, the other person senses the burden of maintaining your good feelings and this, too, is uncomfortable and frustrating.

The skill of expressing your feelings as your own works for the following reasons.

1. It keeps your thinking clear and responsible. It reminds you that you are in charge of your own feelings.
2. It does not disguise feelings in indirect, dishonest ways.
3. It does not imply to others that they are the cause of your good or bad feelings. It neither makes demands nor tries to control your listeners.
4. Because your listeners do not feel that they must bear the responsibility or blame for your feelings, they are better able to listen and to understand. This increases the chances for effective communication and some degree of satisfaction in the relationship.

The following examples show the difference between statements that do not "own" feelings and those which take responsibility.

Does Not Take Responsibility for Feelings	*Expresses Feelings as Own; Takes Responsibility for Feelings*
WIFE: You really make me worry about you!	WIFE: When you seem tired, *I* start to worry. I want you to be happy and rested.
HUSBAND: (*angrily*) Well, stop worrying! Who asked you to worry?	HUSBAND: I am happy. I appreciate your concern for me, but the truth is that I like to work hard. There's no need to worry.

Discussion: In the conversation on the left, the wife implies that her husband deliberately causes her to worry. She suggests that her bad feelings are his fault and demands that he do something so that she can stop worrying. This elicits defensiveness from the husband and confuses the communication. Each misunderstands the other's ideas and reactions.

In contrast, on the right, the wife takes responsibility for her worry and follows this with a preference ("I want you to be happy."). Because her statement does not blame him, the husband is able to respond with a better explanation of his feelings and preferences. The two individuals have a better comprehension of what each other is thinking and feeling.

Directness, Honesty, and Responsibility

Does Not Take Responsibility for Feelings	*Expresses Feelings as Own; Takes Responsibility for Feelings*
EMPLOYEE: This job makes me miserable.	EMPLOYEE: I am not content. I cannot find a way to feel happy or comfortable on this job.
BOSS: (*coldly*) Well, no one else has trouble here. You must just not be cut out for this job.	BOSS: What seems to be the trouble?
	EMPLOYEE: Well, it seems that I don't get a chance to do things that I know or that I do well.
	BOSS: Well . . . let's talk about this in more detail. What sorts of things would you like to be doing?

Discussion: In the example on the left, the employee blames the boss, the situation, and the job for his unhappiness. No one enjoys being labeled as the "cause" of someone else's unhappiness, and most of us react negatively when someone avoids responsibility for the situation. This happens in the above example. The boss becomes defensive, and misunderstanding follows.

In contrast, on the right, the employee keeps the channels of communication open by stating feelings and ideas in a responsible way. It is easier for the boss to respond, to ask questions, and to find out what the employee is thinking.

Does Not Take Responsibility for Feelings	*Expresses Feelings as Own; Takes Responsibility for Feelings*
HUSBAND: You are ruining my weekend. When you're happy, you make me feel good, but, you're moping around and making me very nervous.	HUSBAND: I get upset when you seem depressed. I don't like to see you unhappy, and I don't know what to do.
WIFE: Well, you're the reason I'm moping.	WIFE: I appreciate your concern and I understand that you want to see me happy. But I am worried about my job and there is nothing that you or anyone can do to help. I'll have to work it out on my own, and I'll get over it shortly.

Discussion: In the example on the left, the husband places the responsibility for his unhappiness on the wife and demands that she change her behavior so that he can change his feelings. The wife, in turn, becomes defensive and blames the husband for her feelings. The result is an unpleasant situation, with little understanding or satisfaction.

In contrast, on the right, the husband explains his feelings and reactions directly and responsibly. The wife responds more easily, and both spouses have a clearer idea of how each other is reacting.

In general, the examples on the left are indirect and irresponsible. The speakers place the burden for their feelings on others and demand that their good feelings be maintained and their bad feelings be changed to good ones. Because of these demands, the listeners react defensively. Confusion and upset result, and the chances for effective understanding and communication are reduced.

In the examples on the right, the speakers describe feelings as their own and state their preferences and reactions honestly, clearly, and responsibly. Other people are not blamed or made to feel responsible for the speaker's reactions. As a result, the listeners have more freedom: they can listen, ask questions about the speaker's thoughts and reactions, and explain their own reactions and preferences. This increases the chances of exploring each other's ideas and reaching some degree of understanding in the relationship.

Practice

This section gives you the opportunity to practice the skill of expressing your feelings directly and responsibly.

I. The list below contains both irresponsible and responsible statements. Cross out those that are not responsible and circle those that are:

A. "No wonder my life is so miserable — you go out of your way to upset me!"
B. "When you reprimand me, I feel hurt and angry."
C. "When you seem displeased, I take that personally and think that you're displeased with me."
D. "I'm really touched and happy when you surprise me with a little gift."
E. "You're the reason I'm so mad and upset all the time. If you were a good wife and listened to me once in awhile, I wouldn't be so upset."
F. "It's because of you that I feel inferior all the time. You're always picking on me."

II. Below are pairs of statements. One expresses emotions responsibly; the other does not. Place a check to the left of the one that is responsible.

Directness, Honesty, and Responsibility

A. 1. ___HUSBAND: I'm really upset about what's going on at work. I keep reminding myself of how I feel treated unfairly.

2. ___HUSBAND: Everyone and everything is making me miserable.

B. 1. ___FRIEND: You really hurt my feelings when you didn't ask me to the party.

2. ___FRIEND: When you didn't invite me to the party, I felt very hurt.

C. 1. ___BOSS: When you come in and tell me what I'm doing wrong, I get angry.

2. ___BOSS: You're nothing but a troublemaker. You have the nerve to come in here and tell me what I do wrong.

D. 1. ___WIFE: You're attacking and criticizing me. Why do you always do that to me?

2. ___WIFE: When you tell me things like that, I feel attacked and criticized.

SKILL 4: HELPING OTHERS TO BE DIRECT, HONEST, AND RESPONSIBLE

The skills described in this chapter thus far are intended to help you become more effective in your communication and in your relationships. While the use of these principles is often beneficial to both persons in a given situation, it cannot guarantee that communication will be clear. No matter how "skilled" you become, remember that other people are not aware of the concepts that you now are practicing.

There will be times when you are clear about your purpose and intentions, and the other person is not. She or he may be giving mixed messages, criticizing you, or not stating his or her intentions. Problems like this occur in at least two situations.

1. You are saying and doing nothing. Someone gives you a mixed message or begins blaming and criticizing you.
2. You are clear about your purpose and are using your best skills. For some reason, the other person reacts defensively and negatively.

When either of these situations occurs, it is easy to become upset and to forget about the skills you have learned. It is easy to ignore purposes, consequences, and direct speaking. In fact, the immediate reaction is to counterattack and to use accusations, guilt inducements, and mixed messages of your own. As you know, these responses create confusion and upset. They often precipitate arguments and, in general, decrease the chances for understanding and satisfaction in the relationship.

When these difficult situations occur, it is helpful for you to know how to handle them and how to help others become honest, direct, and responsible. The following section presents three skills to use when the statements and actions of others are upsetting, indirect, unclear, or ineffective.

1. Checking your impressions of others' thoughts, preferences and feelings.
2. Noticing and handling the mixed messages of others: asking for clarification.
3. Responding to others.

Skill 4a: Checking Your Impressions with Others

So far, this chapter has emphasized ways for you to speak honestly, directly, and responsibly. The following skill is to be used when you are not clear about what the other person means. It can be used to encourage honesty, directness, and responsibility in others and, meanwhile, to maintain these qualities in your own communication.

This skill involves the following steps.

1. Do not assume to know the thinking, preferences, feelings or intentions of others.

Assumes	*Does Not Assume*
WIFE: I am really tired. I don't feel like cooking.	WIFE: I am really tired. I don't feel like cooking.
HUSBAND: Well, you're just lazy and you can forget about trying to get me to cook! (*assumes that the wife is lazy and is trying to get him to do the cooking*)	HUSBAND: I can understand that. I don't like chores when I'm tired either.

This step is one part of being honest with yourself. By avoiding assumptions, you are acknowledging that you have only an idea of what the other person is thinking, feeling, or intending to do.

Incorrect assumptions about each other's thoughts, feelings, preferences or intentions contribute to many misunderstandings among people. It is easy to think that you know what someone means, especially when the person is someone to whom you are close. These assumptions distract you from hearing and understanding what the other person is trying to do or say. In some instances, this first step is sufficient to keep communication clear. However, if you are still unaware about the other person's thinking or intentions, use step 2.

2. Tell other people that you are not sure what they mean:
   a. Ask them what they meant or what they were trying to do. Ask what they think, want, or feel. For example, "I'm not sure that I understand. What are you trying to say?" "I don't think that I'm clear about this. What do you want?" "I don't understand your reaction. What are your feelings about this?"
   b. Describe your impression of what they said or did and check to see if it is correct. (Remember to state that it is just an impression or idea. You do not know what is in their heads.) Explore ideas in a pleasant, interested, nonchallenging tone of voice. For example:

   BOSS: I wanted to talk with you about your performance on the job. If you worked harder, you could be one of our best men.

   EMPLOYEE: I'm not sure that I know what you mean. I have the impression that you are pleased with my work. Is that right?

   BOSS: Yes, I am very satisfied with your work. I think that with a bit more experience and effort on your part, you could be one of our best producers.

Frequently, people do not follow these guidelines. Instead of checking impressions or asking others about their thinking, people often do one of the following.

1. They assume to know what the other person means. For example, "I know why you said that! You're picking on my family again!"
2. They react to statements without checking out the other person's thinking, feelings, preferences, or intentions. For example, "All you do is criticize me!" "You're angry and upset." "I know what you want—you expect me to give in."

3. They check out impressions in a dishonest way. They accuse others or ask dishonest questions that contradict or challenge the other person. This can be done with words or by means of a challenging, accusing tone of voice. For example, "How could you be so nasty?" (This is not intended to seek information. It really says, "You're nasty.") "Just what do you think you're doing?" (This really says, "You don't have the right to do what you're doing.") "How do you expect to sell this to the public?" (This does not seek information. It implies, "I don't think you can sell this to the public.") "What do you mean?" (*in a cold, sharp tone*) (This says, "You are wrong," or "I don't like what I heard.")

These common errors elicit negative reactions from others. It is annoying and frustrating to be told what you feel, think, or are trying to do. If you do this to others, they probably will become resentful and defensive. Dishonest questions also elicit negative reactions from others, for they blame and accuse your listener. The only response to these questions is self-defense. In general, failing to check other people's thinking in an honest fashion will contribute to misunderstandings and frustrations in your relationships.

The skill presented in this section is intended to eliminate "mind-reading" and jumping to conclusions. When this skill is used, conversation is more likely to be an exchange and exploration of ideas between people. There is less defensiveness and misunderstanding, and the chances for clear, effective communication are increased. In general, the principle of checking the thinking of others works for the following reasons.

1. It does not assume to know the other person's thinking, feelings, preferences, or intentions.
2. It gives you the opportunity to express your impressions of what was said or done.
3. It gives others a chance to state their thinking and intentions and to correct any misconceptions that exist. As a result, the chances for effective communication are increased.

STEP 1: DO NOT ASSUME. The following examples demonstrate the first step in the checking process. They show the difference between statements that make and act upon assumptions and those that do not assume the other person's thoughts, preferences, feelings, or motives.

Directness, Honesty, and Responsibility

Assumes to Know the Other Person's Thoughts or Motives	*Does Not Assume to Know Thoughts or Motives*
HUSBAND: I'd like to have a party . . . WIFE: Oh no! You're not going to stick me with all that work to impress your business associates. You think women should love to be hostesses, but I don't. You take me for granted! HUSBAND: Wait a minute! You don't even know what I was going to say and you fly off the handle.	HUSBAND: I'd like to have a party this weekend. WIFE: What kind of party? HUSBAND: I was thinking of just having wine and cheese. It won't be much work, and I'll do most of it.
BOSS: I know that you are pretty lazy when it comes to reports, but we need them in . . . EMPLOYEE: Wait a minute! How do you know I'm lazy when it comes to reports? BOSS: Well, you don't like to do them. EMPLOYEE: That shows how much you know about me—nothing!	BOSS: We need all our reports in by July 1st, Tom. EMPLOYEE: OK. I'll get started on them.
HUSBAND: Boy, I sure do a lot of work around here! WIFE: (*assumes that he is complaining*) What do you mean? I do my share around here—all the cooking and cleaning. HUSBAND: What about all of the hours I spend in the yard?	HUSBAND: Boy, I sure do a lot of work around here! WIFE: Yes, I think you do.
LYNN: I'm not going to have any children. They would interfere with my career. RON: You really rebel against being female. But, I know you. Down deep you would love to have babies. You're just trying to be modern. LYNN: (*angrily*) How do you know?	LYNN: I'm not going to have any children. They would interfere with my career. RON: I guess I can understand that.

In the examples on the left, the speakers presume to know the ideas and intentions of the other persons. They speak and react on the basis of their interpretations and presumptions. These same presumptions prevent them from understanding what the other person is trying to do or say. The listeners respond to being told what they think, feel, want, or intend with frustration and impatience. These reactions lower their motivation to explain themselves or to correct the other person's presumptions. As a result, the chances for clear communication and some degree of understanding are significantly reduced.

In contrast, in the examples on the right, no assumptions are made about the other person's ideas or motives. As a result, the communication is straightforward, clear, and more effective.

STEP 2: ASK QUESTIONS. The following examples help to point out the difference between: (1) assuming to know the other person's thinking; (2) asking accusatory, dishonest questions; and (3) checking your impressions honestly, directly, and responsibly.

Presumes to Know the Thinking and Intentions of Others	*Asks Dishonest Questions*	*Checks Impressions: Asks the Other Person*
WIFE: I want to go back to work, but I know you! You think that women should stay home! You're so old-fashioned! HUSBAND: That's not true! You never asked me what I thought! Don't blame me if you're too lazy to go back to work.	WIFE: You don't want me to go back to work, do you? (*accuses, seeks confirmation of her idea*) HUSBAND: I never said that! WIFE: Oh, yes, you did!	WIFE: I want to go back to work, but I have the impression that you don't want me to leave the children with a sitter. Would you mind if I went back to work? HUSBAND: Well, if you'll be more content working, I'd be willing to give it a try.
BOSS: You never discuss your ideas with anyone. If that's how you want it, OK. But people who don't talk about ideas don't get very far! EMPLOYEE: That's fine with me!	BOSS: Have you ever been treated unfairly here? EMPLOYEE: Well, . . . no . . . BOSS: Then why don't you discuss your ideas with me? Do you have some sort of complex? What is your problem?	BOSS: You often come up with good suggestions, but lately it seems that you are reluctant to discuss any of your ideas with me. Is that right? EMPLOYEE: Yes. BOSS: I'd like to be informed of your new ideas and suggestions. Has something happened to discourage you from discussing your ideas?

Directness, Honesty, and Responsibility 53

PATIENT: I'm really worried! Why am I still having these symptoms?
PHYSICIAN: You're overly anxious about this! You'd better settle down. I'll give you some tranquilizers.

WIFE: I had such a bad day at work!
HUSBAND: Well, don't expect me to help you! That's something you have to handle on your own. I can't help it if you can't take it. Maybe you shouldn't be working.
WIFE: Why do I bother talking to you? I thought a husband gave you some support. All you give is criticism!

PATIENT: I'm really worried! Why am I still having these symptoms?
PHYSICIAN: Have you always been this anxious? Don't you think you'd like to see a psychiatrist?

WIFE: I had such a bad day at work!
HUSBAND: Just what do you expect me to do about it? Why can't you be like other women and take your job less seriously?
WIFE: Forget it. I don't even know why I talk to you.

PATIENT: I'm really worried! Why am I still having these symptoms?
PHYSICIAN: I don't understand what you want. My explanations don't seem to satisfy you. Please tell me what I can do.

WIFE: I had such a bad day at work!
HUSBAND: Is there something you want me to do?
WIFE: Well, I'd like you to listen to what happened for a few minutes . . . then I might like to go to a movie to get my mind off work.

In the examples on the left, the wife, boss, physician, and husband assume to know the other person's thinking and intentions. They inform the other people of their thinking and motives. Their listeners are annoyed and frustrated and react defensively. Communication is shut off.

Assumptions also are present in the middle examples. These statements are accusing and challenging but are disguised as questions. Because they are even more dishonest than straightforward accusations, they lead to more frustration and defensiveness on the part of the listener. Misunderstanding and confusion are increased.

In contrast, in the examples on the right, people are asked about their thoughts, feelings, preferences, and motives. Impressions are explained and checked in an honest fashion. Using this skill conveys a sense of interest and understanding to others. It indicates that you are willing to try to comprehend their point of view. This encourages others to restate what they meant. As a result, there is a better chance that you will explore others' ideas and thus have a better idea of what each of you thinks.

Remember: Nonverbal cues are important. When you check with others about their thinking, reactions, or motives, be sure to do it with pleasant, interested expressions and not in an accusing, challenging way. Asking about someone's intentions with harsh or angry nonverbal cues will seem negative, and the other person probably will react defensively.

Practice

This section provides practice in (1) avoiding assumptions of another's thinking, (2) helping others describe what they intend or want, and (3) checking your impressions of his or her thinking, preferences, feelings, or intentions.

I. The statements below represent good examples of the "checking-out" process. After each one, indicate if (1) it assumes to know other's thinking or intentions; (2) it asks the other person what he means or wants; or (3) it checks out impressions of thoughts, feelings, preferences, or intentions.

A. "To me, what you said sounded harsh and critical. Did you mean it that way?"
   1. Does this assume to know the other person's thinking or intentions?
   2. Does it relay an impression and check it out?
   3. What nonverbal cues should be used?

B. WIFE: I'd like to be in the city more often. I miss the excitement.
   HUSBAND: I'm not sure I know your thinking on this. I've wondered if you resent living here in a small town.
   WIFE: I don't resent it, but I would like to get to a big city every month.
   1. Does the husband's statement assume to know his wife's thinking?
   2. Does it ask the wife what she thinks or wants?
   3. Does it check out?
   4. What nonverbal cues should be used?

II. The section below contains groups of three statements. One statement in the group does one of two things: does not assume intentions, or checks out the other person's thinking. The remaining two statements contain assumptions and dishonest questions.

Place a check mark next to the statement that checks out the other person's intentions.

Directness, Honesty, and Responsibility 55

A. 1. ____You are always forcing me to like exactly what you like to do, like going to fairs and antique shows. I'd like to go to the art museum, but you'll never go with me!
   2. ____Don't you want to come to the art museum with me? Don't you care about what I like?
   3. ____I want to go to the art museum. I'd like you to come along.

B. HUSBAND: Please leave me alone right now. I'd rather not talk.
   1. ____WIFE: You don't care about what I did all day. You never listen to my problems, but you always want me to listen to you!
   2. ____WIFE: Okay . . .
   3. ____WIFE: How can you be so selfish? Don't you ever think that I might like to talk? Don't you ever think of anyone but yourself?

C. WIFE: I'd like to have a larger house.
   1. ____HUSBAND: I would, too.
   2. ____HUSBAND: Why are you always complaining about what I *haven't* given you? Don't you see how hard I work to make things nice for you?
   3. ____HUSBAND: There you go again! Always complaining and saying I haven't done enough to make you happy!

III. The statements below assume to know what the other person meant. Rewrite them so they check out impressions with the other person.

A. You don't care one bit about our finances. You never want to sit down and go over the budget with me. You must think that money grows on trees.
   Rewrite:

B. You have interrupted me three times in the last five minutes. If you're not interested in what I have to say, forget it. You're one of the most inconsiderate people I know!
   Rewrite:

IV. In each of the examples below, write a response that asks the other person about his or her thoughts, feelings, preferences, or intentions.

A. YOU: I'd like to talk about our vacation plans. Let's sit down and figure out where we want to go, when . . .

SPOUSE: I've had a rough day . . .
YOU:

B. BOSS: I've really had it with employees who don't work up to their potential.
YOU:

Skill 4b: Handling the Mixed Messages of Others: Asking for Clarification

From an earlier section in this chapter, you have some familiarity with mixed messages and you already have some practice in identifying and replacing them with clear, direct speaking. Using this skill does not guarantee the elimination of unclear messages in your relationships, for you often will be at the receiving end of mixed messages. Many people you encounter will not be aware that they are giving more than one message. Still others, more or less deliberately, use mixed messages to control and manipulate situations and people. This section builds upon the previous skill of checking assumptions and suggests some ways to help you handle mixed messages from others.

This skill of handling mixed messages from others involves the following steps.

1. Recognize a mixed message from another person. Sharpen your skills at identifying these.
2. Repeat to the other person the messages that you hear.
3. Ask the other person to clarify his or her message.

Here is how you might combine these three steps.

WIFE: I hear you say that you want me to be independent, and, in the same sentence, I hear you ask me why I want my own car. I am confused. What are you trying to say?

Whenever you feel confused or frustrated or whenever you wonder what the other person means, let this be a cue to check for mixed messages and ask for clarification.

Using this approach gives other people the opportunity to clarify their thinking to you. It encourages them to become aware of their purpose and how they are coming across. With people who deliberately use mixed messages, you must repeatedly ask for clarification. If they are trying to control or manipulate you, your response probably will not change their intention. Using this skill cannot protect you against power-hungry, domineering persons, but your familiarity with mixed messages will help you to become more aware of manipulations. In this way, you can let others know that you can identify their controlling techniques.

Instead of asking for clarification of mixed messages, people frequently do one of two things.

1. They become confused or frustrated by the message and wonder what the other person means. Rather than attempting to find out, they avoid a confrontation and remain unclear.
2. If people are uncomfortable with being confused, they usually choose one part of the mixed message and decide that this is the "real" message. If they choose the negative section of the message, their reaction is one of upset and defensiveness. On the other hand, if they select the positive aspect of the message and the actions that they expect are not forthcoming, they react with feelings of bitterness, disappointment, and betrayal.

Whatever alternative they choose, the issue becomes a problem in the relationship. Neither approach leads to understanding and satisfaction in the relationship.

This skill of asking for clarification works for the following reasons.

1. It informs other people of the multiple messages that they are giving. As a result of this, their self-awareness is increased and they have the opportunity to examine their purposes and clarify their intentions.
2. Using this skill diminishes the chances for confusion, frustration, and defensiveness on the part of the listener. It increases the chances for effective communication and some degree of understanding.
3. If other people are trying to control you, this skill can let them know that you recognize the multiple messages and expect some clarification.

Remember: it is important that you use this skill in an honest, considerate fashion. Do not use it in an accusatory, blaming way by saying, for example, "There you go—giving another mixed message!

You must really be a manipulator!" Instead, express how the multiple messages are coming across to you. For example, "One day I hear you saying that *I* am Tom's supervisor and the next day I hear you saying that he is to report to *you*. I cannot act unless I know which is your real intention." If necessary, you can be firm and persistent. Ask for clarification until you are certain of what the other person means.

Your tone of voice and facial expressions are also important. Avoid a challenging or accusatory tone of voice and a blaming look and posture (e.g., hands on hips, pointing finger at other person).

The following examples demonstrate the difference between not asking for clarification of multiple, competing messages and doing so.

Does Not Ask for Clarification of Mixed Messages	*Asks for Clarification of Mixed Messages*
HUSBAND: Let's go to the movies with the Smiths tonight.	HUSBAND: Let's go to the movies with the Smiths tonight.
WIFE: The Smiths?! You know how much I dislike Lisa, . . . (*sighs*) . . . but I'll go (*in a negative, whining tone of voice*) if you want to.	WIFE: The Smiths?! You know how much I dislike Lisa, . . . (*sighs*) . . . but I'll go (*in a negative, whining tone of voice*) if you want me to.
HUSBAND: (*thinks that she doesn't like the Smiths but avoids the issue*)	HUSBAND: Wait a minute. I hear a couple of things. You don't like Lisa but you'll go out with them if I say so. Does that mean you will resent it or that you will blame me if you have a bad time?
WIFE: (*harbors resentment; everytime they go out with the Smiths she thinks, "I told him what I think of Lisa and how much I dislike going out with them, yet he continues to ask me to do things with them"; she holds this inside; later it becomes part of an argument about how he does not understand her*)	WIFE: Well . . . yes, I will resent it. I would go out with them to please you, but I would resent it.
	HUSBAND: Well, I didn't know that. I don't want you to be with people you don't like when it's not necessary. Let's go with Bill and Cathy. You like them, right?

Discussion: On the left, the wife expresses both her dislike and her willingness to spend an evening with Lisa. Her husband hears this mixed message but thinks that avoiding the issue is best. As this continues, going out with the Smiths becomes a point of contention in the relationship.

In contrast, on the right, he asks for clarification of her message. It brings the resentment issue into the open and gives the wife the oppor-

Directness, Honesty, and Responsibility

tunity to clarify her intentions. As a result, the issue is resolved and the chances for mutual understanding are increased.

Situation: A disagreement has occurred.

Does Not Ask for Clarification of Mixed Messages	*Asks for Clarification of Mixed Messages*
RON: Of course, I still want to be friends with you. (*does not telephone or ask Bruce to go for coffee or to play tennis*)	RON: Of course, I still want to be friends with you. (*does not telephone or ask Bruce to go for coffee or to play tennis*)
BRUCE: (*decides that Ron no longer wants to be friends and confronts him one day*) Look, if you want to end our friendship, say so! Don't give me this business about wanting to be friends and then you don't phone for a month! What kind of fool do you think I am anyway?	BRUCE: Look, I thought you said that you wanted to be friends, but you haven't phoned and we haven't done anything together for a month. What is it?
RON: I don't know what you're talking about. I've been too busy to call.	RON: Well, I'm still annoyed. I've been waiting for you to make an overture or an apology or something.
BRUCE: I know better than that. Do you think I'm that stupid?	

Discussion: In the example on the left, Bruce jumps to a conclusion about Ron's intentions and makes an interpretation of his behavior. Misunderstanding, defensiveness, and mutual dissatisfaction are increased.

In contrast, on the right, Bruce asks for clarification. Ron begins to sort out his feelings and there is a greater chance for understanding and clear communication.

This example below was selected to show you that mixed messages do not always occur in the same statement or even within the same day. In this situation, the boss gave the employee one message a while ago and then contradicted that statement days later. This illustrates a common occurrence — a delayed mixed message.

Does Not Ask For Clarification of Mixed Messages	*Asks for Clarification of Mixed Messages*
BOSS: Why can't you write more reports? I give you the freedom to set up your own work schedule and I give you a secretary and still there is not the number of reports I want!	BOSS: Why can't you write more reports? I give you the freedom to set up your own work schedule and I give you a secretary and still there is not the number of reports I want!

PAT: "Oh no, you're not going to trick me with one of your mixed messages again. I've caught on to your manipulations and I'm not falling for that again.
BOSS: I don't know what you're talking about.
PAT: Don't play naive with me.
BOSS: I'm not going to sit here and listen to accusations.

PAT: You did not tell me that you had a fixed number of reports you wanted. I'm hearing two conflicting things. One, that I'm free to set up my own schedule. But then you have some fixed expectations that you don't tell me about, so I'm really not free. Will you clear this up?
BOSS: I do have some expectations of you.
PAT: I'd like to know what they are. And I'd also like some clarification of how much freedom I have.

Discussion: In the example on the left, Pat identifies the mixed message but uses it to accuse the boss of manipulation. If the boss is deliberately controlling Pat, this provides an easy cop-out. The boss easily can focus on his accusation and, in this way, can avoid clarifying the mixed message. If, on the other hand, the boss is unaware of giving a mixed message, this accusatory style invites defensiveness in place of clarification and resolution. An unpleasant situation occurs, and the chances for clear communication are lessened.

In contrast, on the right, Pat clearly and firmly asks for clarification. When the boss tries to hedge, Pat reiterates the conflicting message and asks for some resolution. If the boss is being deliberately manipulative, the request for clarification communicates that Pat has "seen through" the boss' device. While this may not end the manipulation and control, it is more likely to convince the boss that some clarification is needed. If the boss is unaware of giving a double message, Pat's reaction increases the boss' self-awareness and encourages some clarification of the multiple messages.

In general, in the examples on the left, the mixed message is handled in a way that does not clarify the issue. Whether it is avoided, whether a conclusion is drawn, or whether the listener uses the concept of mixed messages in a blaming way, the results are similar. If the issue is avoided, one of the two people is confused or resentful. On the other hand, if a mixed message is interpreted or used as an accusation, the listener becomes defensive. The situation deteriorates, and the chances for communication and understanding are decreased.

Directness, Honesty, and Responsibility

In contrast, in the examples on the right, some clarification of the mixed message is achieved. The chances for clear communication and resolution of the issue are increased.

Practice

The following section provides an opportunity to practice the skill of handling mixed messages.

I. The first step in handling a mixed message is to recognize it for what it is. Listed below are statements and actions. Some of these are mixed messages, while others are not.

Place a check next to those that are mixed messages.

A. ____You and your spouse invite another couple to go on a weekend trip. They say, "Oh, sure, we'd love to go," but their expressions and tone of voice sound unenthusiastic.

B. ____A boss tells the employees that he is annoyed with some of the lax behavior that he has seen. He says that it must stop. He sounds angry and firm.

C. ____A close friend tells you that you are the best friend that she has ever had and that your friendship means a great deal to her. Shortly after this, she acts somewhat distant and aloof, turns down lunch invitations, and, when she talks with you, engages in superficial, "phony" chatter.

D. ____Your neighbor says that you are welcome over for coffee any time. Whenever you drop by, she seems friendly and glad to see you.

E. ____Your spouse says that he or she really looks forward to spending time alone with you on the weekend. When the weekend comes, he or she spends most of the time on household chores.

F. ____A mother says to her daughter, "You have to work hard and get ahead, make something of yourself." When the daughter has some successes and speaks of her accomplishments, the mother says, "Don't brag. That's not ladylike. And, besides, you haven't done that much, so don't talk foolishly."

II. The examples below describe mixed messages. Following these are pairs of responses. Check the one that asks for clarification of the double message.

62   A WAY WITH WORDS

A. *Situation:* You have approached your boss about a raise.
BOSS: We are pleased with your work, but we can't give you a raise.
YOU: Why not? Bob just got a raise.
BOSS: Well, he has three kids and his wife doesn't work. You and your wife together make good money.

   1. ___YOU: What does that have to do with anything? That is totally illogical.

   2. ___YOU: I'm hearing several things at once. Do my raises depend on my spouse's salary and not on the quality of my work?

B. *Situation:* Beverly has just graduated from law school and is excited about her new job. Her mother says, "Well, it's all very fine that you're a lawyer and all. But just don't get too excited and involved in your work. You have to start a family sometime. After all, you haven't really accomplished anything until you have a child."

   1. ___BEVERLY: I hear you saying that law school is an accomplishment, but, at the same time, you're acting as if it's nothing. Which do you mean?

   2. ___BEVERLY: That's a real put-down! Just because you had children and are jealous because you didn't go to law school, don't take it out on me!

Skill 4c: Responding to Others

So far, you have learned how to check your impressions of others, how to ask about purposes and intentions, and how to ask for clarification. This section shows you how to apply the skills that you have learned throughout the chapter in everyday situations. The examples in this section focus on what to do when other people are not being direct, honest, or responsible in their words or actions.

The skill of responding to others in ways that will increase their honesty, directness, and responsibility involves the following.

1. Be familiar with the principles discussed in this chapter. Be able to recognize when someone is being indirect or irresponsible. Do not blame them, but be sure to notice it. This can help you to identify manipulations and handle them effectively.
2. People can be dishonest, indirect, or irresponsible in one of these ways: they may blame or accuse you, they may praise you falsely or try to induce guilt, or they may try to control or manipulate you with mixed messages. When someone who matters to you

does this, remind yourself about your purpose and check the consequences of what you want to say or do. As difficult as it may be, do not let the other person distract you from your purpose or from using the skills and principles that you have learned.
3. When relationships are important to you, try to encourage the other people involved to communicate more effectively. You can do this by using the skills discussed in this section.
   a. Ask about the other person's purpose or intention.
   b. Express your reactions and feelings.
   c. Check the other person's thoughts, preferences, feelings, and motives.
   d. Ask for clarification.

This section will provide examples of how to handle two kinds of situations.
1. You are saying or doing nothing, and the other person gives a mixed message or attacks, criticizes, or blames you.
2. You approach the other person with a purpose in mind and use the skills described in this chapter. He or she reacts negatively.

WHEN SOMEONE CRITICIZES, BLAMES OR ACCUSES YOU. When this happens, it is easy for anyone to be surprised and to react defensively. Reacting defensively may have some short-term benefits: the other person may be surprised or intimidated, he or she may give up or withdraw, and you may have protected yourself for the moment. In fact, this may be the effect that you want when you are involved with competitors or rivals. On the other hand, defensiveness also promotes misunderstanding, conflict, and dissatisfaction. None of these qualities are particularly desirable in close relationships, so you should consider both the costs and benefits of being defensive.

Instead of being defensive and self-protective, you can decide to promote clear communication and understanding. This has long-term benefits to the relationship and can be accomplished by encouraging the other person to be direct, honest, and responsible.

The first step is to decide upon the quality of the relationship and the significance of the issue to you. You must decide whether you want the self-protection or the long-term benefits of clear communication and understanding. Decide how much the person or the issue matters to you. If the relationship is important to you, be sure to consider the costs of defensiveness and the benefits of clear communication.

In order to encourage clear communication and some degree of mutual understanding, use these guidelines.

1. Recognize what has happened.
   a. You have been accused, blamed, or criticized.
   b. The other person has tried to make you feel guilty, upset, angry.
   c. The other person has given you a mixed message.
   d. You do not know what the other person intended.
2. Decide on your purpose.
   a. Do you want to start an argument or misunderstanding?
   b. Do you want to keep communication clear?
   c. Do you want more information?
   d. Do you want to maintain the relationship?
   e. Do you want to solve a problem?
3. Ask the other person about what has occurred.
   a. Check your perceptions of his or her thoughts, feelings, preferences, and intentions.
   b. Express your reaction.
   c. Ask for clarification.

As an example, the following conversation might occur.

SPOUSE: You made all those New Year's resolutions about being cheerful and optimistic. And here it is—you didn't get the promotion you wanted and you go off the deep end and make my life miserable!

YOU: (*deciding that your purpose is to keep communication clear*) How did I make your life miserable? (*asks for clarification*)

SPOUSE: Well, last night you said that you were disgusted!

YOU: I said I was disgusted, but I didn't mean for you to think that I went off the "deep end." I do feel disappointed, but that's it. I thought I had done a good job of not bothering you with my disappointment. (*explains your feelings and reactions*)

SPOUSE: You weren't bothering me . . . I just figured that you were upset. Actually, you have kept your resolution of trying to be more optimistic . . . I was expecting you to be more upset.

YOU: (*calmly*) Well, I am not upset. When you comment as you did,

Directness, Honesty, and Responsibility 65

I get discouraged — like you don't appreciate the effort I've made to be optimistic and cheerful. (*expresses feelings and reactions*) I don't know if you wanted me to feel that way or what. (*checks spouse's intentions*)

SPOUSE: Oh no. I want to encourage you.

In contrast to this example, the immediate reaction would be to involve defensiveness and counterattack.

YOU: (*angrily*) What are you talking about? I have been cheerful and optimistic no thanks to you! All you ever do is complain and criticize . . . you would drive anyone crazy!

Notice the difference between these two responses. With the latter approach, an argument is under way. Even if the disagreement is short-lived, accusations and insults are exchanged and the words and the issue may become a sore spot in the relationship.

In contrast, using this skill has the following long-term advantages.

1. It keeps you clear about what has happened. As a result, you are better able to respond effectively to attacks, criticisms, guilt inducements, etc.
2. It reminds you of your purpose in the situation and in the relationship. You are not distracted by the negative statements or actions of others.
3. It encourages others to express and to clarify their thoughts, reactions, and intentions.
4. It eliminates some of the defensiveness on both sides and increases the chances for clear communication and understanding.

The examples below show the difference between not encouraging others to be direct, honest, and responsible versus doing so.

Situation: Married daughter telephones mother.

Not Encouraging Directness, Honesty, and Responsibility	*Encourages Directness, Honesty, and Responsibility*
DAUGHTER: Wayne and I are hoping that you and Dad are not going to buy lots of Christmas gifts this year. This is so childish and so extravagant! You should be saving your money for retirement.	DAUGHTER: Wayne and I are hoping that you and Dad are not going to buy lots of Christmas gifts this year. This is so childish and so extravagant! You should be saving your money for retirement.

MOTHER: We can buy as many gifts as we like — and we can do whatever we want with our money! Besides, when we get old, it's your obligation to take care of us.
DAUGHTER: Oh, no it's not.
MOTHER: (*sharply*) That's what I thought! You are quite a daughter. Is this all the thanks I get for all the sacrificing I did?
DAUGHTER: (*frustrated and upset*) You see, I can't even talk to you! I don't know why I even bother to call!

MOTHER: (*checking her impression*) Are you saying that you don't want us to buy you and Wayne gifts this year?
DAUGHTER: That's exactly what I'm saying! It's too extravagant.
MOTHER: (*expressing her reactions*) "Extravagant" sounds pretty critical to me.
DAUGHTER: I don't want to criticize you . . .
MOTHER: What is it you want to do?
DAUGHTER: I just want to convince you to stop this big gift exchange. Wayne and I can't afford buying things like the rest of you can.
MOTHER: OK, I can understand that.

Discussion: In the conversation on the left, the mother reacts defensively to the daughter's criticism and responds by trying to induce guilt. The daughter feels uncomfortable and frustrated, and the situation deteriorates into misunderstanding.

In contrast, on the right, the mother does not react impulsively. She checks her impressions of what her daughter said, expresses her reaction, and checks the daughter's intention. There is some degree of resolution, and the chances for clear communication and understanding are increased.

Situation: Bob and Nancy are two young attorneys who work together.

Does Not Encourage Honesty, Directness, or Responsibility

BOB: (*frustrated*) Nancy, do you have to dress so stylishly all the time? We are attorneys here. You're due in court today, and you come in here looking like something from a fashion magazine. It detracts from your competence and professionalism.

Encourages Honesty, Directness, and Responsibility

BOB: (*frustrated*) Nancy, do you have to dress so stylishly all the time? We are attorneys here. You're due in court today, and you come in here looking like something from a fashion magazine. It detracts from your competence and professionalism.

Directness, Honesty, and Responsibility

NANCY: That shows how unperceptive you are! I didn't ask for your opinion and I don't want to hear it. You're nothing but a male chauvinist pig, and how I dress is none of your business.

BOB: Yes, it is my business. You represent this law firm, and I don't think you're aware of how you come across.

NANCY: I am well aware of it. (*she is angry and upset; as a result of this encounter, she avoids Bob.*)

NANCY: Are you saying that you want me to dress differently when I go to court? (*checking impressions*)

BOB: Not just in court . . . all the time. Everyone notices how attractive you are and they don't notice your competence.

NANCY: I feel hurt and put down, Bob . . . like you're criticizing me. I'm also very angry. I am an adult and I can judge how to dress. (*expresses reactions*) Was that the reaction you expected me to have? Did you want me to feel angry and hurt? (*checks intention*)

BOB: No, I really meant it for your own good! I would like people to realize that you are a competent attorney and not just a clothes horse.

NANCY: I can accept that; in your opinion, it detracts from my competence. I appreciate your good intentions, but I still want to dress as I do.

Discussion: In the example on the left, Nancy reacts by calling Bob names. He counters with another accusation ("You don't represent this law firm well"), and the situation becomes progressively uncomfortable. Misunderstanding between the two people increases, and the motivation to interact with each other decreases.

In contrast, on the right, Nancy controls the immediate defensiveness that she might experience in response to Bob's remarks. Judging that her relationship with Bob is of some importance, she gives a considered response. She tries to understand what he means and what he is trying to accomplish. Each comes away with a better idea of what the other thinks and feels.

In general, in the examples on the left, defensive responses increase confusion, discomfort, and misunderstanding in the relationship. They lessen the chances for effective communication and some degree of understanding.

In contrast, in the examples on the right, both the mother and Nancy promote understanding by expressing reactions and by checking impressions and intentions. As a result, communication is kept open and each person is able to comprehend some of the thoughts and feelings of the other. The chances of achieving some degree of resolution and mutual satisfaction are increased.

WHEN THE OTHER PERSON REACTS NEGATIVELY TO YOUR PURPOSE. This section discusses situations in which you decide on your purpose, check consequences, and use the skills described in this chapter, but the other person responds negatively. When this happens, it is easy for anyone to feel surprised, defensive, frustrated and thwarted; it is easy to lose sight of what you wanted to accomplish. As we discussed in the previous section, there are advantages and disadvantages to being defensive. Similarly, there are long-term gains and short-term sacrifices involved in working toward effective communication and understanding. Again, decide how important the relationship is to you and weigh the costs and benefits of defensiveness versus understanding. When you want to encourage clear communication, use the following guidelines.

1. Remind yourself of your original purpose.
2. Clarify your intention and restate it to the other person.
3. Ask the other person about what has occurred.
   a. Check your perceptions of his or her thoughts, feelings, intentions.
   b. Express your reactions.
   c. Ask for clarification.

For example, You call your boss to tell him of some scheduling difficulties and he reacts defensively.

YOU: I want to keep you informed about the latest happenings with Dave Jones and myself. We're to have that project completed by the next board of directors meeting, and he has not yet kept one of our appointments. I'm getting pretty frustrated.

BOSS: Well, it's up to you to pin him down.

YOU: I am not Dave's boss and I don't think that's my responsibility. I want you to speak to him.

BOSS: (*angrily*) I get tired of your dumping things on this desk.

YOU: I am not trying to be difficult. I am trying to follow your

Directness, Honesty, and Responsibility 69

instructions. You have told me that, with co-workers, I am not to play supervisor. Besides, I don't think Dave would listen to me. Do you think that is unreasonable?
BOSS: No. But my assigning Dave to that project has been a sore spot with you, and I figured you were getting back at me.
YOU: I am not trying to get back at you, but I do want this situation cleared up.

This decreases some defensiveness and keeps the communication open. As a result, the chances for some degree of understanding and resolution are increased.

Instead of handling the situation in this way, the immediate reaction would be to meet defensiveness with defensiveness and say, "I am dumping things on your desk because your desk is right where this belongs—you're the one to blame for assigning Dave to this project." This second response only would invite more defensiveness and upset from the boss. The situation would rapidly deteriorate into a very uncomfortable one.

In general, encouraging directness, honesty, and responsibility in others has the following advantages.

1. It keeps you clear about your purpose and helps you handle negative reactions from others.
2. It eliminates some of the defensiveness and keeps communication open.
3. It encourages others to express their ideas and to clarify what they said or did.
4. It increases the chances for some degree of mutual understanding.

The following examples show the difference between reacting defensively and encouraging directness, honesty, and responsibility.

Situation: Co-workers are trying to arrange some procedural changes in the office.

Reacting Defensively: Does Not Encourage Directness, Honesty, and Responsibility	*Encourages Directness, Honesty, and Responsibility*
BILL: I want to make this as easy as possible for both of us.	BILL: I want to make this as easy as possible for both of us.

TOM: (*sarcastically*) Sure you do! You make it easy for yourself.
BILL: (*angrily*) Where does it say that you know what I want to do? You are one of the most obnoxious and presumptuous people I know.
TOM: See? You're going to sit there and call me names — and that's how you make things easy for me?
BILL: After your response, you bet — that's the last time I ever try to be nice to you!

TOM: (*sarcastically*) Sure you do! You make it easy for yourself.
BILL: I don't understand, Tom. I don't want to give you a bad time. (*restates intention*)
TOM: No, but what you said sounded too nice. I figured it was phony.
BILL: I meant what I said and I usually don't say things to be phony. (*restates intention*) I want us to get along, but I don't like being accused of being phony. (*restates intention and expresses reaction*)
TOM: I can understand that.

Discussion: In the example on the left, Bill reacts defensively to Tom's assumption and accusation. That increases Tom's defensiveness and the situation deteriorates into an argument. Nothing is resolved; in fact, misunderstanding has been created and the chances for a cooperative relationship are lessened.

In contrast, in the example on the right, Bill does not react defensively. By checking impressions and restating intentions, the chances for achieving some degree of cooperation and understanding are increased.

Situation: Mrs. Thomas hears from a neighbor that her husband has invited the neighbors over for a cookout on Sunday. Mrs. Thomas knew nothing of these plans. She decides to discuss this calmly and rationally with her husband.

Reacts Defensively: Does Not Encourage Directness, Honesty, and Responsibility

WIFE: I was surprised by something Sue said today. But, first, let me check this out. Sue said that you've invited the neighbors over Sunday for a cookout. Is that right?

Encourages Directness, Honesty, and Responsibility

WIFE: I was surprised by something Sue said today. But, first, let me check this out. Sue said that you've invited the neighbors over Sunday for a cookout. Is that right?

Directness, Honesty, and Responsibility

HUSBAND: (*angrily*) Of course, it's right! You were sitting right here when we decided it. Don't act as if you're surprised—and don't accuse me of doing something without your knowledge!
WIFE: I don't remember it that way. We discussed the possibility of a cookout, but we didn't make a definite decision . . . and not for this Sunday. This Sunday is the boys' little league championship.
HUSBAND: Oh no! You're not going to lay the blame for this on me! You had your chance to speak up when we were discussing this—but you didn't. You never mentioned the boys' game.
WIFE: Well, your memory must be shot from all the beer you drink. You can just plan on doing the cooking and serving while I go to the boys' game!

HUSBAND: (*angrily*) Of course, it's right! You were sitting right here when we decided it. Don't act as if you're surprised—and don't accuse me of doing something without your knowledge.
WIFE: I am not accusing you, and I didn't want to make you angry. (*restates intention*) I don't remember making a definite decision for a cookout this Sunday.
HUSBAND: Well, we did.
WIFE: Look, I am not trying to give you a bad time. I just want to know if the neighbors are coming over so that we can plan a different day. (*restates intentions*)
HUSBAND: I invited them because I thought we had agreed. I forgot about the boys' game.

Discussion: In the example on the left, the wife reacts defensively and an argument follows. The husband holds more rigidly to his view of the situation, and the wife becomes more frustrated. Stronger and stronger accusations are leveled, and the situation becomes a problem instead of solving one.

In contrast, on the right, the wife restates intentions in a nondefensive way. This encourages the husband to be more direct and responsible, and some resolution and understanding are achieved.

In general, in the examples on the left, the defensive reactions of Bill and the wife add to the atmosphere of conflict and discomfort. Arguments occur, communication is shut off, and the chances for resolution and understanding are markedly decreased.

In contrast, on the right, defensiveness is decreased while directness is encouraged. Communication is kept open and the two people are better able to exchange ideas and reactions. The chances for mutual understanding and satisfaction are greatly increased.

Practice

This section provides practice in the skill of responding to others.

I. A number of situations are described below. After each situation are several possible responses.

Place a check to the left of the one that seems most effective.

A. *Situation:* Your boss frequently asks dishonest questions when he wants information. He calls you into his office.

1. BOSS: I've been thinking about promoting Jane Wilson to a position in your department. What do you think about that?

a. ____YOU: Well, I'm not sure what you're asking. Have you decided to promote Jane and now are wondering how I will react?

b. ____YOU: Well, she's a good worker, but a lot of guys don't like her.

2. BOSS: You're pretty sensitive about women getting promotions around here. Why do you feel that they are such a threat to you?

a. ____YOU: I do not feel that they are a threat, and I am not sensitive about it, either.

b. ____YOU: I heard you express the assumption that I am sensitive about women getting promotions. What happened to lead you to that conclusion?

B. *Situation:* You and your spouse enjoy different summer recreational activities. You enjoy tennis and your spouse prefers golf. You are expressing your ideas about golf and tennis, and you say, "Golf just takes too long for me. I just can't enjoy myself. I'd like us to play some sport together, but I can't make it golf."

1. SPOUSE: (*defensively*) You've never even tried golf more than twice—so how do you know you don't like it?

a. ____YOU: Wait a minute. You seem upset, we were just talking about golf and tennis and then what happened?

b. ____YOU: What do you mean I've never tried golf? You're the one who won't get near a tennis court with me.

2. SPOUSE: You could enjoy golf if you wanted to. You just don't want to!

a. ____YOU: Maybe that's right—I don't want to play golf, but does it seem that I do that just to upset you?

b. ____YOU: That's right . . .
SPOUSE: That's being stubborn . . . why can't you do what I like once in awhile?

Directness, Honesty, and Responsibility 73

SPOUSE: Yes . . . I figure that you know how much I enjoy golf and you never make an effort to play with me.
YOU: I didn't realize that it was so important to you.
YOU: That goes both ways.
SPOUSE: Forget it. I'm going in the other room for some peace and quiet.

C. *Situation:* Your in-laws frequently criticize how you and your spouse handle the children. Your in-laws come to dinner. Because it is a long, elaborate dinner, you excuse the children after the main dish.

1. MOTHER-IN-LAW: We really shouldn't let them leave the table. We haven't had our dessert or coffee. They can learn to sit still. Besides, they didn't even finish what was on their plates. You two let them be very wasteful!
You decide that you don't want her to upset your dinner.

a. ___YOU: Let's not hear any more lectures on how to raise children.
b. ___YOU: I'm sure that's how you see it. (*quietly, trying to avoid trouble*)

2. MOTHER-IN-LAW: I'm just trying to give you some advice. If you're not careful and strict with them now, you'll have some very undisciplined children! I never let my children leave the table until they had eaten every crumb.
You decide that you want to tell her that you do not want advice. At the same time, however, you do not want her to feel hurt or angry and you do not want to start an argument.

a. ___YOU: Look, I am going to be honest. We appreciate your good intentions, but we don't want advice. We want to raise the kids our way. If we make mistakes, we make them.
b. ___YOU: Oh, that must be why all your kids have weight problems. I'd rather that our kids be skinny.

3. MOTHER-IN-LAW: (*huffily*) Well, that's that. I don't have to put up with this, you know. Come on, George, we're leaving—I am not going to sit here and take this!

a. ___YOU: Good!
b. ___YOU: I don't understand why you are so upset.

4. MOTHER-IN-LAW: You are both unappreciative and rude. I never heard of anyone speaking to an elder in that way!

a. ____YOU: Well, welcome to the modern world.

b. ____YOU: I didn't mean for you to be upset, but I also want you to know that we don't want advice.

II. Here are some situations where you can use most of the skills that you learned in this chapter. Answer the questions as you go along.

A. *Situation:* You are frustrated because one of your co-workers will not listen to your suggestions. You decide that you want to tell your spouse about it. You do not want any advice, but you do want to talk about it.

1. You decide that your purpose is to let your spouse know about your frustrations and to get some understanding and support. You say, "I want you to understand how frustrated I am at work. I would like a little sympathy and support for what I put up with . . . that clown, Roy, still doesn't want to hear any suggestions I make. I get myself very upset by that."

Despite your use of the skills and the clearness of your purpose, your spouse replies, "Well, I know what you're doing wrong. When you get wrapped up in your ideas, that's all that you think about. You probably are not even polite to Roy. Sometimes you're a bit naive. You need to learn how to soften people up. Act a little more sociable and pleasant. You don't bother, and that's why you don't get ahead."

What is your purpose now? (Check the one that you think would be most effective. Before you decide, be sure to check the consequences of your purpose.)

a. ____Criticize your spouse because he or she responded in this way.
b. ____Complain that your spouse does not understand you.
c. ____Act angrily because it seemed that your spouse criticized you.
d. ____Ask for some understanding and support, not advice.
e. ____Blame your spouse because you now feel more frustrated than ever.

2. Which would you do? (Check those that seem most effective. There are three acceptable responses.)

a. ____Forget it (say nothing).
b. ____Assume you know why s/he responded that way. ("As usual, you think you have the answer for everything.")

c. ____Check intentions. ("Were you trying to be helpful?")
d. ____Criticize him or her. ("That is the worst possible thing that you could've said.")
e. ____Restate your intention. ("I want some support and understanding. At the moment, I'm not ready for advice. I'm still having trouble with my own frustration.")
f. ____Complain. ("Now I feel worse than ever.")
g. ____Express your reactions. ("When you said that I'm naive, I felt criticized and misunderstood.")

B. *Situation:* Your boss calls you to his office. With no preparation, he says angrily, "Just because I gave you permission for educational leave, I now have requests from three other employees. I told you to keep it quiet and what do you do? Did you tell everyone? I thought you were more discreet than that. Thanks to you, I now have a mess on my hands."

In fact, you told no one, but word always gets out. You feel that you have been accused unfairly. Decide on your purpose. Be sure to check the consequences.

1. Check the action that you think would be most effective.
a. ____Tell him off.
b. ____Get away until he recovers from his bad mood.
c. ____Accept the blame.
d. ____Refuse to accept the blame.
e. ____Defend yourself.
f. ____Explain that you understand his frustration, but inform him of the facts.

2. What would you do or say? Check those that seem most effective.
a. ____Sit quietly; say nothing.
b. ____State your intentions and your limits. ("I will not accept the blame for something that I did not do. I told no one about the educational leave. I prefer that you check the facts before you come to conclusions and make accusations.")
c. ____Criticize the boss. ("If you're so ridiculous as to make accusations like this without checking them, then you shouldn't be a boss.")
d. ____Assume to know why he said that. ("Just because you're frustrated, don't take it out on me.")

SUMMARY

In order to be direct, honest, and responsible in your communication, follow these general principles.

1. *Purpose*
   a. Decide what your purposes are.
   b. Of these, what is it that you most want to accomplish?
   c. Be sure that you have only one purpose.
2. *Consequences*
   a. Consider the consequences of your purpose. Determine what effect it will have on the other person and on the relationship.
   b. If the effect will be in opposition to what you wanted to accomplish, let this be a cue to you to reconsider your purpose.
3. *Mixed Messages*
   Prime times for giving "mixed messages" are:
   a. When you are unclear about what you want.
   b. When you have hidden motives.
   c. When you are trying to control a person or a situation.
   d. When you are emotionally involved.

In any of these situations, check on your purposes and be alert for any contradictory messages that you may be giving. Confusion or defensiveness on the part of the listener is another possible sign of mixed messages. Learn to watch your listeners' reactions and also use these as cues to check on the message that you are giving. The checking process involves the following.

   a. Ask yourself what messages you are giving with your words and actions. If you are unclear, ask the other person what it seems that you are saying.
   b. Check your purposes. Try to accomplish only one at a time.
4. *Express Purpose*
   Tell your listener what your intentions are. For example, "I'd like some advice from you on how to handle this." "I want some reassurance that I look OK."
5. *Directness and Responsibility*
   This involves two parts.
   a. State your thoughts, feelings, preferences, and intentions as your own. For example, say, "I think . . . ," "I want . . . ," or "I feel . . ."

Directness, Honesty, and Responsibility

    b. Avoid speaking in disguised terms, avoid inducing guilt or trying in other ways to manipulate the person. For example, say, "I want to go out to dinner. Will you take me?" (Instead of, "The kids drove me crazy and I'm so exhausted. I can't possibly fix dinner.")

6. *Check Your Impressions*
   This involves three steps.
   a. Do not assume to know the other people's thoughts, intentions, feelings, or preferences.
   b. Ask others what they mean or what they are trying to do. Ask what they think, want, or feel.
   c. Describe your impression of what they said or did and check to see if it is correct. For example, "I'm not clear about what you're trying to say. It seems that you're displeased with my work here. Is that right? Remember to ask honest questions and to do so in a pleasant, nonchallenging tone of voice.

7. *Asking for Clarification*
   When you feel confused or frustrated, when you wonder what the other person means, this is a cue to check for mixed messages. To do this, (1) repeat the messages that you heard and (2) ask the other person for clarification. For example:
       WIFE: I hear you say that you want me to be independent and, at the same time, you want to know why I want my own car. I get confused. What are you trying to say?"
   This encourages others to clarify their purposes and their thinking.

8. *When Others React Negatively*
   You can expect others to react negatively from time to time. They will give mixed messages and will accuse, blame, criticize, or otherwise try to manipulate you. When this happens, you have the choice of being defensive or trying to promote clear communication. In these situations, weigh the costs and benefits of each choice.

   When you decide against defensiveness and are in favor of promoting clear communication, follow one or more of these suggestions.
   a. Ask about the other person's purpose or intention.
   b. Express your reactions or feelings responsibly.

c. Check the other person's thoughts, preferences, intentions, or feelings; do not assume to know what they are.
  d. Ask for clarification.

REVIEW

This section provides an opportunity to review and practice all the skills learned in this chapter.

Considering Consequences

I. Below are some purposes and possible statements. Some of the statements or actions would be effective in achieving your purpose; others would not. After each one, answer the questions about how the listener might react and decide if it meets your purpose.

A. *Situation:* You are having guests for dinner and there is much work to do around the house.

What you want to accomplish: To persuade your spouse to help you with some chores.

Purpose: Ask spouse for help. ("I'd really appreciate it if you could help clean the house.")
  1. How is your spouse likely to react? How would you feel? (Underline one or more.)

     upset   attacked   criticized
     asked for help   accused of being lazy
  2. How is your spouse likely to behave? (Underline one or more.)

     criticize you   walk away angrily
     he or she will help with the chores   ignore you
  3. Do you want these consequences? (Circle one.)

     Yes   No
  4. Will this accomplish what you want?

     Yes   No

B. *Situation:* You are a supervisor on a job. You set some clear rules for people under you to follow. Two new people began to work under you. They do not follow your rules and they went to your boss to complain. Your boss told them that they did not have to follow these rules and told you to try to be more lenient and understanding of them. You feel that your authority was undermined.

What you want to accomplish: To find out if your boss intended to undermine your authority and give you a bad time.

Directness, Honesty, and Responsibility 79

Purpose: Explain to your boss that you are upset and feel that you were not supported. Ask for clarification of the situation. ("I am upset about this situation, but I don't know what you were trying to accomplish with these new people. I feel that you didn't support me, but maybe you had something else in mind. I'd like you to explain your thinking to me.")

1. How is your boss likely to feel? (Underline any that apply.)
   criticized   disrespected   told off   respected
   asked to explain his thinking   angry   attacked
   aware that you're upset

2. How is your boss likely to behave? (Underline any that apply.)
   criticize you   fire you   try to find out why you're upset
   explain his thinking   walk away   cry
   tell you he doesn't have to explain his thinking to you

3. Do you want these consequences? (Circle one.)
   Yes   No

4. Will this accomplish your purpose?
   Yes   No

II. Each of the examples below describes a situation and purpose in speaking. Beneath each purpose are some statements or actions. One of these is effective in achieving your purpose; the other is not. Check the effective one.

A. Your friend says, "I'm discouraged, nothing seems to be going well. I'm getting tired of my job and I don't like this town."

Purpose: To show interest and concern—let him know you're on his side.

1. ____You laugh and joke around; tell him to look at the bright side of things; point out all the good things about his job; tell him how you love your job.

2. ____You tell him you're sorry that he's discouraged and ask him if there's anything that you can do to help.

3. ____You tell him that he's feeling sorry for himself and that he's immature.

B. *Situation:* Your sister-in-law frequently interrupts you when you are talking and puts down what you say. When you talk about things that are important to you, she seems to change the subject. You just mentioned to the family that you are interested in starting your own business. She says sarcastically, "Oh come on, let's talk about something serious."

Purpose: To let your sister-in-law know how you feel; to let her know your limits.

1. ____YOU: Look . . . I don't like it when you put down my ideas; I won't put up with it. I'd like to get along with you, but I find it hard when you talk like that.	2. ____YOU: (*say nothing, ignore her remarks silently; endure her comments; when she leaves, yell at your spouse instead*)	3. ____YOU: I'll talk about something serious—your obnoxious personality! No wonder you're still not married at your age.

C. *Situation:* A man and woman work together. They are discussing women's rights. He says, "I'm tired of hearing that women are discriminated against. When they are, it is because they are incompetent! I'm tired of hearing how rough it is for them! Men have it rough, too."

Purpose: The woman wants to express the thought that women have some difficulties to contend with that men do not.

1. ____WOMAN: In no way do I think that men have it easy, but I do think that each group has its own unique difficulties. Women have some difficulties that men do not. Would you be willing to listen to some of my ideas?	2. ____WOMAN: Men don't have it as rough as women do! You're blind to the whole situation! And you don't care to see it from the woman's side! But, then, what else could one expect from you?	3. ____WOMAN: You men are all the same! (*walks away angrily*)

D. *Situation:* A husband feels that his wife doesn't appreciate how hard he works both at home and on the job.

Purpose: To persuade her to express some appreciation.

1. ____HUSBAND: Can't you see that I'm fed up around here? I get no word of thanks or appreciation. You are one of the most inconsiderate, selfish people I know. And, one of the laziest! Who does nearly all the work around here, anyway?	2. ____HUSBAND: (*says nothing; keeps it all inside; blows up every few months*)	3. ____HUSBAND: I'd like you to tell me that you appreciate how hard I work. And, I'd like it if I got some thanks for the work I do around the house, too.

E. *Situation:* A married daughter is visiting her mother. The daughter says, "This has been a busy, tough month. I've really been having challenges to face at work. I'm worn out, but I think the worst is over."

Mother's Purpose: To be supportive.

| 1. ____MOTHER: Maybe you aren't doing the right thing at work. You never did know how to get along with people. If you'd make an effort to get along better with your boss, you'd do better. | 2. ____MOTHER: Well, I'm sure you're doing a good job. I'm glad the worst is over. | 3. ____MOTHER: The important thing is, when are you and Bob going to start a family? Then you won't have to work! By the way, Sue Myers just had her second little boy—she's way ahead of you! |

Decide on Your Purpose

Each of the examples below describes a situation and possible purposes that you may have. Imagine that you are in the situation; then do the following.

1. Check any of the listed purposes that you might want to accomplish, if you were in the situation.
2. Decide what you want to accomplish most and write it in the space provided below.
3. Consider the consequences of your purpose. Be certain that it will accomplish what you want in the relationship. If it would appear to accomplish something that you do not want, decide on a different purpose.

A. *Situation:* Your spouse surprised you with a gift. It is a book that she or he thought that you wanted. Although the author's name is similar, it is not the book that you said you would like to have. What do you say? (This is, of course, dependent on what you want to accomplish.)
   1. ____Complain. ("You never listen carefully to what I say! If you had listened, you would have bought the right book!")
   2. ____Point out that this is not the book you wanted. ("This isn't the book I want. I'll exchange it.")
   3. ____Let him or her know that you appreciate the thoughtful gesture. ("Thank you. I appreciate your thoughtfulness.")

4. ___Tell him or her to stop surprising you with gifts. ("Don't buy me something if you're not sure that I want it. Don't do it anymore.")

Which of the ones checked do you want to accomplish most? Write it below.

B. *Situation:* You had an unpleasant and tiring day at work. When you get home, your spouse begins telling you about his or her day. What do you want to accomplish?
   1. ___Express your preference. ("I'd like to be quiet for awhile. Let's talk in an hour.")
   2. ___Act angrily. ("Shut up! I don't want to hear about your day!")
   3. ___Blame him or her for your bad mood. ("I had a rotten day and I was just getting over it. All I needed was for you to start complaining. Now I'm really in a bad mood!")
   4. ___Make him or her feel guilty. ("If you were a good husband/wife, you'd be able to tell when I had a bad day and you wouldn't start yapping at me.")
   5. ___Get some sympathy and reassurance. ("I'd like you to understand that I had a very bad day. Please be sympathetic and reassuring.")
   6. ___End the relationship. ("I can't take it. I'm leaving.")
   7. ___Criticize. ("All you ever do is think of yourself! You are so selfish!")
   8. ___Arrange for some solitude. ("I want to be alone for awhile. I'm going upstairs.")

Which of the ones that you checked do you want to accomplish most? Write it below.

Expressing Intentions

I. The following examples contain pairs of statements. One of them expresses the speaker's intention; the other does not. In each case, check the one that includes an expression of intention.

A. 1. ___FRIEND: Do you want to go out for coffee?

Directness, Honesty, and Responsibility

  2. ___FRIEND: I'd like to talk about something. Do you have time to talk?

B. 1. ___WIFE: We're disagreeing a lot about disciplining the children and I want us to get along better. Can we please sit down and see if we can reach an agreement?

  2. ___WIFE: All we're doing is disagreeing about the children and I don't know what to do!

C. 1. ___BOSS: I want to know why production seems low. This is not criticism of you. Tell me what you think is causing the delays for you.

  2. ___BOSS: Why is your productivity so low?

D. 1. ___HUSBAND: Why don't you wear your blue dress tonight?

  2. ___HUSBAND: I'm just making a suggestion. I like the way you look in your blue dress and I'd like it if you wore that tonight.

E. 1. ___WIFE: I'd like you to reassure me that it's OK that I bought those three new outfits.

  2. ___WIFE: I feel bad that I bought those new outfits, but I needed clothes.

II. Below are listed some purposes in speaking. In the right-hand column are statements that express intentions.

 1. Draw a line from the intention to the appropriate statement.
 2. Underline the part that expresses the intention.

Intention	Statement
A. To tell your friend your limits.	1. "I want to know what you think of my work. Is there anything that you are dissatisfied with?"
B. To persuade your spouse to be more affectionate.	2. "I want to check my impression. Are you angry with me?"
C. To tell employees about new policies.	3. "I would like you to be more affectionate. I really like it when you put your arm around me."
D. To find out what your boss thinks of your work.	
E. To let your spouse know that you want to settle your differences.	4. "I want to explain some policies to you. I don't want to hear complaints today. Please save those for next week."
F. To find out if you and a co-worker can get along better.	5. "I'd like some information. I prefer that we get along on the job. Is that what you would want?"
G. To check an impression.	

6. "You are my friend, but I want to tell you my limits on this. I cannot afford to go out to dinner at some of the places you choose."

7. "I want to stop arguing and work this out. I like for us to get along and I am willing to compromise."

III. The examples below do not express intentions. Rewrite each one so that it tells the person the speaker's intention.

A. YOU: (*in a critical tone of voice*) You have a sore throat and you're smoking a cigarette?
Purpose: To persuade a friend to stop smoking.
Rewrite: "This is just a suggestion . . ."

B. HUSBAND: Do you want to water the flowers while I mow the lawn?
WIFE: Don't ask me if I want to water the flowers! No, I don't want to!
Husband's purpose: To ask his wife if she will water the flowers.
Rewrite: "I want to make a request. Will you please . . ."

Expressing Ideas and Preferences Directly

The examples below contain pairs of statements. One of them expresses the speaker's ideas directly; the other does not. Check the one that is direct and expresses the speaker's ideas.

A. 1. ___"You never think of me! You are so selfish!"
   2. ___"I'd like you to consider my feelings."
B. 1. ___KAREN: Let's plan a day of shopping next week.
        MARCIA: I'm already over my budget, so I can't go.
   2. ___KAREN: Let's plan a day of shopping next week.
        MARCIA: Well . . . I don't know . . . Tom doesn't like it when I go shopping with you.
C. 1. ___HUSBAND: I'd like to move.
        WIFE: I am not interested in moving. I prefer living right where we are.

Directness, Honesty, and Responsibility 85

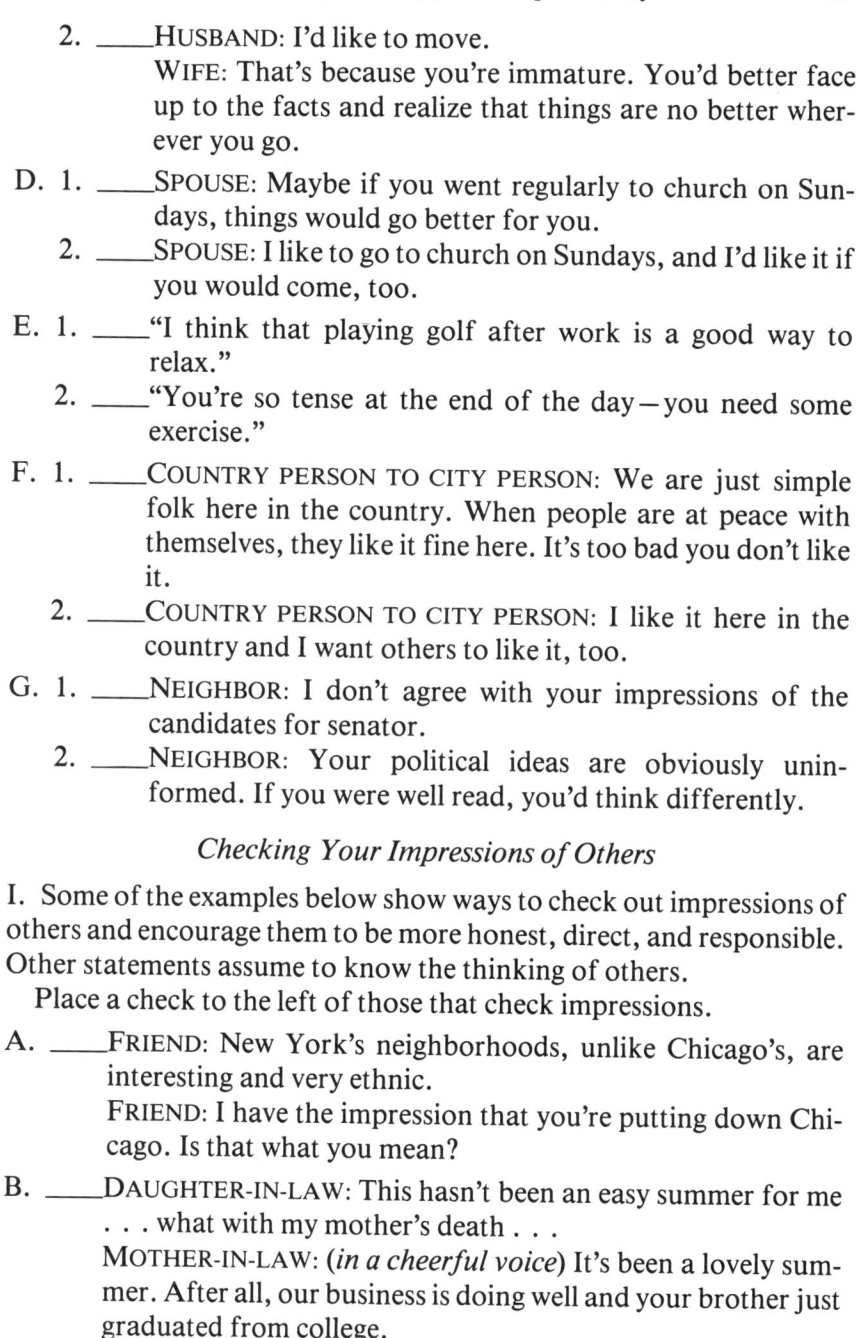

    2. ____HUSBAND: I'd like to move.
         WIFE: That's because you're immature. You'd better face up to the facts and realize that things are no better wherever you go.

D. 1. ____SPOUSE: Maybe if you went regularly to church on Sundays, things would go better for you.
    2. ____SPOUSE: I like to go to church on Sundays, and I'd like it if you would come, too.

E. 1. ____"I think that playing golf after work is a good way to relax."
    2. ____"You're so tense at the end of the day—you need some exercise."

F. 1. ____COUNTRY PERSON TO CITY PERSON: We are just simple folk here in the country. When people are at peace with themselves, they like it fine here. It's too bad you don't like it.
    2. ____COUNTRY PERSON TO CITY PERSON: I like it here in the country and I want others to like it, too.

G. 1. ____NEIGHBOR: I don't agree with your impressions of the candidates for senator.
    2. ____NEIGHBOR: Your political ideas are obviously uninformed. If you were well read, you'd think differently.

Checking Your Impressions of Others

I. Some of the examples below show ways to check out impressions of others and encourage them to be more honest, direct, and responsible. Other statements assume to know the thinking of others.
  Place a check to the left of those that check impressions.

A. ____FRIEND: New York's neighborhoods, unlike Chicago's, are interesting and very ethnic.
    FRIEND: I have the impression that you're putting down Chicago. Is that what you mean?

B. ____DAUGHTER-IN-LAW: This hasn't been an easy summer for me . . . what with my mother's death . . .
    MOTHER-IN-LAW: (*in a cheerful voice*) It's been a lovely summer. After all, our business is doing well and your brother just graduated from college.

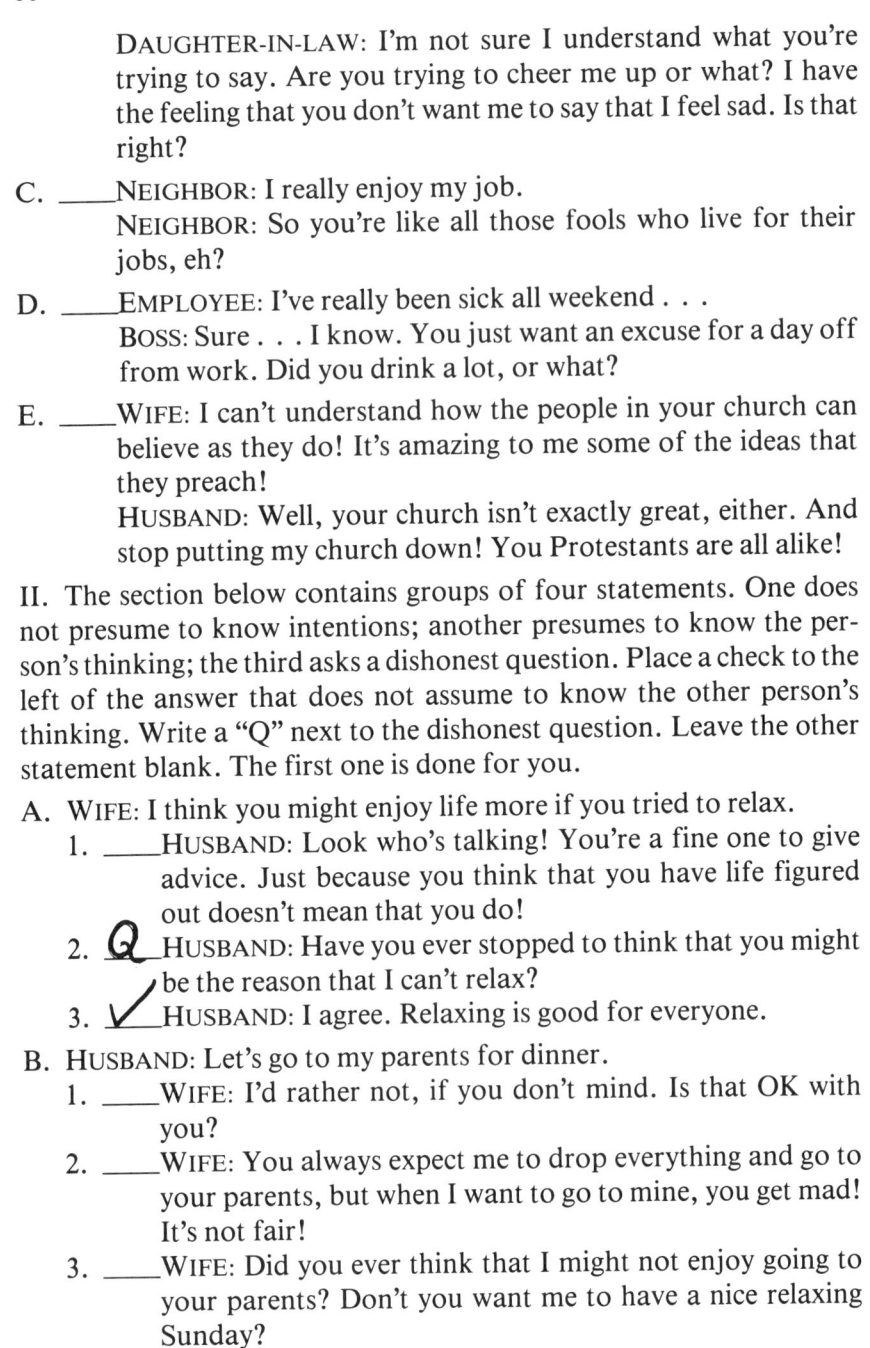

DAUGHTER-IN-LAW: I'm not sure I understand what you're trying to say. Are you trying to cheer me up or what? I have the feeling that you don't want me to say that I feel sad. Is that right?

C. ____NEIGHBOR: I really enjoy my job.
NEIGHBOR: So you're like all those fools who live for their jobs, eh?

D. ____EMPLOYEE: I've really been sick all weekend . . .
BOSS: Sure . . . I know. You just want an excuse for a day off from work. Did you drink a lot, or what?

E. ____WIFE: I can't understand how the people in your church can believe as they do! It's amazing to me some of the ideas that they preach!
HUSBAND: Well, your church isn't exactly great, either. And stop putting my church down! You Protestants are all alike!

II. The section below contains groups of four statements. One does not presume to know intentions; another presumes to know the person's thinking; the third asks a dishonest question. Place a check to the left of the answer that does not assume to know the other person's thinking. Write a "Q" next to the dishonest question. Leave the other statement blank. The first one is done for you.

A. WIFE: I think you might enjoy life more if you tried to relax.
  1. ____HUSBAND: Look who's talking! You're a fine one to give advice. Just because you think that you have life figured out doesn't mean that you do!
  2. *Q* HUSBAND: Have you ever stopped to think that you might be the reason that I can't relax?
  3. ✓ HUSBAND: I agree. Relaxing is good for everyone.

B. HUSBAND: Let's go to my parents for dinner.
  1. ____WIFE: I'd rather not, if you don't mind. Is that OK with you?
  2. ____WIFE: You always expect me to drop everything and go to your parents, but when I want to go to mine, you get mad! It's not fair!
  3. ____WIFE: Did you ever think that I might not enjoy going to your parents? Don't you want me to have a nice relaxing Sunday?

Directness, Honesty, and Responsibility

C. BOSS: John is really doing a good job for us. I think that he is one of our best men.
(This has two appropriate responses; check both.)
1. ____EMPLOYEE: I think he's doing OK.
2. ____EMPLOYEE: I'm not sure I know what you mean. Are you comparing him to me or saying that I'm not doing as well as I should?
3. ____EMPLOYEE: There you go, criticizing me as usual! You can't expect me to produce more if you keep putting me down.
4. ____EMPLOYEE: (*in an angry tone*) Just what do you mean by that? If you must criticize me, why don't you come out and say it?

D. WIFE: I wish you hadn't been transferred to Boston. I like it here.
1. ____HUSBAND: I'm really glad that I was transferred to Boston! Can't you feel the same way I do and stop feeling sorry for yourself?
2. ____HUSBAND: Yes, I know you like it here.
3. ____HUSBAND: I should've known that you'd find something to complain about, as usual. I can never get any support from you! All I can count on you for is unhappiness.

E. CO-WORKER: We seem to be disagreeing a lot. I'd like to straighten this out.
(There are two appropriate answers to this; check both.)
1. ____CO-WORKER: (*in a challenging tone*) What do you think is the cause of our disagreements?
2. ____CO-WORKER: To you, straightening it out means you want me to do it your way! That's all it means!
3. ____CO-WORKER: I don't know what to do to straighten it out. Do you have some suggestions? If you do, I'd like to hear them."
4. ____CO-WORKER: I'm not quite cooled off enough to straighten things out today. But I appreciate your effort. Let's talk tomorrow.

F. WIFE: I'd like to talk with you about my plans to go back to work.
1. ____HUSBAND: Let me watch the news and then we'll talk.
2. ____HUSBAND: We talked yesterday! Wasn't that enough talk-

ing for awhile? Can't I have just one night to rest and watch TV?

3. ____HUSBAND: There you go—interrupting me. You just can't stand to see me relaxing. You like to bother me.

Application of Skills

The following section gives you an opportunity to combine all the skills discussed in the chapter on honesty and directness.

I. Read the situation below and then follow the directions listed beneath it.

Situation: A friend comes to you to say he's discouraged about the difficulties he's having with a few co-workers.

What should you say or do? Read each of the purposes and statements and decide how you would react if someone said this to you. You can choose one or more of the following words or phrases or add some of your own. Write these in the third column next to each statement below:

frustrated	willing to talk to you	hurt
trusting	encouraged	criticized
angry	misunderstood	put down

Purpose	Statement	How the Person May Feel
A. Point out what he does wrong and how he can improve.	"You're too pushy. If you'd be nice, you'd do better."	
B. Complain.	"You always have something to be unhappy about."	
C. Cheer him up by denying his experience.	"Oh, come on, it's not so bad. You're just exaggerating."	
D. Be supportive: ask him what you can do to help.	"How can I help?"	
E. Assume he has another problem.	"How much does this have to do with the fact that you didn't get a raise?"	

II. This example is for you just to read. Below is a conversation. On the left, most of the statements are dishonest, indirect, or irresponsi-

Directness, Honesty, and Responsibility 89

ble; these are circled and labelled. In the column on the right are more effective statements. Scan this just to see the differences.

Statements		Rewrite
HUSBAND: (at 3:00 A.M.) The baby's crying; don't you think you'd better see what she wants?	DISHONEST QUESTION	The baby's crying. Will you please take care of her?
WIFE: I have gotten up with her for the last six weeks! When is it your turn?	GUILT INDUCEMENT / DISHONEST QUESTION	I want to stay in bed. Will you take care of her?
HUSBAND: I have to go to work in the morning! Your job isn't like mine—I have to be on my toes. Besides, you're the one who wanted a baby!	BLAMING	I don't want to, either.
WIFE: That's not true. I wanted a baby, but so did you. You were the one who kept saying that kids were wonderful! When are you going to start doing your share and start learning to take care of her?	GUILT INDUCEMENT / DISHONEST QUESTION	I'd like you to share some of the responsibilities, like getting up at night.
HUSBAND: Why should I? Besides, if you were a good wife, you would want to do this for me. Besides, women are much better at taking care of babies than men are. She won't stop crying for me.	DISHONEST QUESTION / GUILT INDUCEMENT / FALSE PRAISE	I don't want to get up tonight. We'll discuss sharing responsibilities tomorrow.
WIFE: You could take care of her as well as I can. You just don't want to. You just expect me to do all the work!	ASSUMES OTHER'S MOTIVES	I resent having to get up.
HUSBAND: What kind of mother are you? How can you stand to hear her	DISHONEST QUESTION / GUILT INDUCEMENT	I want her to stop crying.

cry like that — just so you can give me a bad time? **ACCUSATION**

Sometimes I wonder how feminine you are. Any other woman would have been up by now. **GUILT INDUCEMENT**

WIFE: Oh, shut up. I'll get up tonight, but you'll be sorry. I'm not going to forget this! From now on, you can do things for yourself! **THREAT**

I'll get up tonight but I am going to tell you my limits on this. I am not going to continue to do everything for the baby plus do all the housework and cooking plus have a full-time job. We will have to work something else out. If you can't help, we'll have to hire someone to do some of these things.

III. This section contains conversations. Underline the statements that are effective and demonstrate use of the skills that we have learned. Put brackets around dishonest, indirect, or irresponsible statements. The first conversation is done for you.

A. BOSS: I want to know what you think of this idea — what if we scheduled our weekly meetings for Friday? Is that a problem for you?
EMPLOYEE: Well, Friday is usually my day on the road. Let me think about it and I'll get back to you. (*one hour later*) I thought about it and looked over my schedule — there's no way that I could fit in a two-hour meeting on Friday. I'd like it to stay on Wednesday.
BOSS: (*coldly*) Well, no one else objected to Friday and the meetings were already set up, so Friday it is. You don't have any serious objections then, do you?
EMPLOYEE: I'm frustrated and angry and I'll tell you why. If you want to change rules, then say so. But I don't like it when you ask me my opinion and then tell me everything was all settled before you asked me.

B. HUSBAND: Why can't you be like Bill's wife? She has children, is a good cook, and still is going to the junior college to take courses in

interior decorating. But you — you're always tired or unhappy and you never do anything exciting. Why can't you do anything on your own? Ever since you've had kids, you've been in a rut. How can you expect me to still find you interesting and attractive?
WIFE: I did these things because I thought that's what you wanted! Four years ago I wanted to go to school and you said, "No." And I had kids because I thought you wanted them . . . I wanted to please you . . .
HUSBAND: You're right . . . but my ideas have changed. I don't want a wife who cares only about the house and kids, is sloppy, buys old-lady-looking clothes, and is boring. I want you to lose weight, buy new clothes, and pay attention to me, not the kids. I'd also like it if you did something independent . . . get a career, do something — you're an intelligent woman, but you're getting damn boring.
WIFE: How can I be independent when you have the car, the money, the status? I really don't understand you. Five years ago, when we were married, you couldn't wait until I quit my job. You complained about the meals we ate out. You kept saying, "If you'd be content to stay home we'd have a good life." Then you started saying that you'd like to have a family. So I quit my job, baked apple pies and cookies, and had two kids — and now that's not what you want! Now, I'm fat and boring. What is it? Are you having an affair with Bill's wife?
HUSBAND: No, but I'll leave you if you don't start changing! Wait a minute — I don't want this mess. I don't want us to be upset with each other. I want us to get along. I just want you to stop this housewife-mother routine you're in. Can we sit down and decide on some changes?

C. WIFE: I want to decide on some new ways of doing things around the house. Now that I have a job, I won't want to cook and clean. I want to hire someone to clean and we will have to eat out a lot. Will you go along with that?
HUSBAND: I don't like to eat out. I like your cooking.
WIFE: I know, but I'm in no mood to cook when I come home . . .
HUSBAND: You're taking your job too seriously. You work too hard! You come home and work on reports all the time. No wonder you're so tense. I don't care about the cooking so much for me

. . . but for your own good I think you should not take your job so seriously. It's good for you to cook and forget about work.

WIFE: I want to forget about work and be like you — sit down and read the paper and have someone else fix dinner!

HUSBAND: Well, don't think I'm going to fix dinner!

WIFE: I didn't mean that. We can eat out or buy things already prepared.

HUSBAND: I don't like to eat out.

WIFE: I don't see any other way. Do you have a suggestion?

HUSBAND: Why can't you cook like you always have? Maybe if you got better organized and cooked on weekends . . . or left work at five o'clock instead of six.

WIFE: I can't leave at five o'clock, and I don't want to cook on weekends. You certainly are self-centered. All you're thinking about is you, not me!

HUSBAND: If you really cared about me, you'd like to cook for me. You know I love good food . . .

WIFE: Look, I've cooked for seven years, and I have done all the housecleaning. Now I'm stopping.

HUSBAND: Well, I figured you'd bring that up. I've done all that yard work and house repair for seven years. What if I said, "No more"? Are you going to do it for the next several years?

WIFE: We'll hire someone to do the yard work. I agree that, if you're tired, you don't have to do that work.

HUSBAND: You just ruined my whole evening by bringing this up. Now I'm in bad mood.

WIFE: I'm going ahead with my plans.

HUSBAND: My stomach is getting upset. Do you want me to get over my ulcer or not?

WIFE: Do you want me to collapse from overwork? Or maybe you don't want my $20,000 a year salary! You can't have both, you know. If I cook, then I can't keep that job.

HUSBAND: Yes, you could — if you were better organized and less tense about everything. You're just a nervous wreck about this job. Everything used to be so peaceful here and you used to be so happy. I can't be happy when you're not happy.

WIFE: I will be happy when I hire someone to cook and clean.

HUSBAND: Just what do you really care about — making me happy or getting ahead in your career?

WIFE: Both.

HUSBAND: Well, you can't have both. You'd better decide, and, I tell you, if your career is more important to you, then maybe you're the kind of woman who never should've gotten married.

WIFE: At least not to you. There are other men who like professional wives and don't want to be babied. Your whole problem is that your mother spoiled you rotten and you still expect the world to revolve around you. But I'm tired of playing your mother. You'd better straighten your thinking out.

HUSBAND: You're driving me crazy! I'm going to need a psychiatrist and it's all because of you.

CHAPTER TWO

Using Nonverbal Cues Effectively

николаевич ONVERBAL CUES ARE THOSE aspects of communication that do not involve words. This includes facial expressions, eye contact, gestures, tone of voice, and body posture. What you communicate nonverbally to others can clarify or contradict what you say, and it shapes the other person's understanding of what you are trying to accomplish. This chapter will describe nonverbal cues and why they are important. It will give you some practice in observing nonverbal cues in yourself and in others and will explain how to use nonverbal cues to communicate effectively.

SKILL 1: LEARNING ABOUT NONVERBAL CUES: WHY THEY ARE IMPORTANT

When you talk with people, they see and hear more than just the words you say. They notice your tone of voice, your facial expressions, the gestures you make; they notice your posture, movements, and your general appearance. These are nonverbal cues, and they shape the other person's understanding of what you mean. These nonverbal cues reflect your attitudes and feelings about yourself, the situation, and the other person. For these reasons, nonverbal cues are very important in communication. The best way for me to demonstrate the importance and the effects of nonverbal cues is to use videotape. As a matter of fact, this is exactly what I do with clients in order to make them aware of how they come across to other people and to show them what changes, if any, they need to make in their nonverbal communication. Since I cannot show you how you come across, I wrote this chapter to at least make you aware of nonverbal cues. By reading and thinking about nonverbal cues, you will notice them more in yourself and in others. When you begin to notice them and become aware of their impact, you can begin improving the effectiveness of your nonverbal communication.

Researchers of nonverbal communication have found that bodily cues communicate how much you like someone and how responsive or involved you are with that person. Nonverbal cues also can show whether you agree or disagree with someone and what your power or status is in the situation. For an example, look at figures 2.1 and 2.2. Imagine that you are speaking to each of the persons pictured. Which one seems to have a positive reaction to you? Which one seems to feel negative about you or what you are saying?

Figure 2.1   Figure 2.2

The person in figure 2.2, of course, seems to be positive and is showing this by his smile, gaze, and the way he is leaning toward you. In contrast, the person in figure 2.1 is looking to the side, leaning away, and has a look of displeasure on his face. In general, when you like someone, you lean toward and look at him or her and your facial expression is pleasant. When you dislike or disagree with someone, you show this by an unpleasant facial expression and by leaning away or turning your body away from him or her. You also may avoid looking at this person and, instead, may gaze at something or someone else in the room.

Body movements and activity mean something, too. Look at figures 2.3 and 2.4. Which of these people seems interested and involved? Which one seems bored or indifferent? The person in figure 2.3 seems involved and interested. He communicates this by his movement and gestures. In contrast, the person in figure 2.4 seems unresponsive and uninvolved in what is happening. It would seem that what is going on is not having much of an effect on him. In general, when you nod, gesture, change your expressions, or make some movement, you seem involved, responsive, and interested in the person or in the situation. If you sit or stand immobilized and your face and expressions do not change, you do not seem to care, you appear uninterested, uninvolved, and unresponsive.

To recognize more of what nonverbal cues can communicate, look at figures 2.5 and 2.6. Which of the people pictured seems to have more power or control?

The person in figure 2.5 conveys more power and control by her relaxed, casual stance, while the person in figure 2.6 communicates lower power by her rigidity and body tension. In general, when you sit or stand in a relaxed and casual way, you seem assured, self-confident, and in control. The more rigid and tense you seem, the less sense of control, power, or status you seem to have.

How you stand or sit in relation to someone also communicates something. Which of the two persons in figure 2.7 seems to like the other more? Which seems more involved? How can you tell?

The person on the right seems involved and interested because he is turned toward and is leaning toward the other person. In contrast, the person on the left has turned her body away from the other and is leaning away as well. It seems as if she wishes to avoid this interaction. In general, standing close, facing, and leaning toward a person communicates liking while distance, turning away, and leaning away communicates dislike.

Voice quality also is important. Your tone of voice, your inflection, and emphasis all help to shape the listener's interpretation of your words. If you were to say something in a pleasant tone and then say the

Figure 2.3

Figure 2.4

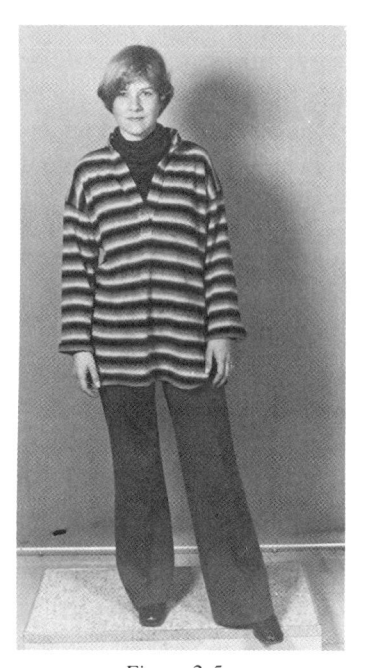

Figure 2.5

Figure 2.6

Using Nonverbal Cues Effectively 99

Figure 2.7

same sentence in an angry tone of voice, you would get two different reactions from your listeners.

To summarize, you communicate a lot by how you look and how you sound. Some expressions, movements, and body positions communicate positive attitudes or reactions. They seem to convey interest, liking, and approval. These cues include:

- Smiling.
- Nodding.
- Looking at the person.
- Pleasant facial expression.
- Turning your face toward person.
- Turning your body toward person.
- Leaning forward toward the person.
- Using a pleasant tone of voice.
- Moving, changing expressions, using gestures.

On the other hand, some nonverbal cues communicate negative attitudes or reactions. Theys seem to convey dislike, disapproval, or disinterest. These negative cues include the following.

- Not looking at the person with whom you are speaking.
- Unpleasant facial expressions: frowns, glares, scowls.
- Showing no facial expressions at all.
- Turning your face away from someone.
- Turning your body away from someone.
- Using an unpleasant, sharp, or angry tone of voice.
- Sitting or standing motionless.

All of these nonverbal cues affect relationships and interactions between people. Positive nonverbal cues encourage people to approach you or interact with you, while negative ones are discouraging and turn people off. The problem for many people is that they do not realize that they are giving any negative cues. They are not aware of the frequent scowls on their faces. They do not know about their harsh tone of voice, their rigid postures, or their lack of responsiveness. It is important for you to become aware of the kinds of cues that you are giving. Try to picture the impression that you are creating. Since all people like to be responded to, practice giving positive nonverbal cues that show your interest, attention, and involvement.

Another important aspect of communication is consistency. This involves matching your words, your intentions, and your body cues so that they all give the same message. For example, if you are trying to be friendly and warm, your words should be pleasant and your voice tone, facial expressions, and body should convey interest and liking. These consistent verbal and nonverbal cues enhance each other and contribute to clear understanding. If, in contrast, your words are positive (e.g., "Tell me all about your trip. I really want to hear about it.") but you are staring at the floor, your tone of voice reflects boredom, and you are fidgeting and tapping your foot, this communication is inconsistent. The other person is faced with contradictory messages from you—you are interested; you are not interested. Research has shown that, in instances like these, your nonverbal cues will be interpreted as the "real" message. In fact, it has been shown that people look most to your facial expressions and vocal cues to determine your motives and to interpret what your words mean (Mehrabian, 1972). More than likely, in the example above, your neighbor would focus on the negative, nonverbal cues that you are giving and would ignore your positive verbal message. Because people rely on nonverbal cues to determine meaning, it is essential that you communicate the same thing with your words, your face, tone of voice, and other "body language." This will be explained in more detail later in the chapter.

In general, it is important to remember that communication is not just what you say but how you say it and how you look and sound when you say it.

Now that you have had a general introduction to nonverbal communication, we will discuss some cues mentioned above in more detail.

Eye Contact

Eye contact means looking at people directly and meeting their gaze. How long and how frequently you look at people, together with the way that you look at them, has a great impact on communication. "Good" eye contact means that you look at the other person appropriately, frequently, and for short periods of time. This does not mean that you stare or glare, nor do you hold their gaze for a prolonged period. Prolonged eye contact may be appropriate for lovers, but, in less intimate relationships, it is intrusive and too familiar. Eye contact is a good thing, but do not overdo it.

Look at figures 2.8 and 2.9 and imagine that you were talking with each of these people. How would you feel about each one? With which one would you feel most comfortable? You would probably feel most comfortable with the person in figure 2.9. Because of his direct gaze, you would feel that he was interested and paying attention. The person in figure 2.8 seems to be avoiding your gaze, and you may wonder what he is thinking.

The importance of appropriate eye contact has been demonstrated in research. The findings indicate that people are more likely to interpret your words as positive if you look at them while speaking. Other studies demonstrate that eye contact between people encourages interaction and increases their comfort and satisfaction with each other. Sustained periods of looking away and not maintaining eye contact can result in angry disruption and termination of communication (Kendon, 1967). In fact, failing to maintain eye contact can be detrimental to a relationship because it cuts off the possibility of seeing and reacting to important nonverbal cues that the other person is giving (Leathers, 1974).

Figure 2.8

Figure 2.9

Facial Expressions

People most frequently look to facial expressions to clarify the meaning of someone's words and intentions. Because the face is so mobile, it can express many things. Pupil dilation, muscle tension, eye and mouth expressions all convey many nuances of meaning. As you know, eyes can look sparkling or dull, cold or hurt. A glance can seem piercing, disapproving, or interested, and the brows and the mouth can reflect surprise or disgust.

Some photographs were selected to give you an idea of the emotions and reactions that the face can portray. Look at figure 2.10. Imagine that you were talking with this person and, at some point, you noticed that his face looks like this. How would you feel? What would you think that he was feeling? Does he seem to be approving of you or agreeing with what you are saying? From his scowl and frown, you would probably judge a negative reaction to you, the situation, or something that is happening.

What about the person in figure 2.11? How would you feel if someone with whom you were talking looked like this? What does it seem that he is feeling? From his expression, you would probably decide that he was confused, puzzled, or did not understand something that you said.

What about the next two photographs? How would you feel if you were talking with the people in figures 2.12 and 2.13. What does each one seem to be feeling? How does each one feel about what you are saying? From his expression and smile, you would judge the reaction of the person in figure 2.12 to be positive. The expression of the eyes and the mouth convey an indifferent attitude in the person in figure 2.13.

To demonstrate how the face shows different levels of intensity, I have chosen a series of photographs. Look at figures 2.14, 2.15, and 2.16. All the people are showing somewhat the same reaction. Which one seems to have the most intense feeling? While all three are showing negative reactions, the reaction of the person in figure 2.14 seems the mildest. Figure 2.15 seems to have the strongest feeling.

Look at figures 2.17, 2.18, and 2.19. Again, the reactions are similar. Which person seems to have the strongest feeling? The man's expression in figure 2.18 seems to show the mildest reaction, while figure 2.17 seems to show the most intense feelings.

This brief introduction has given you some idea of what facial expressions can portray. Practice noticing people's facial expressions and notice the wide range of feelings that can be conveyed. In terms of yourself, remember that people will judge whether you approve or disapprove just by the expression on your face. They also will judge the intensity of your feelings and the depth of your interest and comprehension.

Figure 2.10

Figure 2.11

Figure 2.12

Figure 2.13

Figure 2.14

Figure 2.15

Figure 2.16

Figure 2.17

Figure 2.18

Figure 2.19

Figure 2.20

Figure 2.21

Body Orientation and Posture

Body orientation and posture involve several things: how you stand or sit, how you position yourself in relation to another person, whether or not you face the other person or turn away, and how close or far away you stand. Also included are your torso movements (whether you lean toward a person or back away), the position of your arms (open or closed), and the relaxation or tension in your body.

For an example, look at figures 2.20 and 2.21. Which of the couples pictured seem to like each other more? How can you tell? As before, the people who are turning toward each other seem to show more liking for each other. The other two, by leaning away and turning away, seem to be trying to avoid contact with each other.

In figure 2.22, decide how each person feels. Which one seems more relaxed? Which one seems most powerful? The man is relaxed while the woman looks as if she is tense and somewhat uncomfortable. And because of his relaxation, the man also seems to have more power or control. On the other hand, the woman's tension reduces the power or status that she conveys.

Remember that relaxed posture conveys high power or status. The more tense and rigid that you are, the less control and status that you seem to have. Furthermore, standing or sitting close to someone and leaning or turning toward a person are positive cues that reflect liking and a desire to interact with or include this person. In contrast, standing or sitting far away, leaning or turning away are negative cues and convey that you do not want to interact with the other person.

Start becoming aware of how you and others stand and sit in conversations. See if they are relaxed or tense. Notice how close people stand and how they turn and lean either toward or away from each other.

Voice Quality

Voice quality includes tone of voice as well as volume, rate, and pitch. Articulation, pronunciation, inflection, and silences are also involved. Voice quality is one of the most important nonverbal cues. People most frequently listen to your voice and look to your face in order to determine what you mean. For this reason, it is important that your voice match your intention. Do not sound angry when you are trying to be pleasant; do not sound critical or complaining when you do not intend to be.

Figure 2.22

To give yourself some practice in noticing the impact of voice quality, try to find a radio drama and listen to it. (If you cannot find something on the radio, darken the picture on the TV.) Listen to the voices and decide what each communicates. What picture do you have of each person? If this person were speaking to you, how would you feel? How does the person seem to feel? Notice how the voice quality shapes your interpretation of the speaker's words, intentions, and personality.

Pay attention to the impact of voice quality in your speech and that of others. Try to make your voice fit with what you are trying to accomplish.

Gestures

Gestures are hand movements that are used to qualify or accent your words and other nonverbal cues. They seem to convey responsiveness and involvement, and studies have shown that people who use gestures are liked better by their listeners (Leathers, 1974). As with all aspects of communication, it is important that your gestures be consistent with your words, your intention, and other nonverbal cues. Any discrepancy gives a mixed message to your listeners. This is distracting and makes it less likely for you to be understood accurately.

Movements and Activity

Remember that, at the beginning of the chapter, activity (such as changing expressions, shifting stance, gesturing) was said to reflect responsiveness and involvement. This should be done within reason, of course, for too much movement seems to convey fidgeting and restlessness. Notice the different feeling you get from people who are motionless and immobilized and those who move and change. Start noticing how much activity and involvement you convey. If you have people who will be honest with you, ask them how involved and responsive you seem.

Appearance: Grooming and Dress

Appearance gives some information about your neatness, your status, and sociability, your sex role, your formality or informality, how contemporary you are, and what you think of yourself. Many people underestimate the importance of these cues and are not familiar with the effect that appearance has on communication.

It is important that your appearance match what you want to achieve. You could not do a good job as a mechanic if you showed up in a tuxedo. Nor would you be seen as a competent executive if you appeared at the office looking unkempt. In the same way, wearing bright colors or wild patterns creates a different impression than wearing subdued, conservative colors. It is important to judge what you want to accomplish and to decide what impression would help you to achieve that. Your appearance should be consistent with that purpose and should help you to achieve what you want.

SUMMARY

Nonverbal cues include facial expressions and movements, eye contact, body posture and movements, gestures, voice quality, movement, and general appearance. These cues are very important in communication, and they control and shape people's interpretation of what you mean. In order to communicate effectively, it is essential that your nonverbal cues are consistent with what you are trying to accomplish. The first step in accomplishing this is to become more familiar with nonverbal cues. Then you can increase your awareness of your own cues and those of others.

Now that you have some general information about nonverbal cues, you can practice observing these cues in others. The following section gives further suggestions on how to become a good observer of these cues.

SKILL 2: OBSERVING NONVERBAL CUES IN OTHERS

These exercises are designed to give you practice in observing nonverbal cues and noticing how they affect communication.

I. Practice with Facial Expressions

As we said, the face is an important part of nonverbal communication. This exercise will help you learn about the nuances of meaning that the face can portray.

Several emotions are listed below. Beneath the list are photographs. Look at each picture, and decide what emotion it seems to convey. Write that in the space beneath each picture.

| affection | disgust | happiness |
| anger | self-confidence | skepticism |

II. Visual Practice in Nonverbal Cues

Turn on the television without the sound. Each time you practice this, select one of the nonverbal cues listed below. Pay attention only to the one cue you have chosen.

A. Facial expression and movements.
B. Eye contact.

Figure 2.23

Figure 2.24

Figure 2.25

Figure 2.26

Using Nonverbal Cues Effectively 113

Figure 2.27 Figure 2.28

C. General appearance: grooming, dress.
D. Body orientation: posture; closeness to the other person; turned toward or away; leaning toward or away.
E. Gestures.
F. Activity, shifts, changes of expression.

Mehrabian (1972) has said that nonverbal communication can convey three qualities: approval or disapproval, high or low status (dominance vs. submission), and responsiveness or unresponsiveness.

While you are observing the class of nonverbal cues that you have chosen, think of Mehrabian's qualities and decide what each cue seems to communicate. Answer these questions.

1. Does the person seem to be expressing like or dislike?
2. Does he or she seem dominant or submissive?
3. Does he or she seem responsive or unresponsive, involved or uninvolved?

Next time, select another class of nonverbal cues and repeat the exercise. Continue until you have completed the list. Since it takes careful and practiced observation to notice nonverbal cues, you may want to repeat this exercise several times. Do it until you feel comfortable and skilled at observing and interpreting this "body language."

III. Practice in Noticing Voice Quality

When watching television, close your eyes for five or ten minutes and listen instead. Notice the tone of voice. Answer these questions.

A. Does it seem to convey liking and approval, or criticism and dislike?
B. Does it sound powerful and "in control" or weak and helpless? Is it whining, complaining, or wheedling?
C. Does it convey interest and involvement, or boredom and disinterest?
D. Does the voice sound alive and spontaneous, or dead and flat?
E. What other qualities do you notice—anger, fear, surprise, calmness, sadness, disdain, determination, bewilderment?
F. What does this person seem to communicate with his/her voice?

The more you listen to the voice quality, the more nuances you will notice.

IV. Practice in Noticing General Appearance

Notice the general appearance of others. What do their grooming and choice of clothes communicate? Answer these questions:

A. Does this person seem neat? Does he or she seem to care about him- or herself or does his or her appearance suggest carelessness or sloppiness?
B. Is his or her overall appearance attractive or unappealing? Is he or she striking or average?
C. Does this person's appearance seem consistent with his/her sex role? With his or her social role?
D. What does his or her appearance communicate about socioeconomic status?
E. Does he or she seem contemporary and stylish or out of date? Does he or she seem conservative or somewhat "wild"?
F. Is his or her appearance casual or formal?
G. Based on appearance, what does this person communicate about him- or herself? Does this person seem to think well of him- or herself?

V. Practice in Noticing Consistency between Verbal and Nonverbal Cues

A. It is time for more television practice and, perhaps, even a movie or two just to focus on verbal and nonverbal cues. You have had some practice watching nonverbal channels of communication. Again, choose one at a time. Select one item from this list.
 1. Facial expressions and movements.
 2. Voice quality.
 3. Eye contact.
 4. General appearance: grooming, dress.
 5. Body orientation: posture; closeness to the other person; turned toward or away; leaning toward or away.
 6. Gestures.
 7. Activity, shifts, changes of expression.

Watch the people on television. Listen to their words and answer these questions.
 1. What is the verbal message?
 2. What is the nonverbal message?
 3. Do they match?

Work your way through the list, taking one class of nonverbal cues at a time. Check how well they match the person's verbal message.

B. When you are comfortable with this practice, try it with people around you. Observe friends, neighbors, family, co-workers. Notice their nonverbal cues and how they match or contradict their words.

Now that you have begun noticing nonverbal cues in others, you can start becoming aware of your own nonverbal cues. The following section gives you some practice in this.

SKILL 3: LEARNING ABOUT YOUR NONVERBAL CUES

The best way to learn about your nonverbal cues is to videotape yourself interacting with others and then watch the playback. If you have video equipment at your disposal, use it. Since most people do not, the next best thing is to start "tuning in" on your own body language and start asking for some feedback from others.

I. Practice in Using Body Language

Below is an exercise to see how well you can use your body language to express what you mean. Make a copy of the list below and give it to a friend. In each row, choose one emotion that you want to convey. Use whatever nonverbal cues you want: facial expressions, posture, eye movements. Ask him which of the three emotions you were expressing. The more he or she guesses accurately, the better communicator you are.

Try the same exercise with other friends.

A. boredom	sadness	disagreement
B. surprise	disgust	bewilderment
C. interest	enjoyment	anger

Ask your friends to tell you what you did that seemed angry, sad, interested, and so on.

II. Practice in Noticing Your Voice Quality

Using a tape recorder (if you do not have one, borrow one), tape yourself explaining how a microwave oven (or anything else you wish) works. Make a separate recording for each of the following people.

A. Your parents.
B. A child.
C. A peer (same sex).
D. A foreigner.
E. Someone who is superior to you (e.g., a boss).
F. A peer, opposite sex.
G. Spouse.
H. Someone to whom you have already explained it several times.

Play back all eight of your explanations. Notice the difference in your tone, pitch, and inflections.

III. Self-Awareness

Start becoming aware of how you look and sound. Each day, choose one type of nonverbal cue and monitor that in yourself several times a day. Ask yourself, for example, am I leaning toward the person or away? On another day, tune in on your facial expressions. Am I frowning or smiling? Do I look interested or bored? What about the sound of my voice?

Keep a notebook. Write a page or two for each type of nonverbal cues. As you continue to do this, you will become more and more aware of what you do, how you look, and how you sound.

IV. Asking for Feedback

You will need to get some feedback from others, particularly from people who will be honest with you. Suggest to a friend or to your spouse that s/he pay particular attention to your nonverbal cues. Explain the different types of nonverbal cues that we have discussed. Ask him or her to concentrate on one type at a time and to observe these when the two of you are interacting. After awhile, stop and ask how you looked or sounded: bored, interested, disapproving, confused, etc. See if he or she can specify exactly what you did to create this impression. Ask if you gave any cues that were particularly confusing or frustrating. Encourage her or him to be as honest as possible with you.

SKILL 4: MATCHING NONVERBAL CUES TO YOUR PURPOSE

In order to communicate clearly, your nonverbal cues must help you to achieve your purpose and convey the meaning that you want. To do this, follow these steps.

1. Decide on your purpose and what you most want to accomplish.
2. Select nonverbal cues which will create the impression you want and which will help you to achieve your purpose. For example, if you are trying to be friendly, be certain that your nonverbal communication conveys warmth and liking.
3. If you realize that your nonverbal cues are at odds with your purpose, change them and explain that your other expressions were not what you meant. For example, you are trying to resolve a problem with your spouse and you notice that your voice is sharp. You change to a more pleasant, softer tone and say, "I didn't mean to speak so sharply. I'm not angry. I just want us to settle this."

Using this skill makes it more likely that you will come across as you intend.

Instead of doing this, people often forget their nonverbal cues and fail to match them to their intentions, resulting in contradictory, inconsistent messages. As in the example above, you may not be angry, but, because you are tense, your voice sounds sharp and your facial expressions are grim and unpleasant. Your spouse interprets this as anger and he or she becomes defensive. In this case, your nonverbal cues defeated your purpose.

In contrast, matching your nonverbal cues to your purpose has the following advantages.

1. It presents consistent verbal and nonverbal messages.
2. Because of the consistency, the messages are easier for your listener to interpret and the chances for misunderstanding and confusion are diminished. As a result, your communication is clearer and more effective.

Here are some examples that demonstrate the difference between inconsistent nonverbal cues and those that match your purpose:

Purpose: The husband wants to let his wife know that he is listening and is willing to hear what she has to say.

Nonverbal Cues Do Not Match Purpose	*Nonverbal Cues Match Purpose*
HUSBAND: Sure, I'm listening. I want to hear what you have to say. (*Nonverbal Cues: looks away; turns head away from her; does not smile or nod; tone of voice is sharp*)	HUSBAND: Sure, I'm listening. I want to hear what you have to say. (*Nonverbal Cues: maintains eye contact; facial expression is pleasant; tone of voice is calm, pleasant*)
WIFE: (*angrily*) I'll bet you do! You don't care the least bit about my opinions!	WIFE: (*feels that his words are sincere and expresses her views*)

Situation: Fred frequently teases his co-worker Susan with comments on her physical appearance at the expense of her competence on the job. At first, Susan ignored it. Now she wants to tell Fred to stop it.

Purpose: To express her limits firmly and clearly; to persuade Fred to stop his teasing.

Nonverbal Cues Do Not Match Purpose	*Nonverbal Cues Match Purpose*
SUSAN: Fred, I am tired of your teasing. I want you to stop it. (*Nonverbal Cues: eyes looking downward, head down, half-smile, quiet, somewhat coquettish tone of voice*)	SUSAN: Fred, I am tired of your teasing. I want you to stop it. (*Nonverbal Cues: gazing directly at Fred; firm, angry, expression; firm tone of voice*)
FRED: (*thinks she is being playful, keeps on teasing*)	FRED: (*thinks she is serious*)

Note: The example on the left portrays what happens to many women. They frequently have been trained to give pleasing and submissive nonverbal cues. They are taught to smile, to be quiet, and certainly not to speak angrily and firmly. In contrast, in the example on the right, Susan uses direct and firm nonverbal cues when she wants to come across that way. As a result, Fred is more likely to understand her message.

Situation: A new employee has just been introduced to you and a group of co-workers.

Purpose: You want the new person to feel comfortable and welcome.

Nonverbal Cues Do Not Match Purpose

YOU: (*Nonverbal Cues:* turn body away from the new person; move chair away from his; when you speak to him, lean away; maintain minimal eye contact)

Nonverbal Cues Match Purpose

YOU: (*Nonverbal Cues:* turn body toward newcomer; smile and nod when he speaks)

Situation: A husband and wife have a disagreement.

Purpose: The wife wants to settle the issue. She says, "I'm not blaming you — I just want to settle this with you."

Nonverbal Cues Do Not Match Purpose

WIFE: (*Nonverbal Cues: Voice loud and angry; facial expression set and determined; one hand on hip; finger pointing at husband*)
HUSBAND: You want to settle this all right. You want to blame me!

Nonverbal Cues Match Purpose

WIFE: (*Nonverbal Cues: Voice calm and controlled; face calm; relaxed posture.*)
HUSBAND: OK, how can we settle this?

In the examples on the left, the nonverbal cues are at variance with the purpose. The nonverbal messages that the listeners receive color their impressions, and the speakers' purposes are not achieved. Few people realize the impact of nonverbal cues, but these cues are extremely important in communication. As in these examples, when nonverbal cues are inconsistent with words, the chances for misunderstanding and confusion multiply.

In contrast, on the right, the nonverbal cues match the speakers' purposes. As a result, their communication is clear, consistent, and effective.

Practice

The following section provides the opportunity to practice the skill of matching nonverbal cues to purpose.

I. Situations and purposes are described below; following these are pairs of nonverbal cues. Check the ones that seem most likely to achieve the purpose and communicate the message that the speaker intends.

A. *Situation:* Your spouse is explaining what happened when he or she returned an item to the department store.

Purpose: You know that this is important to him or her, so you want to show some interest.

YOU: Then what happened?

1. ___Look directly at spouse; tone of voice interested; lean forward toward spouse.
2. ___Look down at magazine on your lap; tone of voice flat and bored.

B. *Situation:* You have a minor disagreement with a friend. However, the argument seems trivial and you want to be on friendly terms again.

Purpose: To establish the friendship again.

YOU: There's nothing that keeps me from being friends with you again.

1. ___Voice is pleasant and calm; facial expression and eyes pleasant; posture relaxed.
2. ___Voice is sharp and harsh, seems accusing; eyes narrowed; body is rigid, ready to attack.

II. Three situations are described below. After each situation are two columns. The first one contains possible purposes that you might have, and the second column contains descriptions of various nonverbal cues.

For each situation, connect the purpose to the nonverbal cues that would most likely achieve it.

A. *Situation:* You are interviewing for a job.

Purposes	*Nonverbal Cues*
1. To make a good impression; to appear self-confident.	a. Sit back, put feet on interviewer's desk, act "cool"; try to make tone of voice indifferent and disinterested.

Using Nonverbal Cues Effectively

2. To appear hesitant, uncertain, shy.

b. Stand and sit in a hunched-over fashion; look down, speak quietly and hesitantly.

3. To appear casual, disinterested, as if you don't care.

c. Stand and sit relaxed but not slouched; tone of voice controlled and calm; direct eye contact; pleasant, interested facial expressions.

B. *Situation:* You and your spouse have had a disagreement. He or she tries to smooth things over.

Purposes

1. To show that you do not want to interact and do not want to be involved.

2. To show interest and involvement.

Nonverbal Cues

a. Turn body toward spouse; maintain eye contact.

b. Turn body away; when he or she sits on couch with you, move away subtly.

C. *Situation:* You are to do a yearly evaluation of each employee and discuss it with him or her. You phone Joe Smith for his yearly appointment.

YOU: I need to see you for your yearly evaluation.

Purpose

1. To threaten him.
2. To explain that this is routine.

Nonverbal Cues

a. Matter-of-fact tone of voice.
b. Bewildered tone of voice.
c. Ominous, threatening tone of voice.

SKILL 5: WHEN OTHERS' MESSAGES ARE INCONSISTENT: ASKING FOR CLARIFICATION

Many people will not be as aware of nonverbal cues as you are. For this reason, it is helpful to notice when messages are inconsistent and to ask the other person for clarification. For example, you mention to your spouse that you are thinking about cancelling some weekend plans the two of you had made. S/he does not show much of a reaction and says, "I'm not disappointed. It is no big deal." However, he or she looks disgusted. In order to get some clarification, you say, "You don't look very pleased. If you will be disappointed, I don't want to cancel our plans."

This is the skill that you learned in the first chapter when we discussed how to handle mixed messages. By applying the same skill to nonverbal cues, you give your spouse the opportunity to clarify his or her message and to make communication clear.

In contrast, most people are not aware of mixed messages or inconsistent nonverbal cues. As a result, they make their interpretations based on one part of the message; they jump to conclusions and do not ask for clarification. This markedly increases the chances for confusion and misunderstanding.

In contrast, asking for clarification has the following advantages.

1. It informs the speaker of the inconsistent messages and thus can increase his or her self-awareness.
2. It gives the speaker the opportunity to clarify his or her purpose and message. This increases the chances for clear communication and understanding.
3. When the speaker's mixed message is deliberate or manipulative, your use of this skill lets the other person know that you have recognized the manipulation.

Here are some examples that demonstrate the difference between not asking for clarification and doing so.

Situation: You and your spouse are on vacation. You decide to go off for a long walk alone. You ask your spouse if this is OK. She or he replies: "Of course. I don't mind." (*tone of voice seems a bit cold and harsh; spouse does not look at you*)

Does Not Ask for Clarification	*Asks for Clarification*
YOU: (You go off on your own; your spouse is mildly offended and sulks; when you return, spouse accuses you)	YOU: You said that it's OK, but your voice does not sound very enthusiastic. Is there something that you would rather do?
SPOUSE: Today you promised to play golf with me.	SPOUSE: I thought that we were playing golf today!

Situation: You telephone some friends late Sunday afternoon and ask if it is convenient for you to visit. They reply that it is. You go over and notice that they seem quiet; they do not talk as much as usual. Both seem to be watching the clock.

Using Nonverbal Cues Effectively

Does Not Ask for Clarification
YOU: (*ignore their nonverbal cues; stay for an hour*)
FRIENDS: (*seem increasingly restless*)
YOU: (*leave, somewhat annoyed with them, thinking to yourself, "They were really rude—why didn't they say something if they didn't want me there?"*)

Asks for Clarification
YOU: I think that I'd better be going. I don't want to interrupt your afternoon.
FRIEND: You're not interrupting us.
YOU: You kept watching the clock, and I didn't know if you were hoping that I would leave or what . . .
FRIEND: Well, as a matter of fact, my brother is supposed to be driving up from St. Louis and we're expecting him any minute.
YOU: You should've said something.

Situation: Mary is telling her husband, Don, about an argument that she had with her boss. As she is explaining what happened, her face becomes angry, and her voice is loud and sharp.

Does Not Ask for Clarification
DON: Hey, wait a minute. Don't go getting mad at me! I can't help it if your boss gave you a hard time. What am I supposed to do?
MARY: I'm not mad at you!
DON: Well, then stop yelling.
MARY: I am not yelling.
DON: Yes, you are.
MARY: (*walks away*) You're the one who's yelling.

Asks for Clarification
DON: You sound pretty angry. Are you angry at me?
MARY: No, I'm not angry at you—just at my boss.
DON: I didn't know. You sounded pretty excited.

In the examples on the left, the listeners do not mention the nonverbal cues and come to their own conclusions about what the speakers intend. Each person leaves the interaction with assumptions about the other, and the chances for misunderstanding and confusion are noticeably increased.

In contrast, on the right, the listeners notice the inconsistency between verbal and nonverbal messages. Rather than ignoring it, they mention the discrepancy and ask the speakers for clarification. In this way, the speakers become more aware of how they came across. They have the opportunity to decide more honestly what they want to communicate. They can clarify their intentions, and the chances for understanding and clear communication are increased.

Practice

The following section gives you opportunity to practice the skill of asking for clarification.

I. Before you can ask for clarification, you first must be able to notice inconsistency between verbal and nonverbal messages. This exercise describes situations and statements. Beneath each situation are pairs of statements and nonverbal cues. Place a check to the left of the statement that is inconsistent.

A. *Situation:* A co-worker, Mike, gave a presentation at your staff meeting. You like Mike and you liked his presentation. However, you know that he is to give this presentation to the board of directors, and you have some suggestions as to how he can improve it. You tell him your suggestions and he replies.

1. ___MIKE: Thank you for the suggestions. (*straightens shoulders, stands more rigidly; avoids your gaze, does not smile, voice becomes tense*)

2. ___MIKE: Thank you for the suggestions. (*posture is relaxed, eye contact direct, face and voice seem pleasant*)

B. *Situation:* You and your spouse are discussing plans for the weekend. You would like to drive to your parents for Sunday dinner, and you ask your spouse if he or she would like to go.

1. ___SPOUSE: I'll go if you want to. (*voice sounds flat and distant; corners of mouth are drawn downward*)

2. ___SPOUSE: I'll go if you want to. (*voice is pleasant, matter of fact; direct eye contact.*)

II. Based on the situations described below, how would you go about asking for clarification? Of the pairs of conversations, check the one that asks for clarification.

A. *Situation:* You made suggestions to Mike, a co-worker, about his presentation. He responded by saying, "Thank you for your suggestions." He became rigid, avoided your gaze, and his voice became tense.

1. ___YOU: Mike, did that seem like a criticism? I didn't mean it that way.

2. ___YOU: You're welcome. Anytime you want suggestions, let me know.

B. *Situation:* You proposed to drive to your parents for Sunday dinner. Your spouse said, "I'll go if you want to." His or her voice sounded flat and distant. Your spouse grimaced and turned away.

1. ___You: (*assuming that your spouse wants to go*)
SPOUSE: (*all weekend long, complains that you're spending Sunday with your parents*)
You: Stop complaining. You agreed to this. Don't say I didn't ask you!
SPOUSE: I agreed but against my will.
You: Well, why didn't you say so? I can't read your mind.
SPOUSE: Forget it.

2. ___You: You don't sound too excited, and I don't want to force you to do something that you don't want to do. If you'd rather not go, tell me.
SPOUSE: I'd rather not, but I figured that you would be angry if I said that.
You: No., I'd much rather that you be agreeable to it. I don't want to force you to do something and then have you feeling resentful.

SUMMARY

Nonverbal cues include facial expressions, voice quality, eye contact, gestures, body posture, orientation, movements, and general appearance. By means of these cues, you communicate your likes or dislikes, your responsiveness and involvement, your control or status, and your agreement or disagreement. Your nonverbal cues convey something of your general attitude, either positive or negative. Your attitude, in turn, shapes other people's understanding and interpretation of what you say and do. For example, if your nonverbal cues are positive, your attitude and words are more likely to be seen as pleasant and positive. If, on the other hand, your nonverbal cues are negative, you can be seen as disapproving and critical. Nonverbal cues are especially important when they convey a message that is different from your words (e.g., your words are positive and supportive while your nonverbal cues are negative). In this case, research has indicated that listeners interpret your nonverbal cues as the "real" message. They base their judgments on your facial expressions, voice quality and other nonverbal cues, and, least of all, on your words.

Familiarity with nonverbal cues can help you become more effective in your communication. Remember these suggestions.

1. Check to be sure that your nonverbal cues match your purpose. Be certain that they create the effect that you want. If you want to convey a positive attitude, your nonverbal cues should be positive and consistent.

2. If you notice that your nonverbal cues are not matching your words or are not consistent with your purpose, change them and explain this to your listeners. For example, "I've gotten so excited about what I was saying that my voice sounds harsh and loud. I didn't mean to come across like that."

Knowledge of nonverbal cues also can help you to understand other people better. By noticing nonverbal cues and their consistency or inconsistency with verbal messages, you can gain a better idea of what others intend. Follow these suggestions.

1. Notice what the person is saying. What is the message?
2. Notice what the person is communicating.
3. Is the nonverbal message the same as the verbal one?
4. If the messages are inconsistent, ask the other person for clarification.

PRACTICE IN USING NONVERBAL CUES EFFECTIVELY

This section gives you an opportunity to apply what you have learned about nonverbal cues.

Matching Nonverbal Cues to Purpose

The examples below present a situation and statement, followed by a pair of nonverbal cues. One of these nonverbal cues is consistent with the speaker's purpose and statement; the other is not.

In each case, check the nonverbal cues that would be effective in achieving the purpose.

A. *Purpose:* To find out more about the employee's thinking, not to criticize but to encourage the employee to speak.
   BOSS: Explain what you mean by that last sentence.
   1. ___Tone of voice is cold and sharp; eyebrows are drawn downward in a frown; mouth is scowling.
   2. ___Tone of voice is pleasant and nonchallenging; boss is leaning toward employee.

B. *Purpose:* To tell the salesperson why you're returning the shirt and to persuade him or her to exchange it for you.
   YOU: (*to a salesperson in a store*) "I'm returning this shirt. It doesn't fit. I'd like another in exchange."

Using Nonverbal Cues Effectively

1. ____Tone of voice is pleasant and polite but firm.
2. ____Throw shirt on counter; tone of voice is angry and critical.

C. *Situation:* You are talking with your friend Bob about what he did over the weekend. He says that he went on a canoe trip and had a good time.
Purpose: To show interest.
YOU: That's nice. Where did you canoe?
1. ____You are looking at him; tone of voice seems sincere and interested.
2. ____You are looking down and away from him; tone of voice flat and bored.

D. *Situation:* You want to tell your spouse that the budget is tight and that both of you will have to spend less next month.
Purpose: To persuade spouse to spend less, not to criticize or complain.
YOU: We're just going to have to spend less next month. The budget is tight.
1. ____You stride into room; tone of voice is harsh, almost accusatory; eyes are glaring.
2. ____Tone of voice is matter-of-fact; eye contact is direct; facial expression calm.

E. *Purpose:* To let your spouse know that you want to talk about something; that it is very important and you want to do it immediately.
YOU: I have something very important to talk about with you.
1. ____Tone of voice serious and direct; eye contact direct.
2. ____Tone of voice whining; avoid spouse's gaze.

F. *Purpose:* To find out what someone meant when he said something.
YOU: What did you mean by that?
1. ____Facial expression bewildered; voice calm but questioning.
2. ____Tone of voice sharp, accusing; hands on hips; angry, challenging facial expression.

G. *Purpose:* To encourage friend to continue talking.
YOU: I'm listening.
1. ____Look around room; tap foot impatiently.
2. ____Look at him or her; maintain eye contact; nod head.

128 A WAY WITH WORDS

H. *Purpose:* To be firm and let someone know your limits.
   1. ____Smile; speak quietly.
   2. ____Direct eye contact; speak firmly and clearly.
I. *Purpose:* To settle a disagreement that you had with your spouse.
   YOU: I'd like to settle things.
   1. ____Tone of voice conciliatory but firm; facial expression pleasant; posture relaxed; body turned toward spouse
   2. ____Tone of voice whining; body turned away; gazing at floor.
J. *Purpose:* To seem relaxed and calm.
   1. ____Speak quickly and in a breathy fashion.
   2. ____Speak calmly and at a reasonable rate.

Interpreting Nonverbal Cues

Nonverbal cues are described below. After each cue are listed several possible interpretations. Based on what you learned in this chapter, circle the most likely interpretations.

A. Relaxed posture.
   1. Power, status, comfort.
   2. Low status.
B. Body turned toward other person.
   1. Dislike.
   2. High status.
   3. Liking, positive evaluation, desire to include person.
C. Maintaining eye contact.
   1. Low status.
   2. Positive evaluation, attention, interest.
D. Fidgeting, tapping foot.
   1. High status.
   2. Responsiveness.
   3. Boredom, restlessness.
E. Rigid.
   1. Low status, tension.
   2. Relaxation, attention, alertness.

Checking Out Impressions and Asking for Clarification

On the left are verbal statements and descriptions of nonverbal cues. The column on the right contains some responses that check out im-

Using Nonverbal Cues Effectively

pressions and ask for clarification. Draw a line from the statement on the left to the appropriate response on the right.

Statement

A. "I have something I want to talk over with you sometime. No rush." (*Tone of voice: cold, serious. Facial expression: frowning*)

B. "Go ahead! I'm listening." (*Body posture: He or she is turned away from you. Facial expression: no eye contact, face averted*)

C. "Why did you say that?" (*Facial expressions: eyes narrowed, frowning. Mouth: set, taut, teeth clenched. Tone of voice: accusatory, harsh*)

Response

1. *Check-out:* "When you are turned away from me like that I have the impression that you don't want to listen. Would you rather not talk right now?"

2. *Check-out:* "Your tone of voice sounds very serious. Is there something that you want to talk about right now?"

3. *Check-out:* "Do you want to hear my explanation?"

Choosing a Purpose and the Most Effective Means of Accomplishing It

Imagine yourself in the following situations.

A. *Situation:* You have had a very busy and hard Friday at work. When you get home, your spouse greets you with a smile and says, "I'm in a great mood! Let's go out to eat or invite some people over!"

The first step is to decide what you want to accomplish. Next, decide what you want to say or do and what nonverbal behaviors best communicate this.

The left column contains various purposes and statements; the column on the right lists nonverbal cues. Match each statement and purpose to the nonverbal cues that would be most likely to achieve the purpose.

Purpose and Statement

1. *Purpose:* To get sympathy. "Oh, I've had such a hard day."

2. *Purpose:* To complain and criticize spouse. "Can't you see I've had a hard day? Do you have to be so self-centered all the time?"

Nonverbal Cues

a. Quiet tone of voice.

b. Stares in a challenging way; voice is angry and harsh; throws coat down.

c. Sighs; whining tone of voice.

3. *Purpose:* To state a preference for some quiet and ask your spouse if he or she will comply — "I'm beat right now. I'd like some quiet for an hour and then I can decide. Is that OK with you?"

B. *Situation:* A female co-worker is wearing a new dress.

Purpose and Statement

1. *Purpose:* To put her down. "Where did you get that outfit?"
2. *Purpose:* To tease her. "Oh, no. Not another new outfit."
3. *Purpose:* To pay her a compliment and let her know she looks nice. "I like that dress. Green is a good color for you."

Nonverbal Cues

a. Look her over in an appraising manner, slightly critical; turn corner of mouth downward.

b. Tone of voice is sincere, pleasant.

c. Voice is hollow, insincere.

Applying Knowledge of Nonverbal Cues to Conversation

Here is an opportunity for you to apply what you know about nonverbal cues to a conversation. Use your knowledge of nonverbal cues in two ways.

1. Decide on nonverbal cues that match the purpose and increase the chances of being understood.
2. Use the nonverbal cues as a basis to check out the genuineness of the verbal statement; use the nonverbal communication as a cue to ask for clarification.

At certain points in the conversation, there are questions relating to nonverbal cues. Answer these.

HUSBAND: I'd like to invite the Martins over for dinner this weekend.
WIFE: Oh, OK.

Nonverbal Cues: Tone of voice is matter-of-fact.

Nonverbal Cues: Sighs, voice is tense, flat, sounds as if she's trying to be tolerant.

A. What do the wife's nonverbal cues seem to communicate? Circle those that seem applicable.

excitement   lack of interest   delight   anger

B. Below are some responses that the husband may make. One of

Using Nonverbal Cues Effectively

these does not pay attention to the wife's nonverbal cues; one assumes to know her thinking based on her nonverbal cues; the third pays attention to both verbal and nonverbal cues and checks out impressions. Check the one that attends to the wife's nonverbal cues.

1. ___ "Let's have the Wilsons and Moores over too. You can make one of those dishes you learned in French cooking class. We can serve a good wine. This will really be nice!"
2. ___ "You said OK, but you don't sound too excited about it. Would you rather not do that this weekend?"
3. ___ "If you're going to sound so resentful about it, forget it! I'm not going to have you throw it up to me and remind me what trouble it was!"

The conversation continues in this way:

WIFE: I'll be happy to do it because you asked me to. It's not my preference for spending the weekend, but it's OK.
HUSBAND: Why isn't it your preference?

C. What nonverbal cues should the husband use if he honestly wants to know his wife's thinking? Circle the appropriate ones; cross out those he would use if he wanted to be angry or challenging.

    challenging tone of voice   clenched teeth
    frown   frustrated tone of voice
    interested, questioning tone of voice
    angry tone of voice   pointing finger   glaring

WIFE: I don't look forward to all the housecleaning and the preparation of food. To me that's a chore. I have other things that I enjoy more than entertaining.

D. Look at the purposes and nonverbal cues below. If the wife wants to be pleasant and does not want an argument, which would be most effective?

1. ___ *Purpose:* To complain (whining tone of voice)
2. ___ *Purpose:* To put husband down (hands on hips; sharp, haughty tone of voice; raised eyebrows; acts as if entertaining is beneath her)
3. ___ *Purpose:* To express her own preference but let her husband know that his are acceptable (matter-of-fact, accepting tone of voice)

You have studied nonverbal cues in detail and have learned that nonverbal communication consists of many different "channels." One channel is the face, another is the voice, a third is posture, and so on. In order to interpret nonverbal communication correctly, you will find it necessary to pay some attention to all the channels at once, for it is this combination of all the channels that conveys the overall impression.

A musical group is a good example of how this works. A group of instruments playing together can produce a much wider range of sounds and tones than a solo instrument can. This is because all the instruments combine to produce the total sound. If one of the instruments is changed in some way, the total sound is changed. If two instruments are changed, the total sound is changed even more.

The same thing happens in your nonverbal communication. Each of the "channels"—face, voice, gestures—enhances or qualifies the others, and each channel contributes to the total effect. The result is a "blend" of all your nonverbal cues. The capacity for blending provides flexibility, and this flexibility means that nonverbal cues can convey a wide range of attitudes and emotions. As a matter of fact, this flexibility and capacity for blending are the qualities that make nonverbal cues a rich and important part of communication.

CHAPTER THREE

Appropriateness

APPROPRIATE COMMUNICATION considers social limits and customs, time, place, situation, the person with whom you are speaking, and your relationship with that person. It uses words, behaviors, and ways of communicating that are familiar and accepted and, therefore, are more likely to be understood. This quality of appropriateness increases the chances that your intentions, words, and actions will be understood and interpreted correctly.

The main points of this chapter on appropriateness are:

1. Learning about appropriateness: discussion and examples.
2. Checking social limits and customs.
3. Checking time, place, and situation.
4. Matching what you say and do to the person and to the relationship.

SKILL 1: LEARNING ABOUT
APPROPRIATENESS: DISCUSSION AND EXAMPLES

In this book, *communication* means words, actions, and cues, including manner of dress and appearance. When we speak of appropriateness, we apply it to all these aspects of communication. Communication, including words, appearance, behaviors, and nonverbal cues, is appropriate when it is:

1. Within social limits; it conforms to accepted social customs.
2. Suited to the particular situation, time, and place.
3. Suited to the particular person and takes account of your relationship with that person.

When communication meets these criteria of appropriateness, it increases the chances of being understood. In the section below, these criteria for appropriateness will be discussed, and examples of each will be provided.

Appropriateness as to Limits and Customs

This aspect of appropriateness involves behaving, dressing, and speaking in ways that are accepted by the culture. Familiar words and actions are more likely to be interpreted correctly, and this is a major advantage in communication. When you choose to use words, actions, or expressions that are unfamiliar or unaccepted, you increase the chances of being misunderstood.

The examples below point out the differences between inappropriate words or actions and appropriate ones.

Situation: John works in a conservative firm. The partners do not approve of long hair, moustaches, or beards.
Purpose: To get ahead, get attention, and be well thought of.

Inappropriate Appearance	*Appropriate Appearance*
John decides to show them that he doesn't care what they think. He grows his hair long and also grows a full beard.	John knows that he is "on probation" his first two years. Although he would like longer hair and a moustache, he decides to wait until his job is secure.

Situation: At the office, Bob works with a girl whom he finds very attractive.
Purpose: He would like her to pay more attention to him and go out with him.

Inappropriate Action	*Appropriate Action*
As she walks by, Bob grabs her around the waist and says, "Hey! Stop and talk to me."	Bob creates an opportunity to talk with her. He looks for her at coffee break and asks her to lunch.

Situation: Al has been asked to speak to a community service organization.
Purpose: To make a good impression.

Inappropriate Words	*Appropriate Words*
Al likes to appear sophisticated, so he peppers his speech with sexual innuendos and four-letter words.	Al omits the off-color words and uses speech that is proper and understandable to his audience.

Appropriateness

The behaviors and words on the left do not help the speakers to achieve their purposes. Because the words or actions do not conform to limits and customs, they decrease the quality of the speakers' communication. Other people are more likely to misread their intentions and purposes. In fact, people may focus on the unusual behavior and ignore other aspects, such as John's conscientiousness or Al's well-organized presentation.

In contrast, in the examples on the right, the speakers are more likely to be understood and are more effective in achieving their purposes.

Appropriateness as to Time, Place, and Situation

Appropriateness here involves speaking and acting in ways that are suited to particular situations. What may be appropriate and effective in one situation is ineffective in another.

The examples below demonstrate these differences:

Situation: You have a legal problem that you wish to discuss with an attorney. You have a good friend, Mark, who is an attorney.
Purpose: To get help from Mark.

Inappropriate Time and Place	*Appropriate Time and Place*
On Saturday you drop by his house unexpectedly. You immediately begin telling him about your problem.	You telephone Mark at his office and ask him for an appointment to discuss your problem, making it clear that you are seeking professional services for a fee.

Situation: Sharon, a friend of yours, has been upset lately and has told you some of her problems with her in-laws.
Purpose: To find out how she is; to show your concern.

Inappropriate Time	*Appropriate Time*
You see Sharon on the street talking to another woman. You approach her and say, "How are you feeling today? Are you still upset about your mother-in-law?"	You approach Sharon, make small talk, and wait until the other woman has left. Then you ask how things are going.

Situation: A married couple had a mild disagreement on their way to a restaurant. They are seated within earshot of other people.
Purpose: The wife wants to settle the disagreement.

Inappropriate Place	*Appropriate Place*
As the couple eats, the wife continues to talk about what is upsetting to her. She is speaking excitedly and can be overheard.	WIFE: (*quietly*) I want to settle this issue. Let's talk about it when we get home.

In the examples on the left, the person has chosen the wrong time or place. In each case, the other person (attorney, friend, or husband) is likely to be offended or annoyed and is more likely to misunderstand the speaker's intention. Choosing an inappropriate time, place, or situation makes it far less likely that you will achieve your purpose. In contrast, the examples on the right show how judging the situation and choosing an appropriate time and place increase the chances of being heard and understood.

Appropriateness as to Person and Relationship

This involves gauging what you say and do to the particular person and to the relationship that you have with that person. People, as well as the respective relationships that we have with them, are different in nature. Individuals and relationships range from warm to cool, friendly to unfriendly, close to distant. There are sexual relationships, work and status relationships, social and family relationships. What is appropriate for one person in one kind of relationship is inappropriate for another. What a spouse or lover might say is too personal and private for someone else to say; what a family member may do is too familiar for someone else to do.

The examples below point out the difference between what is inappropriate and appropriate:

Situation: Attractive girl is in dentist's office for check-up.
Purpose: Dentist wants to compliment her.

Inappropriate as to Person or Relationship	*Appropriate as to Person or Relationship*
DENTIST: Well, Ms. Meyers, you're in good shape and your teeth aren't bad, either. (*the dentist is too presumptuous and familiar with the patient and is not responding to the situation; the patient is there to have her teeth checked, not to hear comments on her appearance*)	DENTIST: I'm happy to say that your teeth are fine. (*here the dentist compliments the patient within appropriate limits and responds within the context of the dentist-patient relationship*)

Situation: Tom, a friend of yours, does not like to drink alcoholic beverages. You invite him to a cocktail party at your home.

Inappropriate as to Person or Relationship	*Appropriate as to Person or Relationship*
When Tom asks for a soft drink, you make a big fuss. You tease him and keep after him to try the punch or some other hard drink. YOU: You can't stay at a cocktail party unless you have a cocktail.	Although you have made a special punch for the party, you stock soft drinks for Tom. You don't try to get him to taste your special punch.

Situation: An employee is talking with the boss.
Purpose: To make a suggestion about a new procedure.

Inappropriate as to Relationship	*Appropriate as to Relationship*
EMPLOYEE: This place is run all wrong! I don't know why it doesn't fall apart! What you should do is . . . (*does not acknowledge the relationship of boss to employee and does not acknowledge the boss's higher status nor the possibility that he or she may have already tried what the employee is about to suggest*)	EMPLOYEE: You have much more experience with this place than I do. I have some ideas about trying things differently. Maybe you have already tried them, but I'd like you to hear my suggestions. (*acknowledges the boss's superior status and also considers that he or she may have implemented various suggestions in the past*)

In the examples on the left, Tom, the girl, and the boss probably will feel frustrated, annoyed, and resentful. The words and actions of the speakers only contribute to misunderstanding and dissatisfaction. Assuming that their goal is to maintain a comfortable, satisfying relationship, they have achieved the opposite.

In contrast, the appropriate words and actions on the right minimize the chances for misinterpretation. The possibilities for maintaining comfortable, satisfying relationships are increased.

SKILL 2: CHECKING SOCIAL LIMITS AND CUSTOMS

An essential part of effective communication is expressing yourself in ways that are most likely to be understood. This usually involves behaving, dressing, and speaking in ways that are common and accepted in the culture. To be clearly understood in a rural southern area, you would use different words and expressions than in a large midwestern city. You probably would dress and act differently in these locales. Communities and sections of the country have customs that are unique to each of them; what is acceptable in New York may not be so in Arizona and vice versa. The social customs of farmers are not the same as those of city people, and what is acceptable on a university campus is not acceptable in a conservative small town. Thus, in order to achieve your purpose, it is more effective to be aware of social customs and to stay within the limits of your particular area or situation.

This skill involves the following steps.

1. Observe the social customs and limits of your locale. Notice what elicits a positive and a negative reaction. For example: Where you work, people often bring in a cake or cookies to treat fellow-workers. This is well received. On the other hand, if you work where people are weight-conscious and on diets, bringing in cake or cookies will probably elicit a negative reaction.
2. Ask yourself if what you want to do or say will get the reaction that you want from people. If you think that what you planned to do or say is not within social limits or customs, decide what would be more appropriate. For example, a male employer wants to thank his secretary for some extra work that she did. He thought about taking her to lunch, but this is not commonly done and sometimes starts gossip. He decides, instead, to buy her a small plant for her desk.
3. If you do not know the social limits or customs in a particular situation, ask about them. For example, a friend's father has died. His family is of a different religious denomination than you, and you do not know their customs. You telephone your friend and ask what the family prefers as a memorial.

Another example would be a young man taking a young woman to dinner. In these days of women's liberation, he does not know whether he should open doors for her or not. He wonders if she will be offended by this. He asks, "These days some women are offended when I open doors for them, and some are not. What do you prefer?"

By considering and finding out the social customs and limits, you increase the chances of being understood by others and you also increase the chances of achieving your purpose. This does not occur when people fail to consider social limits and customs. For example, Bill has started a new job in the city. He and his wife are invited to a dinner party. They wear jeans because they enjoy wearing jeans. When they arrive, nearly all the other guests are formally attired. Bill and Sue feel uncomfortable most of the evening. If their purpose was to make a good impression, their failure to observe or to find out about social limits and customs probably has defeated their purpose and elicited a negative reaction instead.

The examples below demonstrate the differences between ignoring social limits and customs and attending to them.

Situation: Jack, a co-worker of yours, mentions at lunch that he is leaving on a golfing trip to Mississippi.

Fails to Consider Social Limits and Customs	*Considers Social Limits and Customs*
YOU: Ugh—Mississippi stinks. I can't think of a worse place to go.	YOU: Hope you have a nice time. (*Or, if you think Mississippi is not a nice place to go for fun, you say nothing*)

Situation: A new physician at a hospital has ideas about programs to try.
Purpose: To persuade others to adopt his or her ideas.

Fails to Consider Social Limits and Customs	*Considers Social Limits and Customs*
The new physician calls in other personnel, tells them that the way they are doing things is stupid and outdated. Orders them to do things the way that she or he says.	The new physician talks with people who have been there longer. Asks them how to go about implementing some ideas. Asks what things have been considered and tried in the past.

By failing to consider social limits and customs, the examples on the left increase misunderstanding and defeat the speakers' purposes. In the examples on the right, the speakers consider social limits and inquire about them. In this way, they increase the chances of achieving their purposes.

Practice

This section provides practice in recognizing and using appropriate social limits and customs.

I. The column on the left contains a description of situations and purposes; the column on the right contains appropriate statements or actions. Draw a line from each situation and purpose to a statement or action that would be appropriate.

Situation and Purpose

A. Your brother is marrying a girl from a different ethnic, religious, and geographical background. You do not know what their customs are regarding showers, gifts, reception, etc.

B. At work you have just been introduced to Dr. John Stevens.

C. You have just taken a new job. Most of the people dress casually. You are in a management position and the other people at your level dress conservatively.

Statement or Action

1. Ask him if he prefers to be called by his title or first name.

2. Dress in your own style but within conservative limits.

3. Speak with your brother, his fiancee, or her family. Ask what is expected or preferred.

II. Below are pairs of situations and conversations. One of each pair pays attention to social limits and customs; the other does not. Check the one that is appropriate.

A. *Situation:* Female professional begins first day at work. She is introduced to her male supervisor.

1. ____SUPERVISOR: Welcome, it's nice to have you here.

2. ____SUPERVISOR: Well, with your looks, at least you should provide some fantasy material for the male employees. That outfit doesn't exactly minimize your charms, either.

B. *Situation:* A man is retiring after twenty years of service to the company. A party is being planned in his honor, and people are contributing to the purchase of a gift. Everyone is asked to contribute. One person who has worked there only a few months responds.

1. ____NEW EMPLOYEE: What is the usual custom? Does everyone give a certain amount or how do we do this?

2. ____NEW EMPLOYEE: This is dumb! Why should I give any money? Some of you have been working with him for twenty years

Appropriateness

and I've only been here five months! So, if you guys are giving two dollars each, I should only have to give a penny!

C. *Situation:* A boss notices that one of his employees seems despondent.

1. ____BOSS: I'm not trying to pry, but if there is something you'd like to talk about, let me know.

2. ____BOSS: Look, Sam, I know the signs. What's going on between you and your wife? Is she seeing someone on the side — or are you? I know it has to do with sex. Come on, what is it?

III. The following examples contain inappropriate actions or statements. Consider social limits and customs by answering the questions at the end of each example. Then write a more appropriate response.

A. *Situation:* You attend a staff meeting with various co-workers. You notice that one staff member is wearing a new outfit.
   YOU: You have on a new dress, don't you? It would be nice if it didn't have that wrinkle in front. Did you forget to iron it?
   1. Will this elicit a positive or negative reaction?
   2. Is this the reaction that you want?
   3. If not, what would be more appropriate?

B. *Situation:* A young woman professional has been asked to speak to a women's club in a small, conservative town on "The Role of Women in Today's Society." She criticizes motherhood and traditional roles and, to show her contempt for tradition, she uses as much slang as she can.
   1. Will this elicit a positive or negative reaction?
   2. Is this the reaction she wants?
   3. If not, what would be more appropriate?
   4. If she does not know how the club members might respond, what should she do?

C. *Situation:* A co-worker is leaving for another job. You do not understand why he is leaving his present one, so you say, "This new job must involve quite a big salary. How much will you be making?"
   What would be a better way to find out why he is taking a new job?

SKILL 3: CHOOSING THE APPROPRIATE TIME AND PLACE

An important part of talking with others is choosing the right situation, time, and place to say what you want. Use the following steps in order to make your decision.

1. Pay attention: notice the place, the people around, the time, what the other person is doing.
2. Decide if this is a time and place that will fit your purpose. For example, you want to talk to a friend and ask some advice. At work you notice that he or she is with other people and seems very busy. You decide that this is not the right time or place to discuss your problem.
3. If you decide that the time and place is not appropriate, decide what would be a better situation. If you are not sure, ask the other person. Wait for a more suitable time and place to try to arrange one. For example, you might wait until your friend is free and then you might say, "There is something that I'd like to talk about with you. It will probably take about a half an hour. Do you have some time when we could talk?"

When the time and place suit your purpose, the other person is better able to listen and understand. Since communication is a complicated process, it is best to have as many things going for you as possible, including a time, place, and situation that fit your purpose.

When people fail to consider the time and place, complications occur. For example, Tom wants to talk privately about a problem and, without thinking, walks into a friend's office. Although the friend seems very busy, Tom launches into a thirty-minute explanation of his problem. In this case, the friend will probably feel imposed upon; he may be preoccupied with other things and may feel annoyed as well. As a result, the friend probably will not be able to listen or understand as well as he would have at a different time and place. Tom feels ignored and misunderstood and his original purpose remains unfulfilled.

The examples below will help to point out the differences between not paying attention to time and place and doing so.

Purpose: To discuss your spouse's clothes buying with your spouse.

Inappropriate	*Appropriate*
YOU: (in front of the other people) We need to straighten out your clothes allowance.	(You choose some time when you and your spouse are alone and he or she is free to talk) YOU: We really need to straighten out our budget, particularly your clothes allowance. Do you want to sit down and talk about it now?

Situation: Your co-worker has just been released from the hospital.
Purpose: You want to point out that the two of you together are expected to increase your productivity next month.

Inappropriate	*Appropriate*
YOU: Look, I've had it with you! All month long, you've been sick and I've had to do all the work around here! The boss told me yesterday that our section is really going to have to increase production. And I'm not going to do it alone. You'd better start shaping up . . . or else. (*inappropriate as to time: fails to consider the person and his or her situation; this outburst may upset him more and decrease his cooperation and productivity*)	YOU: John, I know you've been sick and it takes awhile to recuperate. The boss said that next month we're going to have to increase production. Do you think that next week you'll be up to working with me on this?

Situation: Your spouse has just said that he or she is angry and wants to be left alone.
Purpose: To settle an issue between you and your spouse.

Inappropriate	*Appropriate*
YOU: Don't go anywhere! We're going to sit down and talk this out until it's settled.	YOU: I can understand that you are too mad to talk right now. I do want to get this settled, though, so please let me know when you feel like sitting down and talking it out, OK?

In the examples on the left, the time or place is at odds with the purpose and thus is more likely to distract the listener. In the examples on the right, the time and place are more useful to the speaker's purpose. The other people are freer to hear what is being said. They are not hampered by other distractions and thus can be more responsive to the situation.

Practice

The following section provides practice in choosing the right time, place, or situation for accomplishing your purpose.

I. Each example below describes a situation and a purpose. Following that are times, places, or situations. Circle the one that is most appropriate for accomplishing the purpose.

A. *Situation and Purpose:* A woman does not like the town in which she and her husband are living; she wants to persuade her husband to find another job so that they can move.

   WIFE: I know it's not easy for you to find another job. I also know it's not your fault that I don't like this town, but you don't seem overjoyed with it, either. I'd like to talk about it and see if we want to consider moving.
   1. Place: (circle the most appropriate)
      a. When they are out with friends at a restaurant.
      b. When they are home alone.
      c. When they are at a movie.
   2. Situation or Time: (circle the most appropriate)
      a. Right after husband says that he's had a hard day and wants to be quiet.
      b. When husband is fixing the kitchen faucet.
      c. When they have agreed upon a time to discuss important matters.

B. *Situation and Purpose:* A friend's spouse has died and you want to show your support and concern by calling, visiting, helping, etc.
   Time: (circle the most appropriate)
   1. Six months afterward.
   2. Immediately after the death and in the time that follows.
   3. Wait until he or she is no longer upset; call about a month later.

II. The examples below contain pairs of conversations. One demonstrates the skill of selecting the most appropriate time, place, and situation; the other does not. Check the one that is more likely to achieve the purpose.

A. *Situation:* John approaches Mike. Mike seems very busy, and several people are around.
Purpose: John wants to persuade his co-workers to try a new procedure that he has developed.

1. ____JOHN: Mike, I want to talk to you about a new procedure that I'd like us to try. It goes like this . . .

2. ____JOHN: Mike, I'd like to talk to you about a new procedure and get your opinion. When would be a good time for you?

B. *Situation:* The boss has just returned to his or her desk after a bad session with the board of directors. You were there and know that he or she was backed to the wall.
Purpose: To complain to your boss about some of the difficulties that you have been experiencing recently.

1. ____YOU: I have some problems I'd like to discuss with you, but they're not urgent. When things settle down for you and you have some time to talk, please let me know.

2. ____YOU: (*angrily*) I have really had it around here! Last month you promised to get me these supplies and I haven't seen them yet. When do I get them?

III. The following examples demonstrate inappropriate selection of time, place, or situation. In each case, identify what is inappropriate and describe a time, place, or situation that suits the purpose better.

A. *Purpose:* A mother wants to chat with her daughter and son-in-law.
Action: She telephones at 7:00 A.M., while they are getting ready for work.

1. What would be a more appropriate time to phone?

2. How could the mother find out what would be a better time to phone?

B. *Purpose:* A man wants to explain a business deal to his wife. He wants her full attention and wants her to approve of it.
Action: He begins telling her about the deal while she is fixing

dinner. She is reading recipes and trying to watch several things cooking at once.

HUSBAND: (*hurt*) You're not listening!

WIFE: Yes, I am!

HUSBAND: You're not looking at me! How can you be listening? You don't seem interested. Forget it!

1. What would be a more appropriate time for the husband to accomplish his purpose?

2. How could the husband find out what would be the best time for his wife to listen?

SKILL 4: MATCHING WHAT YOU SAY TO THE PERSON AND THE RELATIONSHIP

Since individuals and relationships are different in nature, it is important to pay attention to the person with whom you are speaking and to the particular relationship that you have with this person. What is appropriate to one person or one relationship is not appropriate to another. For example, what you say to a fellow worker is not appropriate for you to say to your boss; similarly, what you say to someone your own age may sound condescending or presuming to someone who is younger or older than you are. What is fitting for a parent to say to a child would sound patronizing to a friend, and, of course, what you say to your spouse or to a close friend is not what you say to an acquaintance.

In order to adapt your speech and behavior to the other person and to the relationship, follow these guidelines.

1. As the preceding chapters have pointed out, decide what you want to accomplish.
2. Formulate what it is that you want to say or do.
3. Put yourself in the other person's place. If you were that person, how would you feel and how would you react to what you plan to say or do? (Take into account what you know of the person. Is he or she shy, self-conscious, sensitive, arrogant, easily intimidated?)

Appropriateness

4. Consider the relationship that you have with this person. Ask yourself if what you want to say or do is appropriate in respect to the nature of your relationship. Do you know the person well or are you being too familiar? Are you imposing your will upon the person? Are you creating an awkward situation? Are you being respectful of the other person? Are you acknowledging the other person? For example, if you are male and have just met an attractive woman and want to ask her out, you would not want to presume that you have a close, familiar relationship with that woman and behave in a way that she might find disrespectful.
5. If you foresee any difficulties, return to the decision about your purpose. In terms of your relationship with this person and what you know about him or her, decide what would help you accomplish your goal. For example, John has received a big promotion which will be announced to co-workers at a staff meeting. Among the co-workers, he has a close friend. When he stops to consider this friend's reactions (i.e., that the friend is likely to feel hurt if he finds out at the same time as others) and his relationship to this person (they have been quite close and shared many confidences), John changes his plans. He decides to take the friend aside before the announcement and tell him of his promotion.

This skill works because it pays attention to the other person and to your relationship with that person. Since communication can be complicated, it is helpful to gauge your words and actions to your audience. The better that you read the other person and adapt your communication accordingly, the better are your chances of being understood.

When people forget to put themselves in the other person's shoes and do not stop to think about the relationship that they have with the other person, difficulties occur. They say what they think and do not anticipate the other person's reactions. They fail to pay attention to the person or to the nature of the relationship with the other person: business or friendship, close or superficial, trusting or guarded. When aspects like these are disregarded, the other person feels misunderstood, hurt, annoyed, frustrated, or betrayed. The resulting defensiveness disrupts the relationship, confuses the communication, and diminishes the possibility of understanding.

The following examples help point out the differences between communication that is inappropriate to the person and to the relationship, and communication that is appropriate.

Situation: Your child is having trouble in math, and you want to discuss this with the teacher.

Purpose: To tell the teacher that your child seems discouraged about math.

Inappropriate	*Appropriate*
YOU: You're handling this all wrong! You never give Scott any encouragement. No wonder he isn't learning anything! He's never had trouble in math before, so it must be you! (*teacher becomes annoyed and treats Scott badly*)	YOU: I want to mention my observation that Scott seems discouraged about math. Is there some way that he can be encouraged more so that he will try harder? (*teacher has some suggestions which the two of you discuss*)

Questions to Ask Yourself

1. If I put myself in his or her shoes, how would I react? How would I feel. Would I
    - Listen?
    - Be hurt?
    - Be annoyed?
    - Be frustrated?
    - Feel imposed upon?
    - Take it personally as criticism?

2. If I put myself in the other person's place and consider my relationship with this person, how would I feel?
    - Would I feel imposed upon?
    - Is there a role of authority or seniority here?
    - Will the other person think that I am challenging him or her?
    - Am I making undue presumptions?
    - Am I presupposing a familiarity (or a lack of familiarity) that is not there?

Discussion: The example on the left does not consider the teacher's possible reactions and consequent defensiveness, nor does it acknowledge the relationship, namely: the teacher is the expert and you are the parent. It sidetracks the other person and is likely to elicit defensiveness, thus confusing the communication and diminishing the chances of your understanding one another.

In contrast, the example on the right is effective because it takes into

Appropriateness

account the nature of the relationship and the teacher's role of authority and expertise. This sets the stage for clearer, more effective communication.

Situation: An acquaintance has had an eye disease and has lost vision in one eye. You notice that he does not look at anyone directly and frequently keeps his eyes down.

Inappropriate	*Appropriate*
YOU: I notice that you keep your eyes down a lot and don't look at people like you used to. Is that because of your eyes? If it bothers you, maybe you should wear an eye patch over that eye. (*acquaintance behaves strangely, seems offended, and does not answer you*)	YOU: (politely) How are you getting along? (*the two of you engage in small talk for awhile*)

Questions to Ask Yourself

1. If I put myself in his shoes, how would I react? How would I feel? Would I
   - Listen?
   - Be hurt?
   - Be angry?
   - Be annoyed?
   - Be frustrated?
   - Be imposed upon?
   - Take it personally as criticism?

2. If I put myself in the other person's place and consider my relationship with that person, how would I feel?
   - Would I feel imposed upon?
   - Is there a role of authority or seniority here?
   - Will the other person think I am challenging him?
   - Am I making undue presumptions?
   - Am I presuming a familiarity (or a lack of familiarity) that is not there?

Discussion: The example on the left does not take into account the nature of the relationship: The comment is too familiar, too personal, and is presumptuous. Nor does it consider the other person's possible reactions. After hearing this remark, he may feel criticized, self-conscious, or somewhat indignant. In contrast, the example on the right takes into account both the nature of the relationship and gauges the other person's possible reaction. The listener in this case is more likely to read your intentions correctly. In this way, he is not self-conscious and is not forced into giving any personal information.

Situation: Linda, a close friend of yours, has just received a large raise in salary and bought a lovely new home that you and your spouse wanted to buy. She is a good friend, well meaning, and has always seemed genuinely pleased when things go well for you. But things have not been going well for you, and you feel sorry for yourself and jealous of her good fortune.

Inappropriate	*Appropriate*
Say nothing to Linda about her job or house. Act as if nothing happened. When she acts happy, put a damper on the conversation because you are in a bad mood. *(She does not seem as friendly as usual and stops calling so frequently.)*	Even if you have to swallow your jealousy and pride, congratulate her. You may even say, "I feel a little jealous, I guess, but that's just me. You know we've always been the best of friends and I wish the best for you." *(Your friendship continues as before.)*

Questions to Ask Yourself
1. If I put myself in her shoes, how would I react? How would I feel? Would I
    - Listen?
    - Be hurt?
    - Be angry?
    - Be annoyed?
    - Be frustrated?
    - Be imposed upon?
    - Take it personally as criticism?
2. If I put myself in the other person's place and consider my relationship with that person, how would I feel?
    - Would I feel imposed upon?
    - Is there a role of authority or seniority here?
    - Will the other person think I am challenging her?
    - Am I making undue presumptions?
    - Am I presuming a familiarity (or a lack of familiarity) that is not there?

Discussion: The example on the left ignores Linda, her possible reactions, and the long-standing close friendship that you have had with her. She is likely to feel hurt, unacknowledged, and angry, and this may lead to a serious rift in the friendship. In contrast, the example on the right considers the other person and the relationship and increases the chances for maintaining a mutually satisfying relationship.

In general, the examples on the left illustrated words and actions that ignore the other person and the nature of the relationship with that person. Insensitivities like these usually lead to hurt or angry feelings, disagreements, and, sometimes, serious rifts in the relationship.

In contrast, the examples on the right show how to take the person and the relationship into account. In this way, the chances for confusion and misunderstanding are deceased. Instead, the opportunity for some degree of mutual satisfaction and understanding are increased. (This principle of taking the person and the relationship into account is discussed in more detail in the last chapter.)

Practice

This section provides practice in matching the right kind of statement to the person and to the relationship you have with that person. The following examples describe situations and purposes. Following this are pairs of statements or actions. Check the one that is most appropriate and is most likely to accomplish the purpose.

A. *Situation:* A man and woman have been dating for a long time. Their relationship has been close and romantic and has developed to the point of discussing marriage. The man then becomes frightened and wants to stop the relationship. The woman is sensitive, easily hurt, and often self-critical.

  Purpose: He wants to end the romantic part of the relationship, but, since the two work together, he wants to remain friends. He does not want to hurt her.

  1. ___MAN: (*casually*) I want to stop dating, but, since we work together and have so much in common, I'd still like to be friends.

  2. ___MAN: There is no good way to say this and I want to be certain that you don't see it as criticism or as your fault. I am too frightened by marriage and I know that marriage is what you want for us. So, in order for me to be honest with you, I think we should stop dating. You are lovely and desirable and all the things

I've said before, and many men would be good husbands for you. It's me who can't handle this. I'm sorry if I misled you about our relationship. I just didn't know myself well enough.

Questions to Ask Yourself

1. From what I know of this person, if I put myself in her place, how would I feel?
   - Hurt?
   - Angry?
   - Frustrated?
   - Criticized?
   - Betrayed?
   - Disappointed?

2. If I put myself in this person's place and consider the relationship, how would I feel?
   - Imposed upon?
   - Upset?
   - As if the rules of the relationship have changed?

After answering these questions, decide which of the above ways is more sensitive and appropriate to the person and to the relationship. Check it.

B. *Situation:* A man's mother-in-law is visiting. The man, an attorney, returns home from work, and says that he has had a hard and busy day.

Check the most appropriate response by considering the following: From the son-in-law's point of view, how would he feel in each situation? Which statement is more appropriate to the person?

1.____MOTHER-IN-LAW: I really don't know much about what you attorneys do. Were you in court all day?

2.____MOTHER-IN-LAW: Oh, come on. Stop exaggerating! I know better than that. All attorneys are a bunch of shysters and fast talkers. They don't work hard. Now if you were something worthwhile, like a physician . . .

SUMMARY

In order to be appropriate:

1. Observe the social limits and customs of your locale. Notice what elicits a positive and negative reaction.
2. If you do not know the social limits or customs in a particular situation, ask about them. Find out what is appropriate.
3. Be sure that what you want to accomplish is within social limits and customs. For example, you want to invite your boss over to dinner. Ask if it is considered appropriate for senior and junior executives to mix.
4. When you have a purpose in mind, notice the time, place, and what the other person is doing. Choose a situation that best suits your purpose. For example, if you want to have a private talk with a co-worker, do not choose a busy corridor or a time when he or she seems busy.
5. Keep the other person in mind and try to put yourself in his or her place. If you were that person, how would you feel and react? Take into account all that you know about this person. Is he or she shy, sensitive, arrogant, easily intimidated? For example, you have an employee who is very sensitive to criticism. Rather than saying, "You did a terrible job on that, Ron," you might decide to say, "That report was not as well written as your others. I made some suggestions on how to change it."
6. Consider the relationship that you have with this person. Ask yourself if what you want to do is appropriate with respect to the nature of your relationship.
   - Do you know the person well or are you being too familiar?
   - Are you imposing?
   - Are you being respectful?
   - Are you being too distant?

REVIEW

The following section provides the opportunity to practice and apply the skills and principles presented in this chapter.

I. The column on the left contains descriptions of situations. The middle column contains inappropriate responses while the column on the right contains responses that are appropriate. Draw a line from the situation to the inappropriate response and to the appropriate one.

Situation	Inappropriate Response	Appropriate Response
A. You are walking with a friend who trips and falls.	1. YOU: (loudly) Oh no, not ham. I'm not supposed to eat pork! If I'd known that, I wouldn't have come.	a. You are friendly and polite, but maintain some distance.
B. You are married, and you have a new employee of the opposite sex, also married, who is attractive and appealing to you.	2. You use this opportunity to tell him or her that he or she is a weak person.	b. You listen carefully to her symptoms and respond to her in your role as physician.
C. Your spouse comes home from work and complains of feeling upset.	3. You are afraid to intrude; you do nothing.	c. Although you are not to eat ham, you make no comment and fill up on the rest of the meal.
D. Your neighbor's father dies.	4. You ignore it; feel embarrassed, wait until he or she gets up.	d. You ask him if he's okay and help him up.
E. You are a male physician, and an attractive female patient comes to see you, very worried about a physical complaint.	5. You pat her hand, tell her how pretty she is, and say that no one as lovely as she is could have anything wrong.	e. You call the family and ask what you can do. You send an expression of sympathy.
F. You are guests at a dinner party. The hostess is serving ham. You are on a diet and are not supposed to eat pork.	6. You frequently make a point of touching his or her arm, invite him or her for private coffee breaks, and ask personal questions.	f. YOU: I'm sorry to hear that. Is there something I can do?

II. The examples below show inappropriate responses to situations. Some are inappropriate to social limits and customs; others are not appropriate to the situation, person, or relationship; some may be inappropriate in all dimensions.

After reading each example, decide in what ways it is inappropriate.

A. *Situation:* You are at a small party. There is a couple there with whom you are close. The four of you typically exchange confidences, problems, and successes. Recently, you and your spouse were concerned because one of your sons had been caught stealing something at school. You had confided in your friends about this incident but had told no one else.

At the party, your friend says loudly, "Has Johnny managed to keep out of trouble this week or did he steal something bigger this time?"

1. Is this within social limits?   Yes   No
2. Is this the right time and place to ask this?   Yes   No
3. Is this appropriate to the people there?   Yes   No
4. Does it take relationships into account?   Yes   No

B. *Situation:* A woman is writing her annual Christmas letter, which tells about her son and his wife and their lovely new home and car. The letter does not say much about her daughter and son-in-law except to mention, "As for Sue and Bob, there's not much to say. Bob, as ever, is in school—now he's working on a new degree, or something! We just hope he'll settle down and make some money!" She sends a copy of this letter to her son-in-law's parents.

1. Is this within social limits and customs?   Yes   No
2. Is this the right time and place?   Yes   No
3. Is this appropriate to the persons involved (the son-in-law's parents)?   Yes   No
4. Is this appropriate to the relationship with those persons?   Yes   No

C. *Situation:* A female college teacher has an attractive young male student. He has been having some academic problems and is coming in for tutoring. The student is newly married and has been having some typical adjustment problems of newlyweds. The teacher's intentions are to be helpful. The student is shy and reticent. Daily, the teacher asks about the couple's problems, comments on the wife's behavior, and gives the student advice. She presses him for information about their sex life and offers suggestions. When the student seems discouraged, she tells him that marriage is not all that it is cracked up to be, relates stories of how she has been disappointed in her marriage, and complains about her husband.

1. Is this within social limits and
   customs?   Yes   No
2. Is this the right situation for this?   Yes   No
3. Is this appropriate to the relationship
   of teacher and student?   Yes   No
4. Is this likely to lead to misinterpretations
   or upset on the student's part?   Yes   No

D. *Situation:* A mother is going to visit her daughter at her college dormitory. As she approaches, she notices that her daughter has had her hair cut in a new style. There are other girls around. Before greeting her, she says loudly, "Susie, why did you do that to your hair? It's ruined."
   1. Is this within social limits and customs?   Yes   No
   2. Is this the right time and place for
      the mother to express her preference
      for a different hairstyle?   Yes   No
   3. Is this appropriate to the person?
      Has the mother taken into consideration
      her daughter's feelings?   Yes   No
   4. Is this appropriate to the relationship?   Yes   No

III. Some situations are described below. In each case, use the suggested guidelines and decide what response or action is within social limits and customs and is appropriate to time, place, person and relationship.

A. *Situation:* A friend has fallen and been hospitalized with a broken leg.

   Should you make an effort to call or visit? Should you think, "My friend is probably in a bad mood — I won't bother him (her)?"

   If you are not sure what the friend wants, how could you find out? (Check what you want to do.)
   1. ____Wait for your friend to call and tell you.
   2. ____Do nothing.
   3. ____Figure that you're too busy and life is complicated enough, so why bother?
   4. ____Ask your friend what he or she would like — company, phone calls, help with the kids.

B. *Situation:* Your car was in the repair shop for a paint job over a two-week period. Within a month, the spot that was painted begins

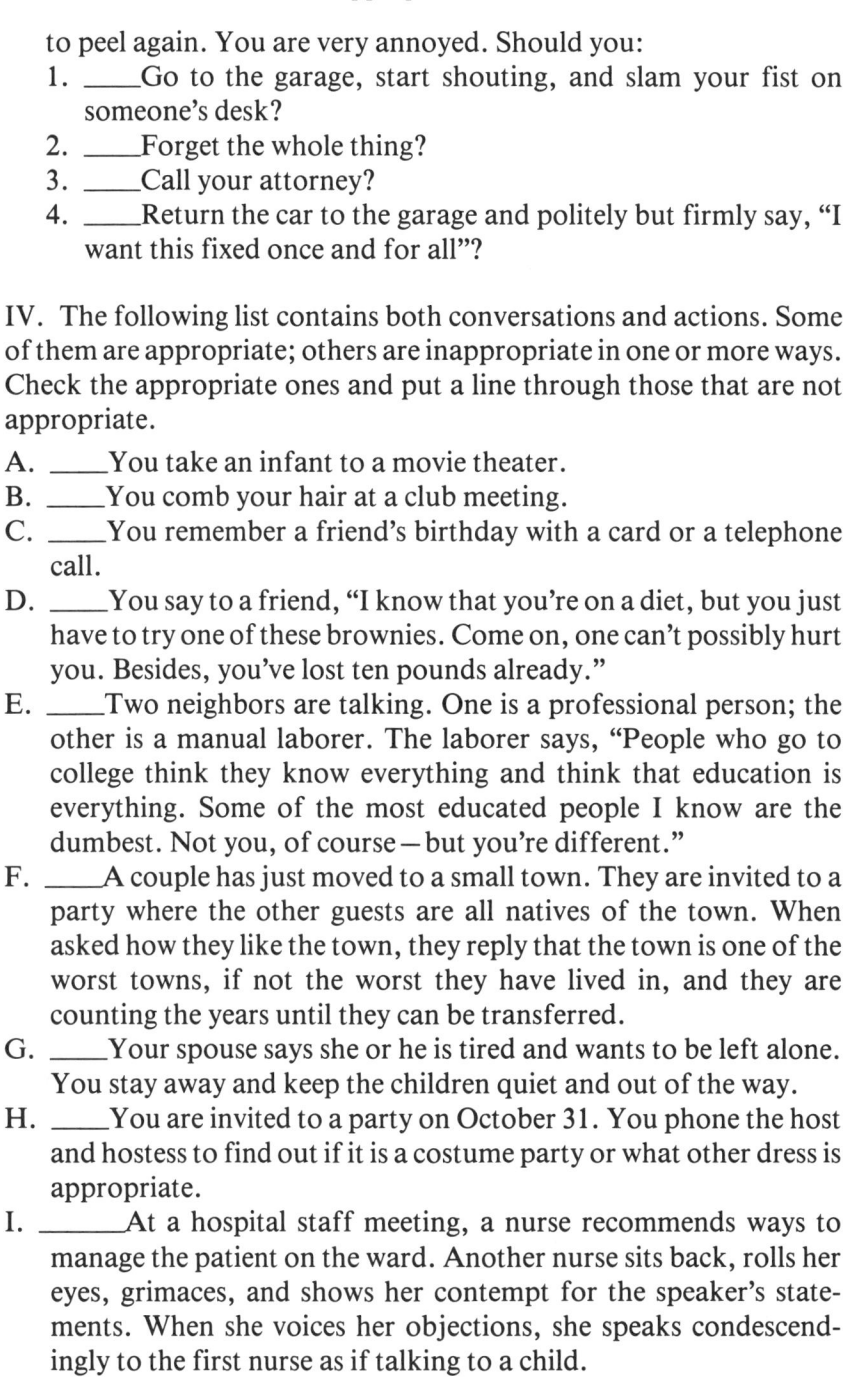

Appropriateness

to peel again. You are very annoyed. Should you:
1. ____Go to the garage, start shouting, and slam your fist on someone's desk?
2. ____Forget the whole thing?
3. ____Call your attorney?
4. ____Return the car to the garage and politely but firmly say, "I want this fixed once and for all"?

IV. The following list contains both conversations and actions. Some of them are appropriate; others are inappropriate in one or more ways. Check the appropriate ones and put a line through those that are not appropriate.

A. ____You take an infant to a movie theater.
B. ____You comb your hair at a club meeting.
C. ____You remember a friend's birthday with a card or a telephone call.
D. ____You say to a friend, "I know that you're on a diet, but you just have to try one of these brownies. Come on, one can't possibly hurt you. Besides, you've lost ten pounds already."
E. ____Two neighbors are talking. One is a professional person; the other is a manual laborer. The laborer says, "People who go to college think they know everything and think that education is everything. Some of the most educated people I know are the dumbest. Not you, of course—but you're different."
F. ____A couple has just moved to a small town. They are invited to a party where the other guests are all natives of the town. When asked how they like the town, they reply that the town is one of the worst towns, if not the worst they have lived in, and they are counting the years until they can be transferred.
G. ____Your spouse says she or he is tired and wants to be left alone. You stay away and keep the children quiet and out of the way.
H. ____You are invited to a party on October 31. You phone the host and hostess to find out if it is a costume party or what other dress is appropriate.
I. ____At a hospital staff meeting, a nurse recommends ways to manage the patient on the ward. Another nurse sits back, rolls her eyes, grimaces, and shows her contempt for the speaker's statements. When she voices her objections, she speaks condescendingly to the first nurse as if talking to a child.

J. A neighbor tells you that she is expecting a baby soon. You and your spouse have always wanted children but are unable to conceive. You say "Great! I'm really happy for you. I'll bet you are excited."

K. ____A group of co-workers go out to lunch together. One of them is seriously concerned that he is having a problem with his heart and is describing the tests and procedures that he is undergoing. He seems concerned and upset. Another person says, "Well, if you're going to die, Fred, a heart attack is a nice way to go, so cheer up. Besides, if you die, I get your job. What's the matter, Fred, can't you joke around? That's your problem, you're far too serious about everything."

CHAPTER FOUR

Acknowledging Others

ACKNOWLEDGING OTHER PEOPLE involves paying attention to and responding to them. This happens when you indicate that you saw what they did and heard what they said. It occurs when you let others know that you notice them and consider them important.

Each of us likes it when another person notices, appreciates, and responds sincerely to us. When you are acknowledged, you feel recognized and worthwhile. If, instead, you are ignored, discounted, or "taken for granted," you are likely to feel hurt, misunderstood, disregarded, or unappreciated. This is not a comfortable feeling, and when it occurs repeatedly you may lose your desire to interact with that person. Failing to acknowledge someone contributes to an atmosphere of misunderstanding, and frustration and dissatisfaction increase.

This chapter defines acknowledgment, points out its importance in relationships, and discusses several ways to achieve this goal. It focuses on these points.

1. Learning about acknowledgment and why it is important.
2. Paying attention to and expressing the positive characteristics of others.
3. Showing interest in others verbally and nonverbally.
4. Being courteous and considerate; avoiding presumptions.
5. Acknowledging others, even when you disagree.
6. Knowing what "incorrect acknowledgments" are and how to avoid them.

SKILL 1: LEARNING ABOUT ACKNOWLEDGMENT AND WHY IT IS IMPORTANT

Acknowledging others involves paying attention to, recognizing, and responding to them. You show interest with words or actions and let people know that you noticed them. Your interest in others conveys the sense that they matter to you. Everyone likes to be noticed, appreciated, and recognized. When we are acknowledged, we feel satisfied and worthwhile.

Acknowledgment can be described as acceptance of and responsiveness to another person. Since people want and, in fact, need responses from others, acknowledgment is a powerful and important part of interactions between people. When you are acknowledged by someone, you have a feeling that you matter to that person. You have a sense of being noticed and significant. This sense maintains your incentive to continue interacting with that person.

If, instead of being acknowledged, you are ignored, discounted, or "taken for granted," you are likely to feel hurt, disregarded, and unimportant. This is not a comfortable feeling, and if it happens repeatedly with the same person you probably will not expect anything positive from interacting with this person. Your motivation to establish or maintain a relationship with this person will decline steadily. Failure to acknowledge people elicits negative reactions and contributes much to misunderstanding and dissatisfaction in relationships.

Acknowledgment involves responding to many different aspects of people, including:

1. Their presence or absence. ("Nice to see you, Ann." "We missed you at the party, John.")
2. Their appearance and nonverbal cues. ("You look nice." "You seem relaxed.")
3. Their actions. ("Thank you for opening the door.")
4. Their statements. ("I heard about what you said, and I think that it's a good idea.")
5. Their experiences. ("I'm glad you had such a good time.")
6. Their intentions and ideas about self. ("I realize that you're trying to be helpful." "I know that you're a hard-working person.")

What you acknowledge depends on you, the other person, and the relationship between you.

Nonacknowledgment occurs when you:

1. Ignore or do not respond to the other person. For example, no mention is made of the special dinner that your spouse prepared.
2. Interrupt.
   HUSBAND: What really concerns me is . . .
   WIFE: Hand me that, please. Those kids made a big mess.
3. Contradict the other person. ("You can't be hungry. You just ate.")

Acknowledgment can, of course, be used selectively. Depending upon the person and the relationship, you may choose not to acknowledge one aspect of a person (e.g., actions) while responding to another aspect such as words. Nevertheless, it is important to remember that repeated failure to acknowledge someone usually elicits strong negative reactions. If you choose to not respond to someone, be aware of the consequences of this action.

Because of the strong impact of acknowledgment, it is an important part of communication. This chapter presents skills to use in responding to others. This first section describes in detail how you can acknowledge or fail to acknowledge various people.

Skill 1a: Acknowledging a Person's Presence or Absence

This skill involves recognizing and responding to people, letting them know that you see them, or telling them that their absence was noticed. It includes smiling, waving, saying hello, nodding your head, or responding when someone greets you. This lets the other person know that she or he is noticed and has some importance in your existence.

You do not acknowledge people when you ignore or avoid them, when you do not respond to them, and when you treat their presence as an intrusion. This creates an impression of disinterest or disregard, and people wonder if you have noticed them, if you disapprove, or if you do not wish to interact with them.

The following examples help to point out the differences between not acknowledging someone and doing so:

Situation: You pass a man you know on the street.

Does Not Acknowledge	Acknowledges
You say nothing and avoid looking at him.	You say "hi", smile, nod to him.

Situation: As you enter a restaurant for lunch, you see your neighbor with the local bank president.

Does Not Acknowledge	*Acknowledges*
The banker is someone that you want to impress, so you say hello to him in a friendly way. You only glance at your neighbor and do not greet him.	You say hello in a friendly way to both of them.

Situation: Husband returns home from work.

Does Not Acknowledge	*Acknowledges*
Wife is busy at her desk, writing, does not look at him or greet him. He comes over to give her a kiss and she says, "Don't bother me. I'm busy."	Wife is busy but looks up and says, "Hi. I'm right in the middle of something—I'll be finished in a minute."

Situation: At work, you walk into the coffee room with a new employee.

Does Not Acknowledge	*Acknowledges*
Introduce him or her to the people that are high in status.	Introduce him or her to everyone.

Situation: A friend has just returned from vacation.

Does Not Acknowledge	*Acknowledges*
You say nothing.	YOU: I missed you. Glad you're back. How was the trip?

Acknowledgment influences the amount of ease and satisfaction people feel when they are together. When people do not feel acknowledged by each other, they are likely to feel dissatisfied and discontent in that relationship and, in fact, are likely to lose their motivation or desire to interact. In contrast, when people feel acknowledged, their satisfaction with the relationship is greater. They have a sense of being recognized, accepted, or appreciated, and their incentive to maintain the relationship is increased.

Skill 1b: Acknowledging a Person's Appearance and Other Nonverbal Cues

This involves recognizing and responding positively to the appearance of others. It can include honest, positive comments about people's physical characteristics, their attire and grooming, or other nonverbal cues. This acknowledgment can also be accomplished by responding with nonverbal expressions that show interest and attention or by a communication of both verbal and nonverbal acknowledgement. For example, smiling back when someone smiles at you, saying to a co-worker, "I like your new outfit," and telling your spouse, "You look particularly nice today." These comments communicate to others that you have taken the time to notice and to appreciate something about them. When things like these are repeatedly ignored or denied, the other person is likely to feel unnoticed and unimportant in your eyes.

It is important to remember, however, that these comments must be honest and sincere. Saying that you like someone's new hairdo when you do not is phony, and it does not contribute to mutual satisfaction and understanding. Dishonest comments are especially risky in close, ongoing relationships. You cannot maintain a facade indefinitely. Eventually, other people will find out about your insincere compliments and will feel betrayed, lied to, and may, in fact, want to end the relationship. Insincere compliments are not shortcuts to satisfaction.

However, noticing and commenting on negative qualities in a derogatory way is not appropriate acknowledgment, either. Saying, for example, "That would be a nice suit if it weren't for that ugly tie" is not acknowledgment. Comments like these only increase defensiveness and diminish trust. They accomplish the opposite of what acknowledgment does and are likely to encourage discomfort and dislike in relationships.

The examples below point out some of the differences between nonacknowledgment and acknowledgment. This first group shows the difference between ignoring and discounting a person's appearance and acknowledging it positively.

Situation: Your spouse works very hard at exercising and keeping his or her weight down.

Ignores	*Acknowledges*
You ignore it, take it for granted, never mention it.	YOU: You really look trim.

Situation: Spouse is wearing a new outfit that enhances his or her appearance.

Ignores	Acknowledges
You do not comment on spouse's appearance but ask how much the outfit cost.	YOU: That looks great. I really like the way you look in that.

The first two examples demonstrate the difference between ignoring and acknowledging. Those below provide a contrast between discounting someone's appearance and acknowledging it.

Situation: A man tells his wife that they are invited to a posh party on Saturday. She buys a special new dress for the occasion. The evening of the party, she puts on the dress and asks her husband how she looks.

Discounts	Acknowledges
HUSBAND: Is that the new dress that you were making such a fuss about? I thought that you were really going to dress up.	HUSBAND: You look very nice. The dress is not as daring as I thought it would be from your description.

Situation: A college girl is dressing for a party. She puts on her best dress and asks her roommate how she looks.

Discounts	Acknowledges
ROOMMATE: (*sarcastically*) That's your best outfit?	ROOMMATE: I think a pants outfit would be better. That navy one you have is complimentary.

Discussion: Repeatedly ignoring or discounting people's appearance gives the impression that you do not notice, do not care, or do not approve of how they look. If you give this impression to someone, he or she is not likely to be comfortable or responsive to you.

These next examples show the difference between insincere acknowledgments and honest ones:

Situation: A woman friend has new hairstyle and asks what you think of it.

Insincere, Dishonest Acknowledgments	Sincere, Honest Acknowledgments
You don't like it but you tell her it looks very nice.	YOU: I'm not sure. It's quite a big change. It doesn't look bad, but I think I like it better the old way.

Situation: Your spouse has gained twenty pounds in the past year and you would prefer that he or she reduce. Your spouse mentions the weight gain and asks if you think a diet would be a good idea.

Acknowledging Others

Insincere, Dishonest Acknowledgment	Sincere, Honest Acknowledgment
YOU: (uncritically) You're fine. Don't worry about a diet. (*spouse does not lose the twenty pounds and, instead, gains ten more; one day, you have an argument*) YOU: And you've gotten to be a big slob these past few years. SPOUSE: (*surprised*) You said I looked just fine all along. Now all of a sudden, I'm a slob. YOU: That's right. You are. I was just too nice to tell you. (*spouse feels hurt, betrayed*)	YOU: I think that a diet is a good idea. I prefer that you get back to your regular weight. SPOUSE: Do I look that bad? YOU: You don't look bad, but I just think that you look better when you are a bit thinner.

Discussion: Dishonest, insincere acknowledgments eventually lead to disappointment and betrayal. This does not mean that you must tell people everything about them that you dislike. Nor does it imply that you are to go out of your way to hurt people's feelings. It does mean that your acknowledgments should be honest and sincere.

The next examples show the difference between negative acknowledgements and positive ones:

Situation: You notice that a co-worker is sitting slouched over, does not smile as he usually does, and is not as impeccably dressed as usual.

Negative Acknowledgment	Positive Acknowledgment
YOU: What's wrong with you? You look like a mess!	YOU: You are not smiling as you usually do. Is there something wrong?

Situation: A friend has adopted a new hairstyle and bought very stylish clothes.

Negative Acknowledgment	Positive Acknowledgment
YOU: It's about time you decided to stop looking like something out of 1950.	YOU: You look really good, and that hairstyle is right for you, too.

In general, when you repeatedly ignore, discount, or criticize people's appearance, they feel unnoticed, disapproved of, or insignificant. Because of this, people will feel frustrated and will have less motivation to interact with you.

In contrast, honest and positive acknowledgments help to create and maintain an atmosphere of being noticed and important. This is an essential part of developing comfortable, satisfying relationships.

Skill 1c: Acknowledging a Person's Actions

Recognizing and responding to people's actions includes saying thank you, expressing your appreciation (e.g., "You do a good job of keeping this place clean"), or responding in other ways to indicate that you notice what they do. By doing this, you let others know that you saw their actions and that you consider them significant.

This does not occur when, through words or nonverbal expressions, you ignore, discount, or deny what another person has done. For example, a husband never comments on how clean the house is or how hard his wife works at keeping it orderly.

The following examples show the difference between ignoring or discounting actions and responding with acknowledgment:

Situation: A co-worker smiles at you and asks, "How are you?"

Ignores, Discounts, Does Not Acknowledge	*Acknowledges*
You do not respond; you look away.	YOU: (*smile*) Fine, thanks. And you?

Situation: A husband gives his wife a blouse as a present. It is not the right size.

Ignores, Discounts, Does Not Acknowledge	*Acknowledges*
WIFE: (critically) Don't you know my size by now?	WIFE: Thank you for such a thoughtful gift. I'll have to get a different size, but I really like it.

Situation: A man has mowed his lawn.

Ignores, Discounts, Does Not Acknowledge	*Acknowledges*
His wife says nothing; takes it for granted.	WIFE: I noticed that the lawn was mowed. Sometimes I forget to mention it, but I do appreciate how hard you work at that.

Situation: You have had a disagreement with a friend, Alan. As far as you are concerned, the disagreement is over and your feelings about

Acknowledging Others

Alan are as positive as ever. You have called him for coffee, chatted with him, and in all ways, tried to be friendly. He continues to act distant and cold. He does not respond to any of your overtures. Finally, you stop by his office and say, "Alan, I don't know what to do. I like you and consider you my friend. Ever since our disagreement, I've tried to be cordial and friendly and you don't respond. What happened?"

Ignores, Discounts, Does Not Acknowledge	*Acknowledges*
ALAN: (*angrily and coldly*) You call that being friendly?	ALAN: OK, I realize that you've tried to be nice. But I was upset by our argument and I have not got over it yet. Some of the things you said in anger still bother me, so being nice seemed phony to me.

The examples on the left are similar to other failures to acknowledge. The speakers in these examples ignore or discount the other person's actions. As a result, the others feel misunderstood, unappreciated, unnoticed, and disregarded.

In contrast, the speakers on the right recognize and respond to the actions of others. This lets the others know that they are noticed, and it confirms their importance in the speaker's existence.

Skill 1d: Acknowledging Another Person's Statements

This involves paying attention and responding to what others say. It means listening, following up on what is said, and responding to thoughts and feelings that people express. For example, you go to a party, and Chris, a friend of yours, says, "I am so tired tonight! I really had a rough day at work."

To acknowledge your friend you might say, "That's too bad. What happened?" This lets Chris know that you heard what she said and are interested in how she feels and in what happened. This does not occur when you fail to respond, change the subject, interrupt, or laugh off or contradict what the other person said. For example:

CHRIS: I'm so tired! I had a rough day at work!

YOU: Come on, you don't know what a rough day is.

In this case, Chris probably thinks that you are not interested and do not care what kind of day she had. In fact, you seem to be "putting her down" and discounting what she said. As a result, she is likely to feel somewhat misunderstood and frustrated. Responses like this fail to recognize and respond to others and are one of the main sources of dissatisfaction and discontent in relationships.

The examples below will help to point out some of the differences between not recognizing and responding to the statements of others and doing so:

Does Not Recognize or Respond to the Other Person

ALAN: I just read a book on gardening.
BOB: Do you know what time the movie starts tonight?

HUSBAND: I feel discouraged. (*looks down, head bent*)
WIFE: I don't want to hear it! Get going! I want to get to the party early!

WIFE: (*excitedly*) Jean and I had a good time today! First, we went shopping, then we had lunch . . .
HUSBAND: Hmm . . . turn the TV to channel 4, please.

HUSBAND: Will you please sit down and go over these bills with me? I want to get this settled.
WIFE: Forget it.

CO-WORKER: I'm cold in here.
CO-WORKER: No, you're not. It's warm in here.

JOHN: I just had somebody do my horoscope. It was really fun!
SAM: Your horoscope! What a waste of time and money.

Recognizes and Responds to the Other Person

ALAN: I just read a book on gardening.
BOB: Did you like the book?

HUSBAND: I feel discouraged. (*looks down, head bent*)
WIFE: What's wrong?

WIFE: (*excitedly*) Jean and I had a good time today! First, we went shopping, then we had lunch . . ."
HUSBAND: Good, I'm glad that you had such a good time.

HUSBAND: Will you please sit down and go over these bills with me? I want to get this settled.
WIFE: I realize it has to be done sometime. I'd rather do it another night, though. How about Thursday?

CO-WORKER: I'm cold in here.
CO-WORKER: It's pleasant to me, but you can wear my sweater if you like.

JOHN: I just had somebody do my horoscope. It was really fun!
SAM: I'm not interested in the occult, but I'm glad you had fun.

In the examples on the left, statements are not acknowledged. Subjects are not followed, questions are not answered, and feelings are ignored or denied. When this happens, people usually feel frustrated, hurt, angry, or misunderstood. This increases feelings of frustration and discontent and sets the stage for unpleasant, dissatisfying interactions.

In contrast, in the examples on the right, people are responded to and recognized. Statements are acknowledged and feelings are accepted as valid. When this occurs, people feel they are noticed and important. They are comfortable in saying what they think or experience, and they are encouraged by your response. This increases the chances for mutual understanding.

Skill 1e: Acknowledging Others' Experiences

This involves recognizing, accepting, or showing interest in the experiences of others, even when their experiences are different from yours. For example:

YOUNG MOTHER: Being a new mother is certainly a big job. I'm really worn out.

NEIGHBOR: I can understand that. It wasn't that way with my third child, because I was used to it. But the first one is really a shock for everyone.

This response communicates interest and acceptance to the young mother. She feels that her neighbor is willing to listen and try to understand what she is experiencing.

Using this skill does not mean that you necessarily agree with the person's experience. Instead, it means that you accept his or her point of view even if yours is different. For example, a husband may say, "I feel like a failure because I didn't get the promotion I wanted." To acknowledge him but disagree, his wife might reply, "I can understand that you may feel like a failure, but I disagree that you are. You may be disappointed, but I do not see that as making you a failure." (Later in this chapter, an entire skill section is devoted to the principle of how to acknowledge and disagree.)

In contrast, interest and acceptance are not communicated to people if you assume that they think, feel, and experience as you do. People frequently forget that others (including their spouse, children, and friends) do not see the world as they do and are not obliged to do so. If people do not accept that others may have reactions or views different from their own, they usually contradict, ridicule, or disallow the other person's experience. For example, in response to the new mother, a less responsive neighbor might say, "How could you feel like that? Being a new mother is one of the most fulfilling times of your life."

It is quite frustrating to be told that you cannot experience things as you do or that you are wrong for feeling as you do. When this happens, you are likely to feel misunderstood and resentful. In fact, failure to accept and acknowledge the experiences of others accounts for much frustration and dissatisfaction between people.

The examples below will help to point out the differences between statements that do not acknowledge the experiences of others and those that do.

Does Not Acknowledge the Experiences of the Other Person

JOHN: We had a really great time in Las Vegas!
JIM: I hate Las Vegas! It's an awful place!
(*Jim denies that John had a good time or that he could like Las Vegas*)

SALLY: I'm redecorating my living room in blue. I like blue.
MARGE: Oh no! That's such a cold color. Your living room will be so depressing!

DON: I really enjoy living on a farm.
PETE: That's because you've never been in the city. You don't know what you're missing.
DON: I have been in the city. I just like this much better.
PETE: That's because you are a hick. You don't see beyond your own simple little world here.

Acknowledges the Experiences of the Other Person

JOHN: We had a really great time in Las Vegas!
JIM: Glad to hear it! What did you do?
(*Jim has had a different experience in Las Vegas but acknowledges John's*)

SALLY: I'm redecorating my living room in blue. I like blue.
MARGE: Blue can be quite attractive in a room.
(*Marge does not agree with the choice of blue but acknowledges Sally's preference*)

DON: I really enjoy living on a farm.
PETE: I know you do. I suppose it's because you were raised here that you like it so much. I don't have the same appreciation of this place that you do, but I can understand that you like it.
(*Pete acknowledges Don's background and experience*)

In the examples on the left, the experiences and feelings of John, Sally, and Don were denied or contradicted. It is disconcerting to be told that you did not experience what you did or that you should not feel as you do. When this happens, you feel misunderstood and react with frustration, discomfort, and defensiveness. This lack of acknowledgment typically lessens the opportunity for mutual understanding and satisfaction.

In contrast, in the examples on the right, the experiences of John, Sally, and Don are responded to and acknowledged. This leads to a sense of ease in the relationships, and the chances for clear communication and some degree of understanding are increased.

This skill of acknowledging and responding to people's experiences is an important one, and you should become quite familiar with it. For this reason, more examples and discussion are presented below.

Does Not Acknowledge Experiences of Others

AL: This has been a tough few months for me. My father's sickness really worried me and with the new baby coming . . . even though I got the promotion at work I wanted, it's been a tough time.
DAVE: (*laughs*) Oh come on. Let's not get dramatic. It hasn't been so bad. Stop feeling sorry for yourself.
AL: (*frustrated*) I'm not feeling sorry for myself.
DAVE: (*laughs*) Oh, yes, you are. Come on, let's cheer up. How about some coffee or a beer?
AL: (*disgruntled*) No, thanks. I'm going home. There I can talk without being accused of being dramatic or feeling sorry for myself.
DAVE: Hey, wait a minute!

Acknowledges Experiences of Others

AL: This has been a tough few months for me. My father's sickness really worried me and with the new baby coming . . . even though I got the promotion at work I wanted, it's been a tough time.
DAVE: I can understand that it has been rough for you. It would be hard for anyone. At least I hope the worst is over. How about getting some coffee or beer with me?
AL: Well . . . OK . . . that sounds good.

Discussion: Often, as in the example on the left, people are threatened by feelings, especially unpleasant ones, and make the mistake of denying another person's sadness or anger. Instead of accepting Al's feelings, Dave plays Pollyanna and tries to remind Al of how good things have been. The "unacknowledged" person (Al) feels misunderstood and contradicted and reacts somewhat defensively. He probably feels frustrated and criticized as well, and he seems to decide that it is not worth it to try to describe to Dave what he is really feeling. This, of course, decreases the chances for exploration of each other's ideas and diminishes the opportunity for mutual understanding. Whenever someone decides that it is hopeless to try to explain his or her feelings to another, that relationship becomes more closed and deteriorates in quality.

In contrast, in the example on the right, Al's experiences are acknowledged and accepted. As a result, there is more chance for exploring and understanding each other's ideas.

Does Not Acknowledge Experiences of Others

WIFE: I was so furious at how your mother was treating you. And what she was saying to me! I am so angry I could scream. What an awful afternoon! I wish we had never gone there.
HUSBAND: Oh, it wasn't so bad. Sometimes you have to do things like that — out of obligation.
WIFE: (*more heatedly*) You don't understand. It was bad. It was a lot of stress and tension for me. And I'm still angry. I have a terrible headache, and I am not going to go through that again — ever. I will not put up with that.
HUSBAND: (*angrily*) There you go, exaggerating as usual. You're making something out of nothing.
WIFE: (*even more angrily*) That's not so. It was something. Now I'm getting even more angry and frustrated. I know how I feel! I was very angry. So don't you stand there and tell me it was nothing. Maybe you were just too blind to notice how your family was behaving! It wouldn't be the first time!
HUSBAND: You're making me upset with your bitching. Be quiet or I'll get more angry — at you.

Acknowledges Experiences of Others

WIFE: I was so furious at how your mother was treating you. And what she was saying to me! I am so angry I could scream. What an awful afternoon! I wish we had never gone there.
HUSBAND: I didn't feel that bad. What was it that you are feeling so angry about?
WIFE: Maybe you didn't notice. But every time I tried to say something, your sister interrupted me. She and you mother acted as if I weren't there. I'd be talking or answering their questions, and they would go right on as if I hadn't said a word. Besides that, you mother treated you like a little kid, your sister acted like a brat, and everybody was talking all at once. No one listened to anyone else. I just got so frustrated!
HUSBAND: Well, I didn't let it bother me.
WIFE: It bothered me.
HUSBAND: It's upsetting to me to talk about it. After all that talking, I need some quiet.
WIFE: And I need to talk and get it out of my system! I was quiet for hours up there.

WIFE: (*sarcastically*) Why are you getting upset? I didn't think anything bothered you! Now you're making something out of nothing!
HUSBAND: I can't take this. (leaves house)

HUSBAND: I understand your need to talk. Can it wait a few hours? Then maybe I could listen.
WIFE: It'll be hard for me to keep quiet but I'd be willing to compromise. I'll respect your need for quiet, if, in two hours, I can say whatever I want and get it off my chest.
HUSBAND: It's a deal.

Discussion: In the example on the left, the spouses' failure to acknowledge each other's experiences leads to upset, accusations, and argument. Notice how each failure to acknowledge escalates the disagreement and fosters misunderstanding. "Nonacknowledgment" breeds more of the same, and the chances for clear communication in the relationship decline.

In contrast, on the right, the husband recognizes the wife's frustration and need to talk, even though his feelings are different. In turn, the wife acknowledges that her husband's experience is different from hers and that he has needs, too. Because of this mutual recognition, both spouses feel understood and are able to work out a compromise that is mutually satisfying.

Does Not Acknowledge Experiences of Others

PATIENT: This leg really hurts, Doc. Isn't there anything you can do?
PHYSICIAN: No, you'll just have to learn to live with it.
PATIENT: It really hurts!
PHYSICIAN: Now, now . . . it can't be that bad. The more you think about it and talk about it, the worse it is. Don't go moping around and feeling sorry for yourself. That's the worst thing to do.
PATIENT: How can you say that? You don't know what I'm feeling. You're not crippled up like I am! I can't even do the things I used to, so don't you stand there and tell me to be tough!

Acknowledges Experiences of Others

PATIENT: This leg really hurts, Doc. Isn't there anything you can do?
PHYSICIAN: Sorry, there's nothing I can do right now. I wish I could do something, but I really can't. (*the doctor acknowledges the discomfort*)
PATIENT: I'm sure you would. It's just that the pain bothers me and I can't do half the things I used to do.
PHYSICIAN: I can't know exactly what you're experiencing, but I know it's hard. I'm sorry that you have to have this unfortunate experience.

PHYSICIAN: Being so bitter and resentful won't help.

Discussion: This example is applicable to many situations in living, besides physician-patient situations, namely: circumstances in which friends or family members are experiencing discomfort, loss, and changes of a psychological or physical nature. Whether you are the spouse, friend, or physician of the person, you do not know what his or her experiences are and have been. In the example on the left, the physician denies the patient's experiences, loss, and pain and implies that the patient is a "weakling" and a bitter person, that he or she is not feeling pain and has no right to feel unhappy about the situation. This leads to further discomfort and frustration on the part of the patient. He or she is likely to go away, feeling misunderstood, resentful and distrustful.

The physician's statements on the right have a different effect. They acknowledge the patient's discomfort and dissatisfaction. Although the physician can do nothing about the pain, the patient has a sense of being listened to and understood. This increases the chances for clear communication and some degree of mutual understanding.

In general, when you ignore, contradict or deny people's experiences, you will elicit vehement reactions. When you tell people that they should not feel as they do, their logical response is to restate their experience. The more strongly you deny their feelings (e.g., "You should not be angry about that," or "Come on, it can't hurt that much."), the more that people are likely to exaggerate their feelings. This easily can escalate into arguments and feelings of extreme frustration.

On the other hand, when you acknowledge the experiences of others, they have a sense of being accepted and understood. This increases the chances for clear communication and ease in the relationship.

Skill 1f: Acknowledging Others' Intentions and Ideas about Themselves

This involves recognition of people's intentions and self-perceptions, even when you do not agree with them. For example:

PATIENT: I know that you are doing what you think is best, doctor, (*acknowledges intention and self-perception*) but I'm still worried about these symptoms.

When others sense that you acknowledge their intentions and self-perceptions, it is easier to explore ideas and express disagreement.

This does not happen when you neglect to recognize or respond to people's intentions or perceptions of themselves. When they are "unacknowledged," people feel misunderstood and frustrated. They are likely to insist even more firmly on their intentions and hold even more strongly to their ideas about themselves. This easily escalates into quarrels and dissatisfaction.

The following examples will help to point out the difference between statements that acknowledge another person's self-perceptions and thinking and those that do not:

Does Not Acknowledge Self-Perceptions of Others	*Acknowledges Self-Perceptions of Others*
HUSBAND: Now when we go out tonight, please act nice to everyone . . . and don't talk too much. WIFE: Nice — I'm always nice! I don't talk too much — just because I don't sit there and act like a mummy — like you do! (*husband denies wife's self-perceptions that she is nice, converses well and is socially skilled*)	HUSBAND: This dinner with the clients is important to me. I know that you can handle social situations, but I'd like you to help me with this and listen to my suggestions. These people like to have a fuss made over them. Let them do most of the talking and ask questions about them.
HUSBAND: You don't look too happy. Something wrong? WIFE: Well, my boss just blew his top at me! HUSBAND: Well, you must have been grouchy or something. What did you do wrong this time? WIFE: I didn't do anything! I'm one of the best workers down there! You'd never understand anyway. (*husband denies wife's self-perception as a good worker and, instead, regards her as "grouchy"*)	HUSBAND: You don't look too happy. Something wrong? WIFE: Well, my boss just blew his top at me! HUSBAND: I'm sure that was not pleasant. You're a good worker, and you two usually get along. WIFE: I know he took out his bad mood on me, and I don't like to be picked on. HUSBAND: I don't blame you for being upset. I wouldn't let it ruin my evening, but that's me.

and someone who always does something wrong)

PHYSICIAN: I can appreciate the discomfort you are having; I don't think there is anything seriously wrong. Come back in a month.
PATIENT: How do I know that I don't have something seriously wrong with me? I've been getting very bad headaches, which I've never had before.
PHYSICIAN: Don't be silly! It is very unlikely that anything is wrong. It's probably tension.
PATIENT: I'm very upset about all of this . . . and I'm not being silly! I'm going to see another physician.
PHYSICIAN: Why are you so anxious?
PATIENT: I want to know what's wrong with me!
PHYSICIAN: I think you're too distraught about this. You need to take some tranquilizers.
(*contradicts the patient's self-perception that he is a mature, sensible person; makes light of his concern and, instead, labels him "silly," "anxious," "tense," "disturbed," and "someone who needs tranquilizers"*)

HUSBAND: (*to wife, who is working on the budget and paying bills*) Here you forgot this, and you didn't do that right.

WIFE: You're right. I won't let it ruin mine, either.
(*husband acknowledges wife's unpleasant experience as well as her usual competence on the job; he does not impose his solution on her but, instead, acknowledges her right and ability to handle it as she likes*)

PHYSICIAN: I can appreciate the discomfort you are having; I don't think there is anything seriously wrong. Come back in a month.
PATIENT: How do I know that I don't have something seriously wrong with me? I've been getting very bad headaches, which I've never had before.
PHYSICIAN: I am quite sure there is nothing seriously wrong, but if you would prefer some further testing and another opinion, I can refer you to someone. Would you like to do this?
PATIENT: Yes, I would. I'd rather get another opinion.
PHYSICIAN: OK, I can understand that. It's a sensible thing to do.
(*acknowledges the patient's concern and also that he is a "sensible" person*)

HUSBAND: (*to wife, who is working on the budget and paying bills*) Here you forgot this, and you didn't do that right.

WIFE: Shut up and get out of here! (*does not acknowledge husband's intention of being helpful*)

WIFE: I'm sure you're trying to help, but I'd prefer to do this alone. (*wife acknowledges intentions*)

Recognizing and responding to a person's intentions and self-perceptions leads to a clearer understanding of what the person was thinking and feeling. When you do not acknowledge people's intentions and self-perceptions, they become frustrated and more determined to persuade you that what they think is right. As a result, arguments and unpleasant situations often develop. Defensiveness occurs, and the chances for effective communication and some degree of understanding are decreased.

Summary

This section has discussed the advantages of acknowledging others and has shown how to acknowledge the following: people's presence, their physical characteristics and other nonverbal cues, their actions, statements, experiences, intentions, and self-perceptions. In any given situation, you can acknowledge or ignore one or more of these aspects. The choice of what to acknowledge and what to ignore depends upon the nature of the relationship, the situation, and how you want to respond. Remember, even if you disagree with someone's statement or self-perception, you can still acknowledge their view of the situation. This makes the communication more effective and the exploration of ideas more comfortable.

There are some specific principles that can help you to recognize and respond to people. The rest of this chapter concentrates on skills that can be used to acknowledge people.

SKILL 2: PAYING ATTENTION TO OTHERS

Paying attention to others involves the following:

1. Look at others and indicate that you notice them by means of nods, smiles, or intermittent eye contact.
2. Listen to what they say and how they say it.
3. Notice specific attributes and actions—for example, hair, pleasant smile, easygoing nature, the special dinner that your spouse fixed, the remodeling that your brother-in-law did, the nice shoes that your boss wears, how relaxed your co-worker seems.

4. Remember to focus on good points. Noticing and commenting on negative qualities is not acknowledgment. For example, "That's a nice outfit, but it's an awful color!" puts the other person down and is not acknowledging.
5. Tell others specifically what you notice and appreciate about them. For example, tell your secretary that his or her cheerful smile is nice to see each morning. (This is more pleasant, accurate, and informative than "You are a wonderful person.") Tell your co-worker that you notice how he or she has reorganized the file room.
6. These statements of what you notice and appreciate must be honest. Do not say that you like the style of your spouse's hair if you do not.
7. If, for some reason, you are going to be inattentive, tell the other person. For example:

HUSBAND: I'm not listening to you right now. I want to finish reading this report, and then I'll be ready to pay attention.

or

CO-WORKER: I'm sorry—I wasn't listening closely. I was thinking about what the boss said.

Often, people forget to notice others and, if they do pay attention, they focus on people's negative qualities. This sets the stage for acknowledging someone in a negative way.

In contrast, using this skill increases the likelihood that you will acknowledge people appropriately and positively. Because they will feel recognized and significant, the chances for effective communication and some degree of satisfaction in the relationship are increased.

Practice

This section provides practice in these seven points of paying attention to others.

I. Noticing positive characteristics

A. You have a friend who can be described in the following way. Check your friend's positive characteristics. He or she:
   1. ____Smokes.
   2. ____Is cheerful and pleasant; smiles, tells jokes.
   3. ____Is considerate, always asks about your day, always listens to your problems.

Acknowledging Others

4. ____Disagrees with you on political issues.
5. ____Is often late—whether you meet for lunch or go to play tennis.
6. ____Has good taste in clothes and always is well groomed.
7. ____Is bald.

Write an acknowledgment statement that tells your friend of one of his or her characteristics that you find positive.

B. Your spouse has the following characteristics. Check the ones that you find positive. He or she:
   1. ____Is very neat and does many chores around the house.
   2. ____Likes to do many of the same things that you like.
   3. ____Does not have the activity level that you do, likes to stay home nights when you would like to go out, and is not as social as you are.
   4. ____Is not as affectionate as you would like.
   5. ____Earns a good salary.
   6. ____Is self-centered, often assuming that you and others like what he or she does and thinks.
   7. ____Has friends that you find boring.
   8. ____Is thoughtful; often buys you gifts.
   9. ____Encourages your interests and your career.
   10. ____Is impatient and short-tempered.

Write an acknowledgment statement that reflects one of these.

II. The examples below contain pairs of statements. One of them mentions positive characteristics; the other does not. Place a check to the left of the acknowledgment statement.

A. 1. ____HUSBAND: Another fancy meal tonight?
   2. ____HUSBAND: I appreciate the time that you spend fixing meals. I know it takes extra effort.
B. 1. ____WIFE: You're usually home on time, and I appreciate that. Tonight you weren't home, and I began to worry.
   2. ____WIFE: (*angrily*) You're late. Why didn't you call?
C. 1. ____MOTHER: (*to son*) It is nice when you phone on Sundays. I look forward to it.

2. ___MOTHER: (*to son*) You're not very thoughtful. You haven't been up to visit more than once in six months.

III. The examples below contain pairs of statements. One of the statements mentions specific positive characteristics in an informative way; the other statement is vague and general. Place a check to the left of the more informative statement.

A. 1. ___WIFE: You are really nice.
   2. ___WIFE: I especially like it when you surprise me like this with flowers. This is very thoughtful of you.
B. 1. ___BOSS: I like the way that you work; you are very conscientious on almost everything you undertake. I appreciate that and am pleased.
   2. ___BOSS: You're a fine employee. We're pleased to have you with us.
C. 1. ___PATIENT: You and all the nurses were wonderful to me.
   2. ___PATIENT: You and all the nurses took time to talk with me. I appreciate that very much.

SKILL 3: SHOWING INTEREST IN OTHERS

There are two ways to show interest in what others are saying or doing.
1. Nonverbal cues of interest and attention
   - Smiling.
   - Nodding.
   - Maintaining eye contact.
2. Verbal cues
   - Following what people are saying. ("I see" or "Yes . . .")
   - Encouraging them. ("Tell me more about what you did.")
   - Telling about your experiences while maintaining the same subject. ("We enjoyed California, too.")
   - Expressing acceptance. ("I'm glad you had such a nice time.")
   - Asking questions and asking for information. For example: "Sam you said that you were taking tennis lessons. How is it going?" "Jane, the last time that I talked to you, you were thinking about getting another job. What's been happening with that?" "I remember you told me that you were very interested in wood working. Have you still been doing some of that?" "I really am not sure what your job involves. Will you tell me some of what you do?"

Acknowledging Others

Using these suggestions will help you to be more aware of showing interest in others.

From time to time, people forget how important their interest and attention is. They may be distracted and look away, interrupt, change the subject, or not ask questions about what the other person has said. Some of the most frustrating people to talk to are those who do not pay attention to what you say or who use whatever you mention as a springboard to tell you their experiences. For example,

YOU: We just got back from San Francisco.

BORE: San Francisco, eh? The last time we were in San Francisco we stayed in Sausalito and went . . . (*continues for the next five minutes; never asks about your trip*)

Responses like these create feelings of frustration and impatience. If you intend to show people that you are interested in them, do not respond like this. Instead, listen carefully and use the suggestions outlined above.

The examples below illustrate the differences between failing to show interest in another person and doing so:

Not Responsive	*Responsive, Shows Interest*
CAROLYN: Our son and his family are coming to visit this weekend. JANE: (*looks away, changes the subject*) CAROLYN: (*feels ignored, plans to change the subject the next time Jane mentions her grandchildren*)	CAROLYN: Our son and his family are coming to visit this weekend. JANE: (*nods*) What do you have planned?
MIKE: I just found a really great stamp for my collection! It was a good buy! TIM: I never could understand how you could waste so much time and money on those stamps. (*denies other's enjoyment*)	MIKE: I just found a really great stamp for my collection! It was a good buy! TIM: I'm glad to hear that.
YOU: We had a great weekend in Chicago. We went to a play and ate at a Greek restaurant. SISTER-IN-LAW: (*not listening*) You say you went to a concert? YOU: No. We went to a play and ate at a Greek restaurant.	YOU: We had a great weekend in Chicago. We went to a play and ate at a Greek restaurant. SISTER-IN-LAW: That sounds nice. Did you like the play? YOU: Yes, and the dinner was good, too.

SISTER-IN-LAW: That's nice. Did you like the Italian food?
YOU: (*becoming frustrated*) It wasn't Italian food—it was Greek! Look, if you don't want to hear this, say so!

PAT: I've started taking piano lessons again. JUDY: Well, I've started taking dancing lessons and that's really fun! Let me show you the first step we learned. PAT: (*feels cut off and frustrated*)	PAT: I've started taking piano lessons again. JUDY: I didn't know you were thinking of doing that. What are you studying?
DAUGHTER: John and I had a great time in New Orleans! MOTHER: You went to New Orleans and didn't buy us a gift. DAUGHTER: (*Thinks to herself: I won't bother to tell her when we go somewhere!*)	DAUGHTER: John and I had a great time in New Orleans! MOTHER: That's a lovely city. I especially loved all the restaurants. DAUGHTER: We did too.

In the examples on the left, the people feel ignored and disregarded and become progressively more frustrated and annoyed. Misunderstandings and feelings of resentment multiply in situations like these.

In contrast, on the right, the people feel recognized and significant. The attention and interest shown, contributes to a sense of comfort and understanding.

Practice

The following section provides practice in showing interest in other people.

I. The right-hand column contains statements that show interest in the other person. Match each statement on the left with the one on the right that is responsive.

A. I can't wait until it's time to start planting my garden.

B. We just had the best time last week-end.

C. I want a microwave oven more than anything!

1. That's nice. What did you do?
2. That's too bad. What's been happening?
3. What is it that you find so satisfying?
4. Why is it at the top of your list?

Acknowledging Others

D. These past few days have been miserable at work. I can't wait to get home at night.

II. The following examples contains pairs of statements. One of the statements shows interest in the other person; the other does not. In each case, select the one that shows interest in and response to the other person. Underline the words that convey this message.

A. HUSBAND: I've been sitting back there, working out our budget and thinking about some plans for remodeling.
   1. ___WIFE: Did you see this schedule for plays? I'd like to go to some of these.
   2. ___WIFE: Good. What were you thinking about?

B. NEIGHBOR: We had a good time. We went to a Japanese exhibit.
   1. ___NEIGHBOR: That sounds interesting. What was it like?
   2. ___NEIGHBOR: None of that Oriental stuff interests me. It's all the same to me.

C. SPOUSE: What I'm concerned about is . . .
   1. ___SPOUSE: Here's that new TV show I was telling you about.
   2. ___SPOUSE: You're hesitating. Tell me what you are worried about.

III. Each of the following examples contains a statement that does not respond to or show interest in the other person. In each case, rewrite the statement so that it is responsive to the other person.

A. FRIEND: I'm reading a book on the codes the Nazis used in World War II.
   FRIEND: I never did like those historical books.
   Rewrite:

B. SPOUSE: Sometimes I think I'd like to do something different . . . maybe get a different job.
   SPOUSE: Would you be quiet and let me read the newspaper?
   Rewrite:

C. SON: Sorry we didn't call sooner. We've both been really busy.
PARENT: Sure, sure . . . you always have excuses. Nobody is that busy.
Rewrite.

SKILL 4: BEING CONSIDERATE: AVOIDING PRESUMPTIONS

Being considerate is one way of acknowledging and indicating to others that they are worthy of respect. This skill involves taking into account the other person's desires, needs, and time requirements. For example:

Statement	*Presumptions*
Donna, a friend, phones you and says, "If it's all right with you, I'd like to drop by after supper for a few minutes. I just thought I'd show you the photos I took at the last party. Is that convenient for you?"	1. The other person may not be free at that time. 2. The other person wishes to do something other than visit or look at pictures.

In this way, Donna does not impose upon your relationship or your time. She gives you the opportunity to let her know if you are busy or if you have other plans. This communicates a quality of respectfulness. You feel that Donna recognizes that you may have other plans or obligations. You feel understood and appreciated.

Sometimes, people impose upon others and make presumptions without considering the other person. For example:

Statement	*Presumptions*
Donna, a friend, knocks on your door and says, "Hi, I was in the neighborhood and thought I would stop by and show you these photos."	1. You are free to talk and to look at the pictures. 2. If you are not free to talk, you can interrupt whatever you are doing.

In contrast, this attitude communicates a lack of respect. Your obligations or desires for privacy are ignored. This can be frustrating and annoying and, if it happens repeatedly, can markedly diminish the chances for understanding and satisfaction in the relationship.

Acknowledging Others

In general, using this skill of being considerate has the following advantages.
1. It communicates a sense of respect to others.
2. It acknowledges their preferences, desires, and obligations.
3. It increases the chances for some degree of mutual satisfaction in the relationship.

The following examples illustrate the difference between actions and statements that make presumptions and those that do not.

Inconsiderate Behavior or Statement	Presumptions	Considerate Behavior or Statement
Phoning at 7:00 A.M. or 11:30 P.M.	1. You are awake, functioning, and willing to talk. 2. You are not in the process of doing something else, such as getting ready for work or getting ready for bed.	Phoning at an appropriate hour and asking, "Is it convenient for you to talk?"
FRIEND: Let me borrow your book on gardening.	1. You have no need of the book. 2. You are willing to lend it. 3. You trust this person to take care of it and return it.	FRIEND: If you would be comfortable loaning your gardening book to me, I would like to borrow it for a few days. I'll be sure to return it at the end of the week.
FRIEND: Come over and play bridge with us tonight. I'll expect you at 7:30.	1. You want to play bridge. 2. You are free to do so.	FRIEND: If you are free and would enjoy playing bridge with us tonight, we would be happy to have you. Would you like to join us?
SPOUSE: I made arrangements to go to the football game with the Spencers. That should be fun.	1. These arrangements will be fun for you. 2. You want to go to a football game. 3. You want to go with the Spencers. 4. You have no other plans.	SPOUSE: I'd like to go to a football game with the Spencers this weekend. Will you go?

The examples on the left make many assumptions. Because these statements are not respectful or acknowledging, you are likely to feel annoyed. If these presumptions continue, your satisfaction with that person and with the relationship probably will decrease.

In contrast, the people in the examples on the right are considerate. The statements acknowledge your time and priorities. This helps create an atmosphere of respect, and the chances for some degree of mutual understanding and satisfaction are increased.

Practice

The following section will provide some practice in identifying considerate statements and behaviors.

I. The right-hand column contains actions or statements that are considerate and courteous. Draw a line from each situation on the left to a courteous response on the right.

Situation	*Response*
A. Parents wish to visit married daughter and son-in-law.	1. They ask the other couple if they are willing to leave.
B. One couple picked up their neighbors; the four drove together to a party. At eleven, the couple who drove wants to leave.	2. They say, "We don't want to impose on you. If you're willing to watch the baby — fine."
C. A young couple has a ten-month-old baby. They are planning a two-week vacation and discuss babysitting with the husband's parents.	3. They call ahead to see (1.) if they are busy and (2.) if they would like to visit.

II. Each example below describes a situation. Following this are two statements or actions. One of these is courteous and considerate; the other makes presumptions.

Check the response that is courteous. Underline the part that acknowledges the other person.

A. Situation: Husband and wife are running their weekly errands.

1. ___WIFE: After the bakery, we'll get groceries, then stop at the bank.
___HUSBAND: I'd like to stop at the hardware store, too.
___WIFE: Oh, no — not there! I'm not going to go there! You always spend so long there!

2. ___WIFE: After the bakery, we'll get groceries, then stop at the bank.
___HUSBAND: Sure, I'd like to stop at the hardware store, too.
___WIFE: Fine. I don't want to go there, but you go there while I'm at the bank.

___HUSBAND: It's just across from the bank.
___WIFE: You can go there after we get home! There's no reason for us to go there — you go by yourself. I don't want to wait for you.

B. *Situation:* Friends invite you over for a drink.

1. ___FRIEND: We have some slides from our trip that we'd love to show you, but you probably are not as interested in them as we are. You won't hurt our feelings if you say you don't want to see them.
YOU: Maybe another time. Tonight I'm in the mood to talk or play cards. OK?

2. ___FRIEND: We have one hundred slides from our trip. Sue, get the projector. This is OK with you, isn't it? Wait'll you see these slides.
YOU: Uh . . . sure.

SKILL 5: ACKNOWLEDGING OTHERS EVEN WHEN YOU DISAGREE

It is easy to acknowledge others when you agree with them or when you disagree on an issue that is insignificant. However, when you disagree with someone on an important issue, it takes a special skill to acknowledge the other person and express your views at the same time. In order to accomplish this, you must recognize your differences, accept the other person's right to think, feel, or act differently from you, and express your acceptance to the other person. This skill involves these steps.

1. Acknowledge the other person's feeling, thoughts, experiences, or self-perceptions. For example, "I can understand that you are annoyed by what happened."
2. Express the fact that there is a difference of opinion and this difference is understandable and acceptable. For example, "Each of us has our own way of looking at this."
3. Express your views directly and responsibly. For example, "Here is my view . . ."
4. If the situation is one that must be resolved, state each of your views and then ask how this can be worked out. For example, "I

want to take a second job, and you think that I would be neglecting the family too much. I can understand your point of view, but I also want that job. How can we work this out?"
   5. Be sure to communicate your acceptance of the other person with appropriate nonverbal cues (e.g., pleasant tone of voice and facial expressions).

When you use these steps, the other person feels accepted, even though your thoughts and opinions differ. This maintains an atmosphere of understanding and keeps communication open.

Instead of doing this, people often criticize others when there is disagreement. They become defensive when someone has a different view; they try to persuade others to think, feel, and react just as they do. Instead of acknowledging, they do one of the following:
   1. They ignore, deny, or contradict the other person's thoughts, feelings, or opinions. ("It's silly to be so upset about that!").
   2. They express their opinion and imply that the other person *must* think the same way that they do. ("If you had any sense, you would see it the way I do!").

Responses like these lead your listeners to feel frustrated and annoyed. They will defend their point of view even more strongly, and the disagreement will become more firmly entrenched. Because of this, their willingness to listen declines, and the chances for effective communication are decreased.

In general, this skill of acknowledging others even when you disagree has the following consequences.
   1. The other person feels that his or her view is accepted and recognized. This maintains a comfortable atmosphere in the relationship and increases the other person's willingness to listen to your ideas.
   2. Because of this acceptance of differing views, there is greater opportunity to explore each other's thinking. As a result, the chances for effective communication and some degree of understanding are greatly increased.

For these reasons, it is particularly helpful to use this principle when disagreement is present and when you are discussing an important issue.

The following examples will help to illustrate the difference between disagreeing and acknowledging the other person while disagreeing.

Situation: A couple is discussing the household chores. So far, the husband does the yard work and the wife does the cooking. They share everything else equally. Recently, the wife has taken a part-time second job and is also active in many community activities. She does not get home most nights until 7:30, and, as a result, she has not been cooking.

Does Not Acknowledge Other Person

HUSBAND: I can't put up with this much longer. I've been having to fend for myself every night for the past two months. When are you going to start cooking again?
WIFE: I'm too tired to cook at 7:30. With two jobs and all these activities, I can't come home and cook, too.
HUSBAND: Well, I don't like cooking. I don't see why you can't come home and fix dinner like you used to. . . . You have to have some responsibility around here! The least you could do is cook for me. What kind of wife are you, anyway?
WIFE: I'm a working wife, and I'm making a very good income, especially with my second job. I'm too tired to cook when I come home.
HUSBAND: Well, somebody has to cook and that somebody is you.
WIFE: Why me? Why not you?
HUSBAND: Me? I'm not the wife!
WIFE: Well, I'm not a typical wife, and I don't want to cook.
HUSBAND: That's just great. Maybe I'm not the typical husband. Maybe I don't want to be married if you don't cook.

Acknowledges Other Person

HUSBAND: I can't put up with this much longer. I've been having to fend for myself every night for the past two months. When are you going to start cooking again?
WIFE: I'm too tired to cook at 7:30. With two jobs and all these activities, I can't come home and cook, too.
HUSBAND: (*calmly*) OK, we have a difference of opinion here. You think that you shouldn't have to work two jobs and then come home and cook, and I can see that; on the other hand, I figure that I do all the yard work. Besides, I don't like to cook, so I want you to do it. How can we handle this?
WIFE: I'd be willing to cook on weekends. On the other nights, we could either go out to eat or you could cook.
HUSBAND: What if we worked together on Sundays? We could cook and freeze things for the rest of the week?

Situation: Husband and wife are relaxing on a Sunday afternoon. He suggests that they go visit their friends, the Scotts.

WIFE: That's a good idea. Let's call them and ask if it's OK for us to drop by.
HUSBAND: There's no need to call. Let's just go.
WIFE: I prefer that we call.
HUSBAND: Look, it's more friendly and casual if we just drop by. What are friends for? If you can't be casual, you're not friends.

Does Not Acknowledge Other Person	*Acknowledges Other Person*
WIFE: You think you're being friendly, but you're wrong. When people drop by our house unannounced, you get annoyed. HUSBAND: Not always! WIFE: No, not always, but sometimes you do. So why is it different when you do it to them? You're just as rude and inconsiderate as the rest of your family. Your parents and your brother always come by without calling, and you get mad!	WIFE: I can understand that you think it's being friendly to drop by. I don't see things the same way. I prefer to call people and give them the chance to say that they are busy. That's more comfortable for me, even with close friends. HUSBAND: I don't think it's necessary. WIFE: OK, but I'm going to call, or else I'll feel like I'm intruding.

In the examples on the left, the husband and the wife express their disagreement. Instead of recognizing and accepting the other spouse's point of view, they disregard or criticize it. The other spouse becomes more frustrated, and each spouse defends his or her position more strongly. The more criticism that is leveled, the more defensive each person becomes. When this happens, people become less and less willing to listen and to understand.

In contrast, on the right, the spouses acknowledge each other's views while expressing their own. This helps to create an atmosphere of understanding and acceptance. Because each spouse feels that his or her ideas are recognized and accepted, there is a greater willingness to listen and to understand. The chances for exploring each other's ideas and arriving at a mutually satisfying solution are greatly increased.

Practice

The section below is designed to give you some practice in expressing disagreement while, at the same time, acknowledging the other person and his or her right to think differently than you do.

I. Below are pairs of statements. One of the sentences expresses the

Acknowledging Others 191

other person's right to an idea different than your own; the other does not. In each case, check the expression that gives the other person the right to his own opinion. Underline the words that seem to convey the idea that it is all right for the other person to think differently than you.

A. Situation: Dave is discussing his preference for neatness with a friend.
   1. ___DAVE: I like things neat and orderly, and I get a great deal of enjoyment out of that. I realize that other people don't feel the same way.
   2. ___DAVE: If I left things as messy as you do, I would be miserable all day. How can you be that way?

B. Situation: In the family, the wife goes to church on Sundays; the husband does not.
   1. ___WIFE: I know you don't like to go to church on Sunday. If you would get up and go to church, you would feel a lot better.
   2. ___WIFE: I prefer to go to church on Sundays, but that's because it's part of me and part of my upbringing. That doesn't mean that you have to feel the same way I do.

C. Situation: Parents are visiting their married daughter and her husband. They begin discussing a political issue, and there is disagreement between the father and the son-in-law.
   1. ___FATHER: Anyone who supports that is naive. You must not have an ounce of sense in you!
   2. ___FATHER: I have a different opinion of this than you do. Of course, you have yours and I have mine for different reasons. Probably we're each a little bit right and a little bit wrong.

D. Situation: Husband is complaining to wife that he feels tired and tense.
   1. ___WIFE: I always feel better after a hard day at work if I go out and get some exercise like playing tennis or taking a walk. That's not to say that you should do the same thing that I do. What do you think would help you to relax?
   2. ___WIFE: If you'd go out and get some exercise after work, then you'd feel better! I can't understand how anybody can sit and do nothing as you do.

II. The following examples include statements that do not give the

192   A WAY WITH WORDS

other person the right to think differently. In each case, change the statements so that they let the other person know that you accept differences of opinion.

A. Situation: A friend of yours has been angry and bitter ever since learning that he has heart disease. You say, "Just because you found out that you have heart disease, you shouldn't be angry! Anger will get you nowhere, and people have no patience with angry, sick people. My brother had a heart attack several years ago, and right now, he's just thankful that he's alive! That's how you should feel."
Rewrite:

B. Situation: You go to visit a friend in a small town. You do not like the community and say, "I can't understand how you can possibly stand to live here. This town is really dead."
Rewrite:

SKILL 6: INCORRECT ACKNOWLEDGMENTS: WHAT THEY ARE AND HOW TO AVOID THEM

Acknowledging someone incorrectly is a frequent error in relationships. Three common mistakes are:

1. Acknowledging something that is not a significant or essential part of the other person's values or self-image. For example, an attorney prides herself on her competence and on her quick thinking. A male client says to her, "I came to you because you're the best-looking lawyer in town." A husband gives his wife a gift that he spent hours selecting. He considered it a thoughtful gift and very much wanted to please her. She opens it, does not comment on the gift, but says, "That wrapping paper was really pretty. Where did you get it?"
2. Responding to what the person wants acknowledged but minimizing or exaggerating it. This can include using hollow superlatives or responding to only one small part of what the person

wants acknowledged. For example, an employee has worked hard for a month on a project. The boss says, "I know you've worked *a little* on this project." A neighbor took care of your children while you and your spouse went shopping. Upon returning, you tell your neighbor, "You are the most wonderful neighbor that anyone could have. No one has ever done anything this nice before, and the kids said that they never had any good food like you made!"
3. Acknowledging something about the person that fits your image of him or her but which is inaccurate or inconsistent with the individual's self-image. For example, a wife sees herself as mature and independent. Her husband prefers to see her as a helpless little girl who relies on him for protection and guidance. He says to her, "You don't fool me. Beneath all that independence, you're just a sweet, helpless little girl."

When you acknowledge others incorrectly, the consequences are almost the same as failing to acknowledge them. When this happens, people feel frustrated and discounted. The qualities or actions that they want recognized are disregarded or minimized, and they are likely to respond angrily and defensively.

These incorrect acknowledgments contribute a great deal to frustrations and misunderstandings in relations. In order to avoid these errors, follow these guidelines.

1. Pay attention. People often ask for reassurance about the things that they want acknowledged. For example, a wife who wants her attractiveness acknowledged may say, "Do you think I'm getting heavy?" If a wife wants her husband to acknowledge the special dinner she fixed, she might say, "Did you like the dinner? I spent all afternoon on it."
2. When you do acknowledge something, notice how the other person responds. If you are acknowledging something that the other person considers trivial or insignificant, he or she may shrug, frown, become silent, or look annoyed. In some way, with words or actions, he or she will indicate that what you said minimized, exaggerated, or did not acknowledge the important issue. For example, a husband wants his wife to acknowledge how hard he works and what a tough job he has. Instead, she minimizes it by saying, "You take everything so seriously and you're so uptight and sensitive. Your job wouldn't be so tough if

you didn't make everything a big deal." Her husband replies, "That's not it. It's not me—it's the job. You don't understand."

A husband wants to be reassured that his wife still cares about him, and she says, "Of course, I do. We're married, aren't we?" He may respond by saying sarcastically, "Oh, that's great." Or, if she says, "You are the most intelligent man in the whole company, I'm sure. You're so smart that I never even understand you half the time!" her husband may say sarcastically, "Oh sure . . . that's it."

3. If the other person gives you an indication that you acknowledged him or her incorrectly or incompletely, ask what you missed. Whenever you get the feeling that the other person wants you to say something but you do not know what, ask directly. For example, a woman tells a male co-worker that she really liked how understanding and gentle he was with an elderly customer. He frowns and says, "Sure, you probably think I'm a pushover." Because he reacted this way to her acknowledgment, she thought that she had responded incorrectly. So she said, "I tried to say I thought you did a good job and not that you were a pushover. What can I say to convince you of that?"

When people are acknowledged accurately and completely, they feel satisfied and better understood. As a result, their motivation to continue interacting with that person is increased, and their incentive to develop and maintain a mutually satisfying relationship is enhanced.

Here are some examples that demonstrate the difference between inaccurate, incomplete acknowledgments and those that are accurate and complete:

Situation: Brian and Lynn work together. Lynn is active in the women's movement. Brian is opposed to women's rights. Lynn has just described an incident where she thought that the boss was paternalistic and condescending to her.

Inaccurate, Incomplete Acknowledgment	*Accurate, Complete Acknowledgment*
BRIAN: You just don't understand the man's point of view at all. The boss was just trying to be protective of you, that's all. LYNN: I don't need to be protected.	BRIAN: You just don't understand the man's point of view at all. The boss was just trying to be protective of you, that's all. LYNN: I don't need to be protected.

Acknowledging Others

BRIAN: Oh, yes, you do. You just don't know it. None of you women could get along without one of us men helping you. You just don't realize how much trouble we take to make things better for you women.
LYNN: (*angrily*) Do me a favor and don't go to any more trouble for me. Why don't you go and protect one of your male friends?
(*Brian acknowledges what fits with his ideas about women and Lynn; he does not acknowledge her self-concept*)

BRIAN: (*recognizing her response*) OK, I guess you feel that you don't need to be protected. But, men usually think that women need some protection. In some ways, I think that they mean it as a compliment.
LYNN: They may mean it as a compliment, but I don't take it as one.
BRIAN: Why isn't it a compliment?
LYNN: If men would say that I could stand on my own two feet and treat me that way, that would be a compliment!

Situation: A husband would like his wife to consider him sexy and attractive. He says, "You don't seem as affectionate and responsive as you used to be. Don't you find me attractive any more?"

Inaccurate, Incomplete Acknowledgment

WIFE: Of course, I do. You look the same as you always did, and you don't even have any gray hairs like all our friends do.
HUSBAND: Great. I look the same and my hair is brown—that doesn't mean that I'm sexy or that you find me attractive.
WIFE: Wait a minute . . .
HUSBAND: Forget it. (*walks away*)

Accurate, Complete Acknowledgment

WIFE: Yes, I do. I think you have a great body and very sexy hair.
HUSBAND: I'd never guess that from how you act. You hardly seem to notice when I'm around.
WIFE: I've been preoccupied with my job and the kids, but I'm going to start paying more attention to you.

In the examples on the left, incomplete and inaccurate acknowledgments create unpleasant situations. Defensiveness and frustration are increased, and both persons become less willing to listen to each other. The situations deteriorate into attacks and both persons feel misunderstood.

In contrast, on the right, the acknowledgments are accurate and complete. As a result, the people involved feel accepted and understood. They are more likely to listen and try to understand the other person's view. The chances for exploring each other's ideas and achieving some degree of satisfaction are greatly increased.

196   A Way with Words

Practice

This section provides practice in recognizing incorrect acknowledgments and substituting accurate, sincere responses.

I. Each of the examples describes a situation and possible responses. One of these statements is accurate, honest, and acknowledging; the other is not. Place a check to the left of the one that is more responsive.

A. Situation: A female university professor enjoys and takes pride in her career. She is not particularly interested in domestic matters. Friends of her husband come over to visit.
   1. ___GUESTS: Oh, what a lovely home you have, and that dinner was delicious. It's good that you didn't let your Ph.D. interfere with really important skills.
   2. ___GUESTS: Bob said that you teach at the university. What do you teach?

B. Situation: Although John is an accountant, he studied classical music for many years and is a good pianist. John's wife has some friends visiting. They are enjoying John's playing. John stops playing and walks into the kitchen where the women are seated.
   1. ___WIFE: We enjoyed your playing.
   2. ___WIFE: Good, I'm glad you stopped playing. You were bothering us.

C. Situation: Wife and husband planned a weekend with two old friends of hers from high school. The four of them had very little in common, and it was an awkward and uncomfortable weekend.
   HUSBAND: I'm glad that's over with.
   1. ___WIFE: What do you mean? That took very little effort on your part.
   2. ___WIFE: Thanks for being so pleasant and cheerful. I realize that you made quite an effort to be nice to my friends this weekend.

II. The following examples contain different types of incorrect acknowledgments. In each case, circle the type of incorrect acknowledgment represented.

A. Situation: A couple has worked on redecorating their home. It is very nice but nothing outstanding.
   GUEST: You have the loveliest home I've ever seen! Those paintings you did yourself are just gorgeous. I know that you have a

good sense of color but this is utterly fantastic. No one could've done a better job!"
Error:
1. Acknowledging something that is not a significant part of person's values or self-image.
2. Exaggerating.
3. Minimizing.
4. Acknowledging something that is inaccurate or inconsistent with the person's self-image.

B. Situation: A man values his career and intellectual achievements. He returns home to tell his wife that he has received a promotion at work. She says, "That's nice." Later that evening, she says, "It is so marvelous how you keep the yard up and all. You're such a good handyman. Most other husbands are all thumbs!"
Error:
1. Acknowledging something that is not a significant part of person's values or self-image.
2. Exaggerating.
3. Minimizing.
4. Acknowledging something that is inaccurate or inconsistent with the person's self-image.

C. Situation: A couple has spent several hours preparing a special gourmet dinner.
GUEST: Well, that was pretty good. Some of those dishes were a little unusual, but they were OK. Next time maybe you can perfect them a bit more.
Error:
1. Acknowledging something that is not a significant part of person's values or self-image.
2. Exaggerating.
3. Minimizing.
4. Acknowledging something that is inaccurate or inconsistent with the person's self-image.

D. Situation: A husband sees himself as a pleasant, thoughtful person.
WIFE: You are one of the most unpleasant, grouchiest, and inconsiderate people I've met.

Error:
1. Acknowledging something that is not a significant part of person's values or self-image.
2. Exaggerating.
3. Minimizing.
4. Acknowledging something which is inaccurate or inconsistent with the person's self-image.

SUMMARY

Recognizing and Responding to Others

Acknowledging others involves recognizing and responding to others with words and nonverbal expressions. This includes acknowledging their presence or absence, appearance and other nonverbal cues, their actions, statements, experiences, intentions, and self-perceptions.

To acknowledge, follow these guidelines:

1. Pay attention to others, look at them, notice what they do or say.
2. Indicate that you notice them by means of nods, smiles, greetings, or eye contact.
3. Notice specific attributes and actions of others. Remember to focus on good points.
4. Tell the other person specifically what you notice and appreciate, but be certain that these comments are honest. Do not say that you like something if you do not.
5. Listen to what people say and how they say it. Follow up what they say; do not change the subject or interrupt.
6. Show interest in the other person by:
   a. Asking questions and asking for information. ("How's that class in woodworking that you're taking?" "You said that you started in business on your own. How did you decide to do that?" "What's it like to be a new father?")
   b. Asking about their ideas, feelings, reactions. ("What did you think of the discussion?")
   c. Encouraging. ("Tell me more about what you did.")
   d. Telling about your experiences while maintaining the same subject. ("We enjoyed California, too.")

Acknowledging Others

    e. Expressing acceptance of the other person's experiences. ("I'm glad you had such a good time." "I'm sorry you feel sick." "I understand that you feel angry.")
7. Take into account the other person's desires, needs, and time requirements. Be considerate.
8. Express the other person's right to have experiences, values, opinions, and thoughts different from yours. Acknowledge their right even when you disagree. For example, "I can see your point. Based on my experience, I have a different view, but that's just me. Each of us has our own way of looking at things."
9. Acknowledge people correctly. Avoid the following common errors.
    a. Acknowledging something that is not a significant or essential part of the other person's self-image. (For example, saying to a female attorney, "You are the best-looking lawyer in town.")
    b. Minimizing or exaggerating what the person wants acknowledged. Recognizing only a small part of what the person wants. (For example, "I know you've worked a little on this project.")
    c. Acknowledging something that is inaccurate or inconsistent with the individual's self-image. (For example, saying to a woman who sees herself as mature and independent, "I know you're just a sweet, helpless little girl at heart.")

Practice in Acknowledgment Skills

This section provides an opportunity for you to review and practice the various skills and types of acknowledgment that you learned in this chapter. There is a separate practice section for each skill that was discussed in the chapter. This is followed by a general section where all the skills can be applied.

PAYING ATTENTION TO OTHERS. The example below describes characteristics and actions that may be appealing or unappealing to you. Following this description, both honest and dishonest statements are listed. Check the honest statements.

I. Of your spouse's appearance, you like his or her hair style, complexion, eyes, and smile.

You are neutral about the way he or she dresses.

You dislike the way he or she has gained weight, when he or she wears jeans or sloppy clothes, when he or she scowls.

A. Your spouse says, "You don't mind if I've gained weight, do you?" What should you reply?

1. ____"By the way, I really like your hair like that.

2. ____"No, I hadn't noticed."

3. ____"I prefer the way you look about ten pounds lighter, but that's just me. You still look attractive, either way."

B. Your spouse says, "I'm going to wear jeans to the Wilsons." How should you reply?

1. ____"That's fine."

2. ____"I think other outfits are more attractive. I would rather that you wear something dressier."

II. In each of the examples below, the speaker is inattentive to you. One of each pair of statements explains the inattentiveness; the other does not. Place a check next to the one that acknowledges the other person.

A. 1. ____SPOUSE: Go away . . . I'm busy.
   2. ____SPOUSE: I'm busy fixing this. I'll listen in a minute.
B. 1. ____CO-WORKER: Excuse me for a minute. I want to jot down a reminder to myself.
   2. ____CO-WORKER: (*while you are talking, looks away, makes notes on pad, doesn't listen*)
C. YOU: We went camping last weekend and had . . .
   1. ____MOTHER-IN-LAW: That's nice . . . (*to your spouse*) I saw your old friend, Jim Bailey, last week. He asked about you and . . .
   2. ____MOTHER-IN-LAW: Excuse me, I'll listen to you but before you tell me about it I have a message for you from Jim Bailey that I don't want to forget.

SHOWING INTEREST IN OTHERS. In the following examples, write some responses that show interest in the other person.

Acknowledging Others

A. FRIEND: We just saw a house that we would like to buy.

B. SPOUSE: There's a chance that I might be transferred to California.

C. The last time you saw your neighbor he was complaining of some problems at work.

D. Someone you know has just returned from a trip to London.

E. FRIEND: Well, I've taken up a new hobby—refinishing furniture.

BEING COURTEOUS: AVOIDING PRESUMPTIONS. The following table contains discourteous actions or statements, the presumptions that these contain, and a place for considerate statements. In each example, read across the row and fill in the last column with a courteous statement or action.

Discourteous Action or Statement	Presumptions	Rewrite: Considerate Statement or Action
A. IN-LAWS: We just thought we'd drop by and take you out to dinner. Come on, get ready!	1. You are free. 2. You want to go out to dinner.	
B. FRIEND: We're so glad that you could come over! I forgot to mention that my sister-in-law is here with her four kids. But I knew you loved kids, so I figured you wouldn't mind all these kids running around.	1. You love small kids running around. 2. You were planning an evening with children.	

C. SPOUSE: Well, for Christmas we won't buy each other gifts — we'll buy a dishwasher. That'll be great! I already looked at them. I have the one that I want picked out.	1. You want a dishwasher. 2. You don't mind foregoing gifts for a dishwasher. 3. You can afford a dishwasher.

GIVING THE OTHER PERSON THE RIGHT TO THINK DIFFERENTLY. The questions below describe situations. In each case, write a statement that would let the other person know that he or she has the right to think differently than you do.

A. Your spouse chooses a color scheme for the den. You dislike it.

B. You go out to dinner with friends, and one of them orders some food (e.g., oysters or cabbage) which you dislike. He or she wants you to taste it.

INACCURATE, INCOMPLETE ACKNOWLEDGMENTS. The following examples contain pairs of conversations. One of them responds appropriately to the other person; the other includes an inaccurate or incomplete acknowledgment.

Check the conversation containing the appropriate acknowledgment.

A. Situation: A club member values himself for being a competent, strong leader.

1. ___FELLOW CLUB MEMBER: You are such a good president because you're cheerful and pleasant, and you start each meeting with a good joke.

2. ___FELLOW CLUB MEMBER: You handled that meeting very well.

B. Situation: Student has worked hard at preparing a speech for class. He does a good job.

1. ___FRIEND: That was a good speech. You did a good job.

2. ___FRIEND: You are so lucky. Everything comes so easily to you.

Acknowledging Others 203

C. Situation: A woman has a high-pressure job in a corporation. She has a managerial job, makes a good salary, and is pleased with her competence and profession.

1. ____FEMALE NEIGHBOR: I know you work so hard. I'll bet you'll be so glad when you can take time off to have a baby.

2. ____FEMALE NEIGHBOR: I know you work hard, and I'm sure you're quite pleased with the job that you do.

General Review and Practice in Acknowledgment

This section provides an opportunity to review and apply all the principles and skills of acknowledgment.

ACKNOWLEDGING THE PRESENCE, ABSENCE, OR ACTIONS OF OTHERS
I. The examples below present pairs of statements. One of them recognizes and responds to the presence, absence, or actions of another; the other does not. In each case, place a check to the left of the statement that is responsive to the other person.

A. Situation: A husband gives his wife a gift, a dress.
 1. ____WIFE: (*in a complaining tone of voice*) This dress isn't the right size. Don't you remember my size?
 2. ____WIFE: Thanks, I really appreciate your thoughtfulness. It just so happens I need a different size, so I will exchange it. It's a lovely dress, and it's nice that you picked it out for me.

B. Situation: You did a favor for a friend.
 1. ____FRIEND: Thanks for picking that up at the store. I really appreciate it.
 2. ____FRIEND: There's something else I'd like you to get for me.

C. Situation: Parents return from Hawaii.
 1. ____CHILD: I'm glad you're back from your trip.
 2. ____CHILD: What did you buy me in Hawaii?

D. Situation: Neighbor drops by with some cookies that she baked.
 1. ____YOU: Thanks for bringing over those cookies. How about some coffee?
 2. ____YOU: You interrupted me in the middle of my favorite TV program, so I don't have time to talk.

II. In the examples below, someone does not respond to or recognize the other person. In each case, rewrite the comment to form a more appropriate response.

A. Situation: An employee typically does good work. In the past week, he has turned in two reports that are not as good as his others.
Boss: John, you need to improve your reports.
Rewrite: (suggestion: acknowledge his usual good reports)

B. Situation: A husband had a bad day. He comes home from work, sits down to read newspaper.
Wife: Hi, how was your day?
Husband: (*makes no response, does not look up or acknowledge wife's presence*)
Rewrite:

III. Listed below are a mixture of statements and actions that are responsive, while others do not follow the principles of acknowledgment. Circle those that are responsive; cross out those that are not acknowledging.

A. Respond to another person's question or statement.
B. "I appreciate your help/gift/advice."
C. Ask questions about what a person said.
D. Change the subject.
E. "Huh?" "What?" "I wasn't listening."
F. "I can understand that."
G. Interrupt the other person.
H. Do not answer.
I. "So what!"
J. "I'm not sure I understand. Would you explain that again?"
K. "That's a good point."
L. Contradict, ridicule, or deny what a person says.
M. "That's stupid!" "How silly!"
N. "That's wrong!"
O. Someone seems excited and happy. Ignore it.
P. "I see your point; I may not think exactly as you do but I appreciate your suggestions."
Q. "You seem upset. Is something wrong?"

R. When your spouse walks into the room, start reading the newspaper.

ACKNOWLEDGING APPEARANCE AND OTHER NONVERBAL CUES. Some situations are described below. Beneath each situation are two columns. The left-hand column contains examples of negative acknowledgments or failures to respond, while the right-hand column is designed for appropriate acknowledgments. In each case, read the situation and the inappropriate response. Then write a responsive statement in the right-hand column. The first two are done for you.

A. Situation: Your sister-in-law diets, exercises, and is proud of her trim figure.

Inappropriate	*Appropriate*
"Not many women are so lucky to have such a small frame."	"Your figure is great, and I know that you work at it."

B. Situation: Your co-worker seems happy; he is laughing and smiling.

Inappropriate	*Appropriate*
"What's with you? Can't you be serious?"	"You look like you're in a good mood."

C. Situation: A female friend has pretty long blond hair.

Inappropriate	*Appropriate*
"I'll bet your hair would look nice cut short!"	

D. Situation: A co-worker is wearing a nice-looking jacket. You do not particularly like the color, but it is still a nice jacket.

Inappropriate	*Appropriate*
"Too bad that jacket is that color."	

E. Situation: A neighbor is wearing a new diamond ring. She shows it to you.

Inappropriate	*Appropriate*
"I hate diamonds. They are so gaudy. Give me an emerald any day."	

F. Situation: Your spouse walks in, sighs heavily, and takes off his or her coat with a dejected air.

Inappropriate   *Appropriate*

Say nothing.

ACKNOWLEDGING THE STATEMENTS OF OTHERS

I. Each of the examples below contains a group of "responding" statements. In one of the statements, the speaker recognizes and responds to the other person; in the other example, he or she does not. In each case, place a check to the left of the statement that acknowledges the other person.

A. LEE: I'm so excited! We just had a talk on "Suicide Prevention" and I'd like to join their volunteer group and be trained to help at the crisis center.
   1. ____JOAN: Oh, you have better things to do than that. Most of the people that threaten to kill themselves aren't going to do it, anyway! They're just big babies. Are you going to the Garden Club luncheon on Saturday?
   2. ____JOAN: I don't know much about the crisis center. What do they do there?

B. JIM: Beth and I were thinking of going to the art museum tomorrow. You are welcome to come along, if you're free and you'd like to see it.
   1. ____BOB: We're busy.
   2. ____BOB: Thanks very much for inviting us, but my parents are coming to visit tomorrow, so we're not free. Sometime, we would really enjoy doing that . . . you and Beth have a good time.

C. KAREN: Oh, have I had a hard week!
   1. ____DIANE: Oh, come on. You just feel sorry for yourself.
   2. ____DIANE: I must tell you this! Have you heard that Sue Johnson left her husband?
   3. ____DIANE: I'm sorry to hear that. What happened?

D. JACK: Hi, Tom, you're tan! Have you been somewhere?
   TOM: We've been to Florida. I told you we were going for two weeks.
   1. ____JACK: Oh, I forgot.
      TOM: We had a really great time. We . . .

Acknowledging Others 207

> JACK: Well, that's great for you people who can take off from work. But in my business and the kind of guy I am, there's no way that I would ever take a vacation for that long.
> 2. ___JACK: Oh, I forgot, that's right. Did you enjoy yourself?
> TOM: We sure did.
> JACK: Where did you go?

II. Each of the examples below represents a conversation in which one person is not recognizing or responding to the other. In each case, please rewrite the comment to make it acknowledge the other person.

A. SON: Jane and I will be going on a trip in April. We've decided to go to the Bahamas.
PARENTS: Consider yourself lucky! We could never afford vacations when we were first married. In those days, we had to work hard for everything, not like you young people.
Rewrite:

B. PAULA: I'm so excited about having a baby. Don and I have been wanting to have a child for a long time.
NEIGHBOR: Did I tell you that my daughter was accepted into medical school?
Rewrite:

ACKNOWLEDGING THE EXPERIENCES OF OTHERS

Each of the examples below contains a pair of statements. One of the statements recognizes and responds to the experiences of another person; the other does not. In each case, check the statement that acknowledges the other person.

A. WIFE: I'm hungry. Let's stop and get something to eat.

1. ___HUSBAND: You're not hungry. We just ate a few hours ago.

2. ___HUSBAND: I'm not hungry right now after that big breakfast. I'd like to drive another fifty miles or so before we stop. Do you think you can hold out a while longer?

B. HUSBAND: I can't stay home from work even though I have a cold. That office really falls apart when I'm not there.

1. ____WIFE: I can understand how you feel. I just want you to take care of yourself, but it's up to you to decide. Do whatever you think is best.

2. ____WIFE: Don't be silly! Everything will go along just fine without you! Nobody is that important! What's more important is for you to stay home and take care of that cold!

C. PAT: I really enjoy modern art! We just saw the most fascinating exhibit at the Art Institute.

1. ____SUE: How could you possibly like that junk? That just shows you what majoring in art will do to you!

2. ____SUE: I don't understand and appreciate modern art as you do, Pat. Maybe sometime if we go to the art museum together, you could give me a brief explanation of what there is to appreciate.

ACKNOWLEDGING THE SELF-PERCEPTIONS AND INTENTIONS OF OTHERS. The examples below contain pairs of conversations. One of them shows recognition and responds to the other person; the other does not. In each case, place a check to the left of the conversation that acknowledges the other person's thoughts, intentions, or self-perceptions.

A. JOHN: I sure liked my first job better than this one.

1. ____TERRY: That's because you're only remembering the good things about it. Everything in the past always looks good.
JOHN: No, that's not true! I really did like the atmosphere and people I worked with better!
TERRY: Well, If you'd stop comparing this job with the last one and if you'd stop complaining so much, you might fit in around here and like it better!

2. ____TERRY: I can understand that. It is always hard to come to a new situation from a familiar place. What did you like about the other place?
JOHN: Well, the people seemed friendlier . . . and less critical. You've been friendly, but you're about the only one who has.

B. SUE: I wish I didn't have to live in this town. I wish Bill would get transferred soon.

1. ____ANN: Is there something specific about it that you don't like?

2. ____ANN: You're always complaining.

Acknowledging Others 209

SUE: I really can't find anything to do on weekends. And the shopping is lousy.

SUE: I am not. I'm just trying to explain . . .

ANN: You're just one of those who always looks at the negative side of things.

C. MARTHA: I just love antiques. This was really a buy!
   1. ____TINA: I don't know much about them, so I can't appreciate them as you do. Can you explain to me why that one was a good buy?
   2. ____TINA: It looks like a piece of junk to me.

D. LAURA: I really miss working. I plan to go back to work as soon as I can.
   1. ____DIANE: You can't feel like that! Who would ever leave a six-week-old baby! You'll be sorry.
   2. ____DIANE: I can understand why you might be bored at home. I guess you miss the excitement and satisfaction of your career.

Remember: In acknowledging other people, avoid telling them how they should feel and what they should do. Avoid using phrases that communicate this to them, for example, "You can't feel that way." "It would do you good to . . ." "You should . . ." "That's the worst thing to do."

GENERAL APPLICATION OF SKILLS AND PRINCIPLES. Each conversation below contains nonacknowledging replies. These are circled for you. Using the skills that you learned in this chapter, write a more responsive statement to the right of the one that is circled.

Statement

A. WIFE: I do not want your friends, the Jacksons, here for the weekend. I don't enjoy their company. If you want to visit with them, you can drive over to their place.
HUSBAND: What do you mean you don't like them? They're very nice . . . if you'd just try to like them, we'd have a lot of fun.
WIFE: No, I've tried. I don't like them. He treats me as if I were a little girl. Besides, when they come,

Response

(Suggestion: acknowledge wife's experience.)

the three of you talk about "the good old days" in high school and in your hometown and I have nothing to contribute. I find that very boring.
HUSBAND: Oh come on. They are not like that. You're exaggerating.

B. Situation: Joan is new in town. She is invited to have lunch with the other wives of her husband's firm. The following conversation occurs:
MARTHA: Do you have children, Joan?
JOAN: No.
MARTHA: Well, with all that time, what sorts of hobbies do you have?
JOAN: No hobbies — I have a career and I'm quite busy with it.
MARTHA: Oh, really? Well, one of these days you'll have children and then you'll know what busy is. (Suggestion: acknowledge statements about job.)

C. PHIL: We really enjoy traveling.
SAM: We never travel. We'd never leave the kids alone. Home is a much better place to be. (Suggestion: Acknowledge their enjoyment of travel even when you disagree.)

CHAPTER FIVE

Providing Relevant, Descriptive, and Precise Information

PEOPLE ARE MORE LIKELY to understand when you give them an idea of "where you are coming from" and what you are trying to do. In order to do this, you must say what you think and how you feel; you must explain to people how your thoughts and feelings are relevant to them. You express these thoughts and feelings in ways that are clear and understandable; you avoid distracting your listeners and making them defensive.

This is not as complicated as it sounds. This chapter gives you some simple, specific guidelines to follow.

SKILL 1: PROVIDING RELEVANT INFORMATION

If you want to be understood, it is important for you to give your listeners as much relevant information as possible. When you do this, your listeners have a clearer idea of "where you are coming from" and what you are trying to accomplish. In order to provide essential and relevant information, be sure to express:

1. What happened.
2. What you think or feel, how this affects you, and what your reactions are.
3. How what you are saying relates to the other person.

For example:
YOU: I had a bad day at work (*what happened*), and I feel miserable (*your reaction*). I'd like to do something pleasant to distract myself. If we go to a movie, I think I'll feel better. How about it? (*how it relates to the other person*)

SPOUSE: Well, OK. A movie's not a bad idea.

This includes the essential information and gives your spouse an idea of what is going on with you. It is a special case of one of the first skills we learned, expressing your intention or purpose.

Instead of doing this, people often express some of these components (like what happened or how it relates), but they leave out the rest. It may sound like this.

YOU: I had a bad day at work, I didn't accomplish what I wanted, and I feel miserable. (*feeling and reaction*)
SPOUSE: (*thinking that you want to be left alone*) Don't worry, I won't bother you. I'll go out and work in the yard.
YOU: (*to yourself*) That's great! Won't even talk to me when I've had a bad day. Just wait until she (or he) has a bad day. I'll act just like that!
YOU: Let's go out to a movie.
SPOUSE: I'd rather stay home.
YOU: (*angrily*) The least you could do is try to be nice. Maybe I need some cheering up. Did you ever stop to think of that?

In both examples, you stated only a portion of what was going on. This lack of information misled your spouse, and his or her misinformed reaction, in turn, confused you. The communication is very unclear, and both people have mistaken notions of what the other was feeling. Omitting important ingredients, as in these examples, usually leads to misunderstanding and ineffective communication.

Expressing essential and relevant information is necessary because people cannot read each other's minds. It is especially important to provide this relevant information when it is easy to be misunderstood, namely, (1) when the other person does not know you well or (2) when the two of you know each other well but are discussing an issue that is sensitive or emotionally charged.

Giving your listener relevant and essential information has these advantages.

1. The other person has a better idea of your thinking, feeling, reactions, and preferences.
2. The listener has less chance of formulating incorrect assumptions.
3. The other person has all the information and a better basis for making a decision (for example, whether to go out or stay home).

Providing Relevant, Descriptive, and Precise Information 213

The following examples show the difference between incomplete statements and those that provide more complete information.

Does Not Provide Information

BROTHER: I really dislike these family get-togethers! There's nothing I hate more than coming over here.
SISTER: (*offended*) Well, I'm sorry that you find our company so displeasing.
BROTHER: I didn't mean you!

HUSBAND: Maybe we should move to Florida. It might be a good idea.
WIFE: (*shocked*) And leave all our friends? And take the kids out of school? Never! How could you even consider that?

BOSS: (*in a serious tone of voice*) I have some things I want to talk over with you.
EMPLOYEE: (*worried, thinks to himself*) What did I do wrong?

HUSBAND: We need to stop spending so much.
WIFE: Don't blame me! You're the one who is always buying things.

WIFE: Let's get away this weekend.
HUSBAND: Oh, maybe some other weekend. I'm tired.

Provides Information

BROTHER: I really dislike these family get-togethers! I like to see you, of course, but I don't particularly enjoy seeing all of these second cousins that I don't even know.
SISTER: Well, I can see what you mean.

HUSBAND: I'm just thinking aloud and I'm not seriously considering this. Maybe we should move to Florida. It might be a good idea.

BOSS: This is no big deal. I have some things I want to talk over with you when you have time.
EMPLOYEE: I'm free at four. Is that OK?

HUSBAND: I'm thinking aloud about our buying. We need to stop spending so much. I realize that I spend a lot, so I'm talking about me even more than you.

WIFE: This is very important to me. I really want to get away this weekend. I really need a break from the routine.
HUSBAND: OK. If it means a lot to you, let's do it. Where do you want to go?

In the examples on the left, the speakers express only portions of their thinking. Their listeners must guess at what they mean and how it relates to them. Usually, as in these examples, they come up with the wrong idea. The sparse and incomplete information elicited hurt, defensiveness, and counterattacks. The communication was confused and each person misunderstood the other's ideas and purpose in speaking.

In contrast, in the examples on the right, the important and relevant information was provided. The listeners were better prepared and, as a result, had a better idea of where the speakers were "coming from." This increased the chances for more accurate exploration and understanding of each others' ideas.

Practice

This section provides practice in providing relevant and essential information.

I. In the pairs of statements below, one statement contains essential and relevant information; the other is incomplete. Place a check in front of the statement that is more easily understood by the listener.

A. 1. ___WIFE: I really don't like going to your parents for Sunday dinners.

    2. ___WIFE: This may seem trivial to you, but it's important to me. I really don't like going to your parents for Sunday dinners every week. Can we work out something else?

B. 1. ___BOSS: I asked you here so that you can tell me what benefit there is to this new program you started. What good is it? Why do it?

    2. ___BOSS: Before I go before the board of directors, I need some way to sell your new program to them. Tell me what advantages it has.

C. 1. ___HUSBAND: Somehow I don't feel like eating. Nothing seems appetizing.

    2. ___HUSBAND: Everything tastes great. I'm just not hungry, so don't be surprised if I don't eat much.

D. 1. ___FRIEND: Thanks for inviting me to coffee, but I'd better decline. I am upset about a number of things. It would be best for me to be alone and work them out.

    2. ___FRIEND: I don't want to go to coffee.

E. 1. ___WIFE: I'm bored. Nothing is exciting. It's just the same old routine, day after day. And I'm fed up.

    2. ___WIFE: I'm bored and restless, but it has nothing to do with you. This weather has been so bad that I just feel cooped up.

II. The column on the left contains statements that do not present the speaker's thinking adequately. The column on the right contains statements that provide relevant and essential information. Draw a line from the incomplete statement on the left to the more complete one on the right.

Incomplete Information

A. TEACHER: I think your paper would be better if you changed the first few paragraphs.

B. WIFE: I could use some help in the garden.

C. HUSBAND: Just keep the kids quiet and away from me.

Essential Information

1. I had a frustrating day at the office, so if I should be a bit irritable, that's why. Don't take my crankiness personally—it's not meant for you. Just please keep the kids quiet and away from me.

2. I don't mean this to sound like the paper is not good. But I do think that it would be smoother if you changed the first few paragraphs.

3. It is not necessary for you to do this. But if you have the time and energy, I could use some help out in the garden.

SKILL 2: BEING DESCRIPTIVE

This section shows how to substitute description for the following.
1. Accusations, blame, and interpretations.
2. Vague and evaluative terms.
3. "Preaching" and unfavorable comparisons.

Skill 2a: *Being Descriptive Instead of Blaming and Interpreting*

Being descriptive in your communication involves stating exactly who, what, when, where, and how. For example, a husband might say to his wife, "On weekends, you cook a great deal of food, and I eat more than usual. Since I'm trying to lose weight, I'd like you to help me cut down by not making any of my favorite desserts. Especially because they are so good." This example contains the important components—the husband describes what happens, how he feels, and how his wife can help. Because the wife is not blamed or judged in a negative way, she does not become defensive and she is better able to understand what her husband is trying to say. This facilitates the communication between them and increases their chances of understanding each other and solving the problem at hand.

Instead of being descriptive, people usually do one of the following.

1. They use judgmental terms, accuse other people, or call them names. This happens when someone uses words that have a negative connotation. The following are some words that have a negative connotation: "stupid," "obnoxious," "rude," "inefficient," "stubborn," "slow." You have heard many of this type and probably can come up with a list of them. Here is an example of how they are used in conversation:

HUSBAND: It is so dumb. You waste so much time cleaning the house. (Instead of, "When you clean, you do not have time for me. On the weekends, I like to do things with you. I feel that our time together is more important than cleaning the house.")

2. They blame others for disappointments, frustrations, or upsets. They do not take responsibility for their own feelings and reactions. For example:

WIFE: "It's all your fault that the kids don't confide in us. If you didn't have such an awful temper, they might be less afraid to speak up." (Instead of, "I'm concerned about the kids. Neither of them confides in us. They may be scared off by your temper; I don't know. Whatever it is, I'd feel better if they confided in us. Let's find a way to change this.")

3. They interpret other people's thoughts, behaviors, or motives. For example:

CO-WORKER: You're just trying to be different. You're nothing but a troublemaker! (Instead of, "Each time that the seven of us seem close to an agreement, you find some small detail to disagree on. We need to settle this.")

The examples above are not descriptive, nor do they provide useful information to the listener. Instead, they make accusations and judgments and elicit hurt, anger, and defensiveness. The listener is distracted by these words and is less likely to hear and understand. In fact, statements like those above usually elicit a defensive, judgmental response and the situation ends in an uncomfortable exchange of harsh words and counteraccusations.

Accusations and interpretations like those above are "put downs." They easily can be interpreted as emotional attacks and they create an unpleasant atmosphere between people.

This skill of substituting descriptive words for accusing, blaming, and interpretive terms works for the following reasons.

1. It describes who, what, when, and where. In this way, it provides clear and specific information. It specifies how you are affected as well as the consequences.
2. Because it does not blame, accuse, or interpret, the chances of provoking a defensive reaction are decreased.
3. As a result, the probability of being heard and understood are increased and effective communication is facilitated.

The following examples help to illustrate the difference between using negative and judgmental terms and being descriptive.

Negative and Judgmental	*Descriptive*
HUSBAND: Your mother never wants to hear what I have to say. She is so rude! WIFE: How dare you call my mother rude? Your mother is one of the most inconsiderate people I've met. She never wants to hear what anyone says!	HUSBAND: Your mother frequently interrupts me in the middle of my sentences. When she does that, I get very frustrated. WIFE: I know what you mean.
WIFE: Why are you so sloppy? HUSBAND: I'm not sloppy! The problem is that you are a perfectionist and a chronic complainer. You're never happy.	WIFE: I prefer that you not leave the newspapers scattered on the living room floor. Will you try to pick them up? HUSBAND: I'll try to remember but you may have to remind me again.
CO-WORKER A: If you don't stop being so disorganized, we're never going to get this project finished. You're deliberately doing this to get me in trouble with the boss. CO-WORKER B: (*counterattacking*) Well, if you'd be on time when we're supposed to work, we'd get a lot more accomplished! Besides, you're so paranoid about everything!	CO-WORKER A: I know, John, that you do not typically make a schedule for yourself, but I work better that way. Since we have to work on this project together, I'd like to suggest that we draw up a tentative schedule for ourselves. Would you be willing to do that? CO-WORKER B: OK.

The examples on the left are accusatory, distracting, and uninformative. The listeners do not know what is meant by "rude," "sloppy," or "disorganized." They only know that they do not think of themselves in those terms and they do not intend to be any of those things. They feel hurt, resentful, and frustrated and react with defensiveness and counterattacks. When this happens, the content and the level of discussion are changed, the subject and the focus are shifted, and the main point is overlooked. Instead of solving the problem, there is an argument, and this accomplishes nothing. In fact, the personal attacks and resulting defensiveness create an unpleasant atmosphere and make it far less likely that some degree of understanding and resolution can occur. Exchanges like these are a waste of time and energy and produce only negative results.

In contrast, the examples on the right are descriptive and, in some cases, follow the description with a statement of the speaker's preferences or suggestions. This gives the listener more information without accusing, blaming, or interpreting the behavior and motives of the other person. As a result, the chances for mutual understanding and some resolution to the situation are markedly increased.

Remember the importance of nonverbal cues. An accusing look or tone of voice conveys negative feelings, even when your words are descriptive. Be sure to check your nonverbal messages.

Practice

This section provides practice in:

1. Recognizing judgments, accusations, and name-calling.
2. Recognizing words that interpret the behavior and motives of others.
3. Describing and substituting descriptions in place of negative and judgmental terms.

I. The examples below contain pairs of statements. One in each pair contains descriptive words; the other includes accusations, judgments, or interpretations. Check the descriptive one of the pair and underline the accusatory, judgmental, or interpretive words in the other. The first one is done for you.

A. 1. ____WIFE: You are really *irresponsible* and *inconsiderate*. This is the second time this week

2. ✓ WIFE: When you don't call to say you'll be late and I ruin the roast, I get really angry and frus-

Providing Relevant, Descriptive, and Precise Information 219

that you've been late for dinner and haven't called. The roast is overdone and dinner is ruined!

B. 1. ___PARENT: Your mother and I would like you to get good grades. I think that if you study you can make B's easily.

C. 1. ___BOSS: I'm trying to explain the new policy and you keep interrupting me. I'm getting annoyed. I want to finish.

D. 1. ___FRIEND: How can you be so stupid? You should've gotten over our disagreement by now. You must be neurotic.

trated. If I don't know when you're coming home, I can't prepare dinner.

2. ___PARENT: You're such a disappointment to your mother and me. There was no reason for you to get a C in that class. How could you do that to us?

2. ___BOSS: I know that you are trying to give me a bad time. You always do that. You are rebellious and can't handle authority figures.

2. ___FRIEND: You still seem very cool to me. You don't speak to me and you don't call me for lunch or for coffee. I would be happy if we could forget that argument we had and be friends.

II. Below is a list of words and phrases. Some of these words or phrases are negative, accusatory, interpretive, or judgmental. Circle the ones that fit this description. (Two are already done for you.) These are words and phrases that you might try to eliminate from your speech.

A. try
B. rude
C. work
D. help
E. "Why can't you ever succeed at anything?"
F. promise
G. thoughtless
H. messy
I. call
J. "I'd like it if you'd call me to play tennis."
K. "You must have an inferiority complex."
L. stupid
M. obnoxious
N. practice
O. find
P. cruel
Q. "No wonder you don't have any friends!"
R. "I don't like it when you call me at work."
S. "Why are you so sloppy? All your friends are so well-groomed."
T. call
U. selfish
V. sickly
W. write

III. Three situations are described below. To the right of each situation is a statement that makes an accusation or interpretation. Using the rules of description that you learned in this section, rewrite each statement in the third column. You might find it useful to employ the skill of describing preferences directly and responsibly (from chapter 1). The first one is done for you.

Situation	Interpretive or Accusatory Statement	Descriptive Statement
A. A husband notices that his wife does not pay all bills on the first of the month as he prefers.	HUSBAND: You are so lazy and irresponsible. You never pay the bills on time, and you are putting us in a mess financially.	HUSBAND: I get anxious when you don't pay the bills on time. I would like you to take care of them before the first of the month. (*remember: tell who, what, when, where, and how*)
B. A mother-in-law notices that her daughter-in-law gets colds easily and seems very tired. She wants to tell her to take better care of herself.	MOTHER-IN-LAW: My, dear, you are such a weakling. You seem so sickly all the time.	
C. A wife does not like it when her husband doesn't listen to her. She started to tell him about her day and noticed that he was reading the newspaper and not looking at her.	WIFE: There you go again—ignoring me as usual. You probably like the paper more than you like me!	

Skill 2b: Being Descriptive, Specific, and Nonevaluative

Eliminating interpretations and accusations is one step toward clear communication. In order to provide others with relevant and clear information about your thinking, it is important to be specific. This means that you substitute specific descriptions for vague, evaluative, and emotional terms. For example,

WIFE: You seemed to notice that I went to a lot of trouble with dinner tonight. I really like that. (Instead of the vague "You were so nice tonight.")

or

HUSBAND: I appreciated the fact that your mother telephoned before she came over today. (Instead of "Well, for once, your mother was considerate.")

Specifically describing thoughts, feelings or events is not a skill that is commonly taught and practiced. Instead, people usually learn to use vague, evaluative, emotionally toned words or phrases that do not provide much information. When this happens, conversations can go like this.

WIFE: You were so nice tonight!
HUSBAND: (*unsure of what she's saying*) Well, I'm always nice.
WIFE: Not like you were tonight . . . usually you're not this nice!

HUSBAND: Well, for once, your mother was considerate!
WIFE: What are you talking about? My mother is just as considerate as yours!

Nice and *considerate* are examples of vague and emotional words. They relate to the speaker's ideas of what is "nice" or "considerate," and the other person, of course, does not know what is meant. As in the example above, the husband thinks that he is "nice" most of the time, and, as a result, he does not understand what it is that his wife is trying to say. All he has is a vague notion that he somehow won her approval tonight, and he did not win it on other nights. He probably is slightly irritated or hurt and may think to himself, "Of course, I was nice! When am I ever not nice? Is she implying that I'm not nice other nights?"

Similarly, in the example involving the wife's mother, the wife reacts to the term *considerate*. It implies a judgment and evaluation of her mother: namely, that she usually is not "considerate." Since she does not know what her husband means, she reacts defensively.

This is a marked contrast to descriptive statements (e.g., "I really appreciated the fact that your mother called before she came over"). These provide information and keep defensiveness and distraction to a minimum.

It is impossible to eliminate all evaluativeness, for, at some point, there are some things that you like and some that you dislike. However, the issue of responsibility enters here. It is one thing to say, "You're a mean person," and quite another to say, "I get uncomfortable when you do that." The latter sentence tells about your feelings while the first evaluates the other person. Likes, dislikes, and preferences have their place in the world, but try to state them as yours and not as an evaluation of the other person.

This skill of substituting specific description for vague, evaluative terms has these advantages.

1. It provides the other person with clear information about what you like, prefer or think. It describes clearly who, what, when, where, and how.
2. Because the words are more specific, the listener has more information. Defensiveness and distraction are also minimized.
3. The conversation is kept "on the track" and is task-oriented. This increases the possibilities for mutual understanding as well as some resolution of the problem.

Remember: nonverbal cues also are important. A look or tone of voice can convey disapproval even when the words do not.

Vague, Subjective	*Specific, Descriptive*
EMPLOYEE: What do I have to do to get a promotion? BOSS: Well, you have to be productive. EMPLOYEE: (*hurt*) Well, does that mean that I'm not productive now?	EMPLOYEE: What do I have to do to get a promotion? BOSS: In order to get a promotion, you have to develop and start your own program and bring in about five new clients.
HUSBAND: You certainly weren't too helpful while I was painting. WIFE: What do you mean? I tried to stay out of your way. HUSBAND: That's how much you know. I didn't want you to leave me alone. WIFE: What did you want me to do? HUSBAND: If you don't know, forget it. If you really cared about me, you'd know.	HUSBAND: When I am painting, I feel better if you come over and take a look at it. You know, give me a little encouragement. WIFE: I didn't know that. I usually try to stay out of your way.
BOSS: This last proposal of yours is the first good one you've had. EMPLOYEE: I've been here five years, and that's the first good proposal? Either I'm stupid or you're very critical!	BOSS: Usually your proposals lack target dates, but this one includes them. That's why I like it a lot.

Providing Relevant, Descriptive, and Precise Information 223

DALE: That wasn't a very smart thing to do at the meeting.
PAT: (*hurt and angry*) Since when do you know what's smart?

DALE: I would not have spoken out as you did at the meeting.
PAT: I know, I just felt like doing that.

The examples on the left use unclear words that are uninformative and confusing. Besides being vague, words like "good," "helpful," and "smart" judge and evaluate the other person. This usually leads to defensiveness and distraction. The issue is sidetracked, and the chances of exploring ideas and achieving some understanding are decreased markedly.

In contrast, the descriptive examples on the right give more information about the speaker's ideas: their preferences, disagreements, standards for promotion, and suggestions. These conversations are more likely to lead to exploration of ideas. The chances for understanding and some degree of resolution also are increased.

Practice

This section provides practice in recognizing vague and evaluative words and substituting description for these.

I. The examples below contain pairs of statements. One of these is descriptive and tells who, what, when, where, and how; the other statement is vague and uses subjective, evaluative words. Check the statement that is descriptive. In the other, underline the words that are vague and evaluative. The first one is done for you.

A. 1. ____BOSS: It would be <u>better</u> if you had more initiative. What you <u>should</u> do is be more interested, then you'd make a <u>good</u> impression.

2. _✓_BOSS: John, I'd prefer it if you started some projects on your own rather than asking me. Work up a proposal and bring it in. That will show some initiative.

B. 1. ____FRIEND: (*in a friendly tone*) I know that you and your wife are having a rough time these days and both of you are considering divorce. I just want to remind you that, even in this day and age, divorce is painful.

2. ____FRIEND: (*disapprovingly*) This idea about getting a divorce is no good. Just because you and your wife had a fight is no reason to come unglued. You're being very childish and impulsive about this.

II. Below is a list of words and phrases. Circle the ones that are evaluative. Two are already done for you.

A. gain
B. situation
C. talk
D. "You're a wonderful person."
E. would
F. better
G. silly
H. nice
I. dumb
J. ridiculous
K. write
L. mention
M. good
N. "I appreciate it when your reports are this prompt."
O. worse
P. "You're a big disappointment."
Q. lazy
R. work
S. include
T. inefficient
U. irresponsible

III. Situations are described below. Following each situation is a statement that includes descriptive words. In each case, underline the words that tell who, what, when, and where.

A. Situation: Mark notices that Carol, a co-worker, does not speak up in meetings unless called on. Mark wants to suggest to her that she speak up more often.

MARK: I notice in our meetings that you don't speak unless the chairman specifically asks you a question. I'd like you to speak up more frequently.
CAROL: Well, I'm not sure that I have anything important to say.
MARK: Whenever you talk, the point you bring up is usually right on target.

B. Situation: A husband wants his wife to sit and watch television with him.

HUSBAND: On week nights after supper, you're usually working on some project. You're either sewing, baking, or playing the piano. Some nights I'd like you to sit with me and watch television.
WIFE: I thought you liked some privacy.
HUSBAND: Not always. About once a week I enjoy being alone but not other nights.
WIFE: How will I know which night you want privacy?
HUSBAND: I'll tell you.

IV. Two situations are described below. Following each is a conversation that uses vague, evaluative terms. These terms are underlined. Beneath that is a space for you to write in a more effective and descriptive statement.

Providing Relevant, Descriptive, and Precise Information 225

A. Situation: A wife wants to get away this weekend and spend a few nights in the nearest city. She does not want to sit at home.

WIFE: Life around here is boring. All you ever do is watch TV and I need something more exciting. I want to go off to the city this weekend and do something worthwhile for a change.
HUSBAND: You can do something worthwhile right here at home. You shouldn't have to go to the city. You're just restless.
WIFE: You're just a "stick in the mud."

Rewrite: (How can the wife describe to her husband what she would rather do?)

B. Situation: A mother wants to tell her son that, even while he is in college, she and his father prefer that he get a job to make some spending money. They do not like his depending on them for everything.

MOTHER: For your own good, you should get a job and start being responsible. If you don't stop being so irresponsible, you'll be nothing but a failure. We can't keep on babying you and providing for you.
SON: Thanks a lot. (*walks away*)
Rewrite:

Skill 2c: Being Descriptive: Avoid "Preaching" and Unfavorable Comparisons

In being descriptive, it is important to state who, what, when, and where without "preaching" or using negative comparisons. This means saying, for example, "I'd like more variety in our meals" (instead of, "What you should do is have more variety. That's what good cooks do," or "You are not as good a cook as my mother is.") By description, you provide information without having your listeners feel preached at, measured, or compared to others.

Instead of being descriptive, people often preach or use unfavorable comparisons. They say, for example, "What you should do is _____," "You are not as good as _____," or "Anyone with brains would _____." This communicates disapproval and negative evaluation. When people feel disapproved of, they usually feel hurt, criticized, angry, or resentful, and, most of the time, they become defensive. An atmosphere of disapproval, evaluation, and resulting defensiveness only fosters distrust and dissatisfaction in a relationship.

Preaching and comparisons can lead to errors in your thinking. One way to put people down is to judge their worth by comparing them to a standard or what they "should" be. You also can put people down by comparing them negatively to others. Someone always will be smarter, taller, better looking, richer, or more popular than the person you know. So comparing your spouse or friend to others can encourage you to be critical of the people you know. Furthermore, thinking and telling a spouse, "Why can't you be as nice as _____?" does not explain what you want him or her to do. Instead of giving information, it elicits frustration, defensiveness, and, possibly, some jealousy or resentment as well. In general, preaching and unfavorable comparisons provide little or no information. They can be interpreted as "put downs" or emotional attacks, and, as a result, they elicit a maximum amount of defensiveness and distraction.

In general, this skill of substituting descriptions for negative comparisons has the following advantages.

1. It gives more information to your listener.
2. It reduces the possibility of defensive and frustrated reactions from your listeners.
3. It minimizes distraction and it keeps the conversation "on track." This increases the chances for exploring ideas, being understood and achieving some resolution.

The examples below help to point out the differences between communication that uses comparisons and communication that is descriptive.

Using Comparisons or "Preaching"	*Being Descriptive*
PARENT: Why can't you be as smart as your brother?	PARENT: I'd like it if you worked harder at your school work and got good grades.
CHILD: (*frustrated*) Because I'm dumb, that's why!	

Providing Relevant, Descriptive, and Precise Information 227

HUSBAND: Why can't you get down to 102 pounds and be thin like your sister?
WIFE: (*defensively*) Why don't you get a divorce and marry her?

BOSS: You are far less organized than John. You need to adopt some of his habits and be more like he is.
EMPLOYEE: (*angrily*) Since when do I have to be compared to John? Is he the standard around here? Well, maybe John is the only good businessman around here. That tells me where I stand!

HUSBAND: I'd like it if you lost some weight.
WIFE: I'd like it, too. I could try dieting, but I'll need a lot of encouragement.

BOSS: You take two or three weeks on reports, and I'd prefer that your reports be in within the week.
EMPLOYEE: I'll have to work on a much tighter schedule to do that.
BOSS: I think that efficiency and organization are important qualities to have.

Preaching or using comparisons, as in the examples on the left, presents some hazards, and the frustrated, defensive replies illustrate these well. Using comparisons invites the reaction, "So you think she is better than I am!" This can lead to resentment, rebellion, or rejection. When spouses, children, friends, or employees feel that they do not measure up to your standards, they may give up trying. This will only lead to less and less satisfaction in the relationship.

Description, on the other hand, is straightforward, informative, and keeps defensive reactions to a minimum. It is much more effective, for example, for the husband to suggest that his wife diet instead of comparing her unfavorably with her sister. In general, description minimizes distraction and is more likely to lead to understanding and resolution.

Practice

This section gives you an opportunity to practice being descriptive and recognizing preaching or unfavorable comparisons and eliminating them.

I. The following examples contain pairs of statements. One is descriptive; the other is comparative. Place a check next to the statement that is descriptive without using comparisons.

A. 1. ____WIFE: Can't you relax? You're just a worrier, and you shouldn't be that way. If you want to succeed, you'll have to learn how to relax.

2. ___WIFE: John, you seem to be smoking a lot these days. Are you worried about something?
B. 1. ___HUSBAND: When I come home from work, you don't greet me and sit down and talk. I'd like it if you'd meet me at the door, tell me you're glad to see me, and then sit down with me.
2. ___HUSBAND: Why can't you be pleasant and cheerful like other wives are?
C. 1. ___HUSBAND: You are too emotional and too dependent on me. Why don't you try being as self-sufficient as Judy Clark? Now there's a mature, responsible woman for you.
2. ___HUSBAND: I'd like it if you would pay your own bills and decide what to fix for dinner on your own. Instead of calling me at the office to ask what you should do, decide these things on your own.

II. Below are examples of conversations where the people are preaching or using nondescriptive, comparative words. Underline all the words and phrases like this that you find. The first sentence is done for you.

A. HUSBAND: <u>You should</u> make a New Year's resolution to <u>be a better</u> cook and hostess.

WIFE: (*hurt and angry*) What do you mean? What's wrong with how I cook?

HUSBAND: You cook fine. It's just that you don't plan meals as well as you should. You often have something similar two nights in a row. My mother never did that — she used a lot more imagination than you.

WIFE: Thanks a lot. So my meals are boring compared to your mother's. Well, maybe you should just go back and live with her . . .

HUSBAND: I didn't mean that.

WIFE: Maybe you would also like me to be as hardheaded and obnoxious as your mother is.

HUSBAND: Now, just a minute . . .

WIFE: You're the one who says that. You're the one who gets upset and says that you've never met anyone who's as opinionated as she is.

HUSBAND: I know, but . . .
WIFE: And, as for being a hostess, maybe you'd like me to be as much a homebody as your sister is. All she does is cook and clean. Is that how you want me to be.?
HUSBAND: No, I didn't mean that.
WIFE: Well, as long as we're on New Year's resolutions, let me tell you that you're a long way from what I wanted in a husband. I wanted someone who would be understanding and supportive. You aren't nearly as understanding as a husband should be. And you certainly aren't very encouraging, either!

B. SON: I want a car, and you say that you can't afford one. Why aren't you generous like Carl's parents? They bought him a car when he turned sixteen.
FATHER: Well, Carl is a lot more appreciative and grateful than you are. Your mother and I have done a lot more for you kids than other parents have.
SON: That's not true.
FATHER: I've never heard Carl complain about his parents. He's always congenial and polite. Why can't you be as mature as he is? Maybe if you were, you'd get along better with people and be more successful, like you should be.

III. Situations and purposes are described below. The left-hand column shows how a person might handle the situation by preaching or using comparisons. Fill in the right-hand column by writing descriptive statements that do not preach or use comparisons. The first one is done for you.

A. *Situation and Purpose:* A wife wants her husband to spend more time with her.

Using Comparisons	*Descriptive*
WIFE: Why don't you spend more time talking with me? I wish that you would be more understanding, like Jim Smith is. Marilyn says that they are always sitting down and talking.	WIFE: I would like to spend more time together. I don't like it when we don't see each other for two nights in a row, for example. I'd like us to set aside some time every night, just to talk.

B. *Situation and Purpose:* A wife thinks that her husband is cool, aloof, and uninterested in guests. He doesn't greet them at the door, and he doesn't act interested in the conversation. Her boss is coming for dinner, and she wants her husband to be cordial, talk with him, and act interested in the conversation.

Using Comparisons   *Descriptive*

WIFE: My boss is coming over, and I want you to act warm and pleasant for a change. You should know by now that I can't get a promotion unless both of us make a good impression socially. Anyone with sense knows that.

C. *Situation and Purpose:* A husband often forgets birthdays, anniversaries, Valentine's Day, etc. His wife likes it when he remembers these days with something small, even just a card or a rose.

Using Comparisons   *Descriptive*

WIFE: My brother always brings Donna something on special days. Why can't you be like other husbands and show me that you care about me?

SKILL 3: LEARNING HOW LANGUAGE AFFECTS THINKING: BEING PRECISE AND AVOIDING EXAGGERATION

Language reflects and expresses your ideas, and, in turn, it helps to shape your thinking. Words label the people and events in our world and determine how and what we think about them. Words also determine how we behave in relation to people, objects, or events that we encounter. For example, we do one thing with a fork and something else with an ashtray. We expect different services from our attorney than we do from our mechanic. We think and act one way around someone labeled a "genius," but our thoughts and actions are quite different around a "mental patient." Because of the effects that words or labels have on our thoughts and actions, it is important to use precise and accurate labels. Precise and clear words and labels contribute to and maintain a realistic, accurate view of people, relationships, and the world in which we live.

Providing Relevant, Descriptive, and Precise Information 231

It is easy for people to use exaggerated and overstated language, and it is equally easy for them to fall into the trap of absolute "either-or" labels. This means that they see and label things as either "good" or "bad," "black" or "white." Thinking like this ignores many differentiations and shades of meaning that exist between the two opposites. It leads to a rigid, overly simplified way of looking at the world. Absolute, exaggerated, or overstated language contributes to and helps to maintain a limited and unrealistic picture of people and events. A picture like this can make it difficult to function effectively and to get the things that you want in life.

One way to achieve precision is to substitute descriptive words for exaggerated or simplified labels. For example, if a friend has done something that you dislike, think of it and describe it as such ("something that I disliked") rather than exaggerating it into "He did something awful," or, "He is an inconsiderate person." These exaggerations distort the picture and overstate the importance and magnitude of the friend's action. Similarly, if you exaggerate and label your spouse as "selfish," you are focusing on faults and ignoring other possible qualities. If you repeat this overstatement often enough, you probably will come to believe it and will think of your spouse as "selfish," despite thoughtful or kind actions that he or she may do.

In the same way, if you say that a friend is "always late," you probably are exaggerating the number of times that he or she is tardy and minimizing the number of times that he or she is prompt. By exaggerating the negative qualities of your friend or spouse, you miss an accurate perspective and maintain a biased one instead. The same principle applies to situations. If you have labeled an event as "terrible" or "awful," you miss out on other aspects of it and your perspective is very limited. As you continue to repeat this exaggeration, you will believe it and will come to see yourself as inadequate in relation to that particular situation.

You also can have an unrealistic view by overstating good qualities. If you say and think that someone is "always wonderful and kind," you will expect that person to live up to that label all the time. When a "fantastic new boss" does not give you a raise or when a "wonderful friend" forgets your birthday, you can feel disappointed and betrayed.

To give you an idea of how precise thought and language works in everyday situations, two examples are presented below. The one on the left shows exaggerated, imprecise language while the one on the right demonstrates accurate, precise description.

Imprecise	*Precise, Descriptive*
WIFE: I've had it. You are no help to me at all. You are so lazy and selfish that I can't stand it! You never do a thing around here. HUSBAND: If I never do anything, then who is it that mows the lawn and paints the house? Or maybe those don't count. If you're the one who does all the work around here, maybe you'd like to take on the yard work, too.	WIFE: Look, I'm upset. You said that you'd help with the cleaning, but I ended up cleaning the garage and the basement all alone . . . and I'm angry about that. I feel that you let me down. HUSBAND: I guess I did say that and then forgot about it. I'm sorry. I can understand that you feel angry.

In the example on the left, the wife exaggerates her negative feelings. She uses overstated superlatives to express herself, and her statements lead the husband to respond with exaggerated and defensive reactions. The situation deteriorates, and the chances for understanding and resolution are drastically diminished.

In contrast, the examples on the right demonstrate more precise thinking and the husband is better able to hear and understand. The chances for exploration and some degree of resolution are increased.

Here are some steps to follow to increase the precision of your thought and language. Apply these guidelines to your thoughts and statements.

1. Ask yourself, Are these the facts? Is that exactly what I mean and exactly what happened? Is this exaggerated in either a positive or a negative direction?
2. Check to be sure that you have stated the frequency accurately. Is it really "always" or "never," or is it, more precisely, three times this past month?
3. Be certain that the strength or degree of the words is accurate. Is it "awful"? Was it the "worst" time that you have "ever" had? Do you really "hate" your neighbor?

Below is an example of how to use this skill to check and revise the accuracy of your statements.

HUSBAND: (*to himself*) My wife never thinks of me. All she cares about is herself. I'm going to tell her that—just how inconsiderate and selfish she is.

Providing Relevant, Descriptive, and Precise Information 233

Before he speaks, he decides to check his accuracy. He asks himself:
1. Are these the facts? Is this exactly what I mean? Is this exactly what happened? Am I exaggerating?
2. Am I stating the frequency accurately? (Does she "never" do this?)
3. Is the strength of the word what I mean? (Is she really "inconsiderate" or does she just forget sometimes? Do I tell her what I want?)

On the basis of this checking out, the husband revises his thinking to, "For the last two weeks, my wife has been saying that she wants to get a babysitter and go away for the weekend. I have been very tired from work, and I also have chores I need to do around the house. She wants a break from the kids, but, when she says this, I feel hassled.

Based on this revision, he talks with his wife. Their conversation may go like this.

HUSBAND: When you say that you want to get away on the weekend, I feel hassled. I'm tired from work, and I also feel that there are some chores that I should do around the house. I'd rather relax here.
WIFE: I didn't know you felt that way. When you didn't answer my questions about going away for the weekend, I thought that you were just giving me a bad time.
HUSBAND: Will you be satisfied staying home this weekend? We could go out for dinner on Saturday and could plan a trip for some other weekend. Is that OK?

Conversations like this resolve problems. Instead of speaking in this way, people often use imprecise and exaggerated language. They say "always," "never," "hate," "the worst," and "awful" when these are not accurate descriptions of what happened. For example, they may say "always" when the actual occurrence is once in awhile or twice last week. They say "hate," "ugly," and "terrible" when, more precisely, they dislike someone or something. It is difficult for people to understand and respond to strong words like "ugly" and "disgusting," especially when these words are applied to them or to someone or something close to them. Words like those mentioned above are emotionally powerful and usually elicit exaggerated and defensive reactions.

When people do not check the accuracy and precision of their thought and language, their thinking remains muddled, and the situation is exaggerated and misrepresented to listeners as well. Suppose that, in the example above, the husband did not check the precision of his thoughts.

HUSBAND: You never think of me! You are one of the most selfish and inconsiderate people that I know! If you were the least bit considerate, you'd know why I don't want to go away for the weekend! But not you! All you care about is what you want to do!"

WIFE: Oh, I know why you can't go away for the weekend. You just don't care about me or what I feel! You don't care that I have had two awful weeks with the kids, and they're driving me crazy! All you care about is yourself. And you're too lazy and too stingy to take me away for a weekend.

The wife's reaction to her husband's language is defensive, angry, and equally overstated. The chances for any mutual understanding and resolution of the issue have dropped markedly as a result of this encounter. From this example, you can see how interactions of this type resolve nothing. Instead they lead to misunderstanding and conflict and can seriously undermine relationships. Inaccurate thinking and language parallel each other and lead to biased views and actions. In the example above, if the husband persists in labeling his wife as "selfish and inconsiderate," he will see her that way and he will behave in that way as well. He may look for things in her actions that will support his notion of her selfishness, and he may ignore or discount thoughtful things that she does. Besides affecting perceptions and behavior, imprecise thought or language usually defeats your purpose. It distracts the other person, keeps your thinking muddled, and gets communication "off the track." In the end, nothing is accomplished.

Contrast this second example with the first, more precise conversation where the husband and wife discuss their respective ideas about the weekend. By checking both his thinking and his language, the husband arrives at a more balanced perspective. Instead of an emotional attack on his wife, he describes the situation and his reactions. A reasonable, problem-solving discussion follows, and a solution is found.

Using this skill of checking the accuracy of your statements has the following advantages.

1. Since language reflects your thinking, your words provide clues to your thinking.

Providing Relevant, Descriptive, and Precise Information

2. Since language shapes your thinking, precise words can help to clarify your thinking and keep it realistic as to facts, frequency, and degree. Using this skill decreases exaggeration, and encourages a more balanced perspective of the situation.
3. Precise, unexaggerated language is far less likely to elicit defensiveness and distraction from your listeners. For this reason, it is easier to understand and is more likely to lead to an exchange and exploration of ideas.
4. It keeps the conversation "on track" and is more likely to result in some degree of understanding and some resolution to the problem.

The following examples help to point out the differences between inaccurate, imprecise statements and accurate ones.

Imprecise, Does Not Check Accuracy

HUSBAND: As usual, I failed again. I never do anything right. I didn't get the promotion. I never get anything I want.
WIFE: That's not true. All you're doing is feeling sorry for yourself.
HUSBAND: I am not feeling sorry for myself. Things always go wrong for me.
WIFE: (*frustrated*) You're exaggerating.
HUSBAND: (*frustrated*) I am not exaggerating! You just don't understand. I give up. (*both walk off; husband is depressed and disgusted*)

Precise, Checks Accuracy

HUSBAND: I didn't get the promotion. I'm really disappointed.
WIFE: I'm sure you are.
HUSBAND: It's not the end of the world. I have to remember that I'll have other chances.

Discussion: In the example on the left, the husband exaggerates matters to himself and to his wife. Not only does it distort his own conception of the situation, but it also is frustrating to the wife. This double exaggeration ends in confusion, misunderstanding, and feelings of dissatisfaction.

In contrast, in the example on the right, the husband's thinking is clear and accurate and he expressed himself precisely. This facilitates effective communication between the spouses and increases the chances for understanding and satisfaction.

Situation: Kate has asked Martha if she would like to come over and play bridge.

Imprecise, Does Not Check Accuracy

MARTHA: There is no bigger waste of an evening than playing cards!
KATE: (*offended*) If I knew that you felt that way, I wouldn't have asked you. Don't worry—I won't bother you again!

Precise, Checks Accuracy

MARTHA: I don't like to play bridge for relaxation. I have to concentrate on it so hard that it is not fun. I'd rather not.
KATE: I didn't realize that you felt that way about it.

Discussion: The difference between stating, "I don't like to play bridge for relaxation," and, "There is no bigger waste of an evening," is quite noticeable. The implication that bridge is "bad" and "waste of an evening" is a "put down" of Kate's interest and she reacts defensively. In contrast, saying precisely, "I don't like to play bridge for relaxation" leads to more discussion and a fair amount of understanding between the two women.

Imprecise, Does Not Check Accuracy

HUSBAND: I can never get any peace and quiet around here after work. But you are so selfish and inconsiderate, you never even think of that.
WIFE: Me, selfish? You're the one who never takes the kids out of the house so that I can have a rest!

Precise, Checks Accuracy

HUSBAND: I'd really like to be able to have a half hour of quiet when I come home from the office. Is there any way that we can arrange that?
WIFE: I didn't realize that you wanted that time to yourself after work, or I would have kept the children away from you. I'll send them down to the basement and then they can have their playtime with you after dinner.

Discussion: This example demonstrates the effects of exaggeration and overstatement. The husband does not check his perception of the wife's selfishness and communicates this exaggerated perception to the wife. She becomes upset and defensive, and the problem, instead of being resolved, is compounded.

In contrast, on the right, the precise statement helps to facilitate some understanding and resolution of the issue.

In general, these examples show how imprecise, exaggerated language reflects and maintains sloppy thinking. This, in turn, has a negative effect on actions, communication, and relationships as well. The conversations that contain exaggerations and emotional attacks either lead to an escalation of the attacks or to the withdrawal of one or both parties. Either way, there is conflict and hurt feelings. No resolution is found, and, instead, there are negative consequences to the relationship.

In contrast, checking the accuracy of your language encourages and reflects clear thinking. It helps to keep a balanced perspective of people and situations and promotes exchange of ideas. This increases the chances for some degree of understanding and resolution.

Remember: as with other skills, this one does not guarantee success and satisfaction in your relationships. Some people whom you encounter will exaggerate a great deal and will use this as a weapon in many situations. Emotional attacks, biases, and unbalanced perspectives are their way of handling life and people. No matter how precise you are or how well you explain accuracy to them, they will continue to exaggerate and attack. With these people, use what you learned here to recognize their overstatements for what they are. When they attack you and call you "immature" or "irresponsible" (or whatever other words are in their repertoire), do not take it seriously. Use this skill to become proficient at recognizing people who try to survive or get their way by exaggerating and overstating.

Practice

The section below gives you an opportunity to practice the skill of checking the accuracy of your statements.

I. Below are three columns. The first one contains statements of facts, the second contains exaggerations of the facts, and the third column contains an accurate representation of them. Match each situation in column 1 to the exaggerated statement that goes with (column 2) and then to an accurate statement of the facts (column 3).

Facts	*Inaccurate Statements*	*Accurate Statements*
A. A husband tells his wife that she made a delicious dinner. Then he adds, "Next time we have asparagus, make a little cheese sauce. I like it that way."	1. WIFE: Look . . . everything with the kids goes along perfectly well until you butt in . . . then all you do is mess things up! That's when they get noisy . . . it's your fault!	a. MOTHER: I know you didn't mean to do that, Tom. It's OK. b. HUSBAND: I know that you enjoy talking, but I'd like some quiet now. Maybe we can talk later.

B. A wife and husband are having a disagreement over how to discipline the children. The husband thinks that the kids are too noisy. The wife doesn't mind the noise.

C. A wife likes to talk with her husband and discuss daily happenings. Tonight they have been talking for thirty minutes.

D. As all children do, Tom frequently drops or breaks things. He accidentally tips over a lamp.

HUSBAND: My fault! This place is a madhouse. You let the kids scream at the top of their lungs!

2. MOTHER: You are the clumsiest child I've ever seen. Can't you do anything right? Nothing is safe from you.

3. WIFE: As usual, you can never be satisfied with anything! You always have to find something to complain about.

4. HUSBAND: Can't you ever be quiet? I don't think you've ever been quiet for longer than a minute!
WIFE: That's not true. At least I'm not the total bore that you are. You never have a thing to say.

WIFE: OK.

c. WIFE: I don't mind the noise.
HUSBAND: But I do. When I'm home, I'd like them to follow my rules.

d. WIFE: Glad you enjoyed dinner. Next time I'll try to remember that you like cheese sauce.

II. Below are listed pairs of statements. One of them is inaccurate in facts, frequency, or degree; the other is accurate. Check the one that is more precise.

A. 1. ____BOSS: You have been late three times this month. I want you here on time!

2. ____BOSS: You are constantly tardy, and I am tired of it. Do you think that, for once, you could get here on time?

B. 1. ____FRIEND: I don't like the weather in this part of the country.

2. ____FRIEND: This is an awful town! I hate everything about it. I can't wait to move.

C. 1. ____YOUNG MAN: I can't ever get the women that I like to go out with me. I'm a total failure . . . I must be ugly or queer or something!

2. ____YOUNG MAN: Sometimes I cannot get dates with women I like.

D. 1. ____WIFE: (*thinks to herself*) My husband is so lazy.

2. ____WIFE: (*thinks to herself*) My husband doesn't work around the yard very much.

E. 1. ___STUDENT: I have only spoken a few times in front of a group of people. It is new and uncomfortable for me. I suppose that if I had more practice, I might feel more comfortable about it.

2. ___STUDENT: I just can't talk in front of groups. I fall completely apart.

III. Two situations are described below. Following each one is an exaggerated statement. Using the skill you have just learned, check the accuracy of facts, frequency, and degree and write a more accurate statement that is likely to help the speaker achieve his or her purpose.

A. Situation: A husband is working around the house. His wife is resting. They usually share the chores, but today she has a cold.
Purpose: To get wife's help in hanging a picture.

HUSBAND: Would you get over here and help me? You've done absolutely nothing all day but sit around and pamper yourself. I'm the one who always has to do all the work around here, week in and week out.
Skill: Are the facts stated correctly? Is the frequency accurate? Is the strength of the words accurate?

Below, write a more accurate statement — one that is more likely to achieve the husband's purpose.

B. Situation: Todd has run into some difficulty with his supervisor. In three previous jobs, Todd has gotten along reasonably well with supervisors, although there were minor skirmishes and disagreements with all of them. In his present job, the supervisor watches his work closely. Todd is uncomfortable with this and wants to know why the supervisor evaluates him so closely.
Purpose: To make the relationship more pleasant and comfortable and to find out if the supervisor thinks negatively of him.
In a moment of frustration, Todd says without thinking:

TODD: I can't take this around here. You're the only supervisor I've ever had trouble with . . . my last supervisor was a great guy and a wonderful administrator and everything ran perfectly. But you're always looking over my shoulder and making me so nervous that I can't think at all. I can't take this. What's the matter? Do you think I'm too stupid to do the job on my own?

Using the skill just learned, check the following.
1. Are the facts correct?
2. Is the frequency accurate?
3. Is the strength of the words accurate?

Below, write a more accurate statement — one that is more likely to achieve Todd's purpose.

SKILL 4: CHECKING OUT HOW YOU COME ACROSS

Even when you are precise and descriptive, it is important to find out how you come across to others. From their point of view, what did it seem that you said, did, or meant? It does not matter if your words were specific and accurate. If your listener did not understand you, your communication did not achieve your purpose. It is your responsibility to make yourself clear and to be certain that others understand. Otherwise, you may assume that you were understood correctly when that is not the case.

You can accomplish this by asking straightforward questions. For example, "Does that make sense?" "What did it seem that I said?" "What did it seem that I was trying to do?" "How did that come across to you? Does it seem reasonable?"

This skill is useful at these times.

1. When it is important for you to be understood as accurately as possible (for example, discussing a problem with spouse).
2. When you are emotional or intensely involved. Using this skill is a good way to check how you came across.
3. Whenever the other person seems to have misunderstood your intention or words. If the other person, contrary to your expectations, becomes defensive, if he or she withdraws or seems hurt, angry, or upset, this is a good indication that you were misunderstood.

Here is an example of how the skill might be used in a conversation.

YOU: (*to a friend*) Why don't you take tennis lessons? It might help you with your weight.
FRIEND: (*angrily*) Thanks a lot.
YOU: Wait. I must've given the wrong impression. What did it seem that I said?

Providing Relevant, Descriptive, and Precise Information 241

FRIEND: You were telling me to lose weight. I know I've picked up a few pounds this last month.
YOU: I didn't mean that at all. I was only trying to be helpful. I know that you worry a lot about keeping your weight down, and I thought that exercise might help you to burn up calories without having to cut down on food.

By checking out how you come across, you can obtain a better idea of how the other person perceives your message. This helps to keep communication clear and gives you an early opportunity to clear up any misunderstandings.

Frequently, people do not check out how they come across. Instead, they assume that others have understood what they said or did and know their feelings, intentions, and motives. They go on speaking without checking out the impression that they created and without checking the other person's perceptions of what was said, done, or intended. In this case, something like the following can occur.

FRIEND A: Why don't you take tennis lessons? It might help you with your weight.
FRIEND B: (*angrily*) Thanks a lot.
FRIEND A: Don't get offended so easily. I'm just trying to be helpful.
FRIEND B: You're helpful, all right. Just because you're skinny is no reason for you to tell the rest of us what to do. (*walks off*)

This skill of checking with the other person about how you came across works for the following reasons.
1. It conveys to the other people that you want to know their perceptions. This acknowledges their right to reactions and impressions that are different than yours.
2. It gives you the opportunity to find out if the other person understood what you said and perceived your thoughts, feelings, and intentions accurately.
3. When the other person responds, you have the opportunity to clarify your motive and your words. This helps to clear up any misunderstandings and increases the chances of accomplishing what you want.

The following examples help to point out the differences between failing to check out the impression that you created and doing so.

Not Checking Out

WIFE: Will you help me in here when you have a minute?
HUSBAND: No! I'm busy.
WIFE: (*offended*) Never mind, I'll do it myself. (*angrily*) Just don't ever ask me to help you with anything.

TERRY: You're talking awfully loud, so I know that you're excited.
SUE: (*coldly*) Well . . . never mind.
TERRY: What were you saying?
SUE: I don't want to talk about it now. Forget it.

Checking Out

WIFE: Will you help me in here when you have a minute?
HUSBAND: No! I'm busy.
WIFE: (*offended*) Never mind, I'll do it myself. (*angrily*) Just don't ever ask me to help you with something.
HUSBAND: Wait a minute . . . did I seem unreasonable to you?
WIFE: Yes. You sounded like you didn't want to be bothered. And I was just asking for a little help.
HUSBAND: Well, I'm sorry. I answered impulsively. I meant that I was right in the middle of paying the bills. I'll come in a few minutes when I'm finished.

TERRY: You're talking awfully loud, so I know that you're excited.
SUE: (*coldly*) Well . . . never mind.
TERRY: What are you saying?
SUE: I don't want to talk about it now. Forget it.
TERRY: Wait a minute . . . what did it seem I said?
SUE: That I was talking very loudly and excitedly and that I should stop it!
TERRY: I didn't mean that you should stop it. I know you were enthusiastic about your idea because you frequently speak more loudly when you are excited about something.
SUE: Well, was I being obnoxiously loud?
TERRY: No, not at all. But I didn't think that you would want to be overheard.

Providing Relevant, Descriptive, and Precise Information 243

In the examples on the left, the speakers assumed that the listener understood what was said. Then, when the listener reacted with upset or defensiveness, the speakers retorted with equally defensive statements. The misunderstandings escalated, and the chances for exploring each other's ideas and achieving some degree of resolution declined markedly.

In contrast, in the examples on the right, the speakers notice that their listeners seem upset, hurt, angry, confused, or withdrawn. When this happens, they ask the listeners what it seemed that they had said. This gave the speakers a chance to clear up any misunderstanding. Confusion and defensiveness were minimized, and the chances for effective communication were increased.

Remember: nonverbal cues are important. If, when checking out how you came across, you look angry or speak in a critical tone of voice, you will seem blaming and challenging. If you honestly want to know how you came across, your nonverbal cues must be pleasant and encouraging.

Practice

This section provides practice in the skill of checking out how you come across.

I. The conversations below contain statements in which one person checks out how he or she came across. Underline these check-out statements.

A. HUSBAND: I've really had it. Everything is so monotonous and routine. It's really a drag. I'm really bored and sick of everything.
WIFE: (*coldly*) Well, thanks a lot.
HUSBAND: Wait a minute . . . did it seem that I was including you in what I was fed up with?
WIFE: It sounded like that to me!
HUSBAND: I didn't mean you. I said "everything," but I meant everything about work and the grind of rushing around and getting ahead and doing chores on weekends and trying to spend time with the kids. You and I have very little time together, and I feel like I have no time for myself.
WIFE: At first, I thought that I was one of the things that was bothering you.

B. WIFE: (*hurt and frustrated*) I don't know why I bother to talk with you! You act like I'm so dumb and that I don't understand anything.

HUSBAND: I do not think you're dumb!

WIFE: Yes, you do.

HUSBAND: What did I do to give you that impression?

WIFE: While we were talking about the problem on your job, you kept saying that I didn't understand the situation. Every time I made a suggestion, you said that it wouldn't work. So I feel that you don't even want to hear what I have to say!

HUSBAND: I'm sorry. I am frustrated with the situation at work, and I really don't want to hear anyone's advice or suggestions. That has nothing to do with you, and I don't think that you or your ideas are dumb.

II. The column on the left presents situations while the column on the right contains suitable "check-out" questions. Match the situation with a "check-out" statement that the speaker might make.

Situation	Check-Out
A. Teacher presents a new idea to class and lectures for ten minutes on it.	1. "Do you think I came on too strong? I didn't want to seem angry and rude to everyone."
B. Mother receives a gift from her daughter and says, "Oh, this is too expensive. You shouldn't have spent all this money. You should be watching your budget!" She notices that her daughter is silent and doesn't say much the rest of the afternoon.	2. "Will someone please summarize what I said, so that I'm sure I made it clear?"
	3. "Did I sound unappreciative before? I'm sorry if I did—I didn't mean to."
C. John and Dave leave a staff meeting where Dave disagreed with everyone fairly strongly.	

SKILL 5: ASKING FOR SPECIFIC AND DESCRIPTIVE INFORMATION

Although you may apply the skills of description and accuracy, other people will not be familiar with them and, instead, they will leave out portions of their thinking and will use vague, unspecific, or evaluative terms. When this happens, it is helpful to ask the other person for specific and descriptive information. Use these guidelines.

Providing Relevant, Descriptive, and Precise Information

1. If the person leaves out relevant information, ask for it. Try to find out what happened, what his or her feelings and reactions are, and how this relates to you. For example, "I don't quite understand. What happened?" "I'm not clear about this. How did that affect you," or, "How do you feel about that?" "I'm not sure how this relates to me. Is there something that you want me to do?"
2. If the person is using vague or evaluative words, ask for a more specific explanation. Use who, what, when, where, how questions. Encourage the person to describe what happened. For example, "I'm not sure that I understand. What did I do that seemed rude?"
3. It is especially important to ask for this information in a pleasant way. If you ask these questions with a challenging tone of voice, for example, you are likely to elicit defensiveness and will get very little descriptive and specific information. Remember that you are trying to get information in order to solve a problem or issue. Keep your nonverbal cues consistent with this purpose.

Of course, some situations that you encounter will be difficult and complicated. For example, the other person may be blaming or accusing you or he or she may be preaching or exaggerating. In these special situations, you do try to get more descriptive and specific information but the technique involves several more steps. A method of handling these problem situations is presented in the next chapter.

This skill can be used in many situations in order to gain more information about the other person's thinking. It is helpful to use because it encourages others to express themselves more descriptively and specifically and it elicits more useful information. As a result, the conversation is usually more productive, and the chances for some degree of understanding and resolution are increased.

The examples below show the difference between not asking for more information and doing so. They also show some of the situations in which the skill can be used.

1. When the other person does not provide complete information.

Does Not Ask for More Information

EMPLOYEE: I really don't like these new procedures that were started.

Asks for More Information

EMPLOYEE: I really don't like these new procedures that were started.

BOSS: That's nothing new. You never like anything.

BOSS: What seems to be the problem with them?

2. When one person does not explain how what he or she says relates to the other.

Does Not Ask for More Information

WIFE: I sure don't like your working nights as you do. I get pretty lonely.
HUSBAND: (*angrily*) What do you expect me to do about it?
WIFE: I don't expect you to do anything about it! Just forget that I said anything. (*walks off*)

Asks for More Information

WIFE: I sure don't like your working nights as you do. I get pretty lonely.
HUSBAND: You never mentioned that before. I thought that maybe you liked having the evening to yourself.
WIFE: Well, I don't.
HUSBAND: What can I do about it?
WIFE: Nothing. I just am complaining, I guess . . . and I wanted you to know that I miss you at night.

3. When the other person uses vague, evaluative words instead of being specific.

Does Not Ask for More Information

HUSBAND: Why can't you be considerate and thoughtful sometimes?
WIFE: I am. You just never take the time to notice it.
HUSBAND: Oh, come on. You are one of the least considerate people I've seen.
WIFE: That's your opinion. Personally, I think that you take the prize.

Asks for More Information

HUSBAND: Why can't you be considerate and thoughtful sometimes?
WIFE: If I were considerate and thoughtful, what would I do?
HUSBAND: Well, you might bake a cherry pie to surprise me once in awhile. You know that I love that.
WIFE: Besides the cherry pie, is there anything else specifically that you'd like me to do?
HUSBAND: Well, I was a bit frustrated tonight when you didn't ask me how my talk with the boss went.

In the examples on the left, the listeners react immediately and defensively to what the speakers said. They do not check out their understanding of what was meant and they do not ask for more spe-

Providing Relevant, Descriptive, and Precise Information 247

cific and descriptive information. The interaction becomes increasingly defensive, and denials, threats, or counter-accusations follow. Nothing is accomplished, and, as a matter of fact, misunderstanding between the people increases.

In contrast, in the examples on the right, the listeners do not become defensive, but, instead, they encourage the speakers to clarify and specify what they meant. This provides more useful information. The interaction is more productive, and some understanding and resolution of the issue is achieved.

Practice

This section provides practice in helping someone to be more descriptive and specific.

Pairs of conversations are presented below. In one of the conversations, the interaction is productive. Questions are asked, and useful information is elicited. In the other, the people react without asking for more information and nothing is accomplished.

Place a check mark in front of the conversation that seems more productive. After you do this, go back and underline the statement or statements that ask for more specific information.

A. 1. ____HUSBAND: That friend of yours, Mrs. Brown, is here all the time on weekends. She really bugs me.
WIFE: Well, I don't invite her over here! Besides, I never complain when your friends stop by!
HUSBAND: Oh, yes, you do, and every time that Sam comes here, I hear about it!

2. ____HUSBAND: That friend of yours, Mrs. Brown, is here all the time on weekends. She really bugs me.
WIFE: Do you mean that you want me to discourage her from coming by?
HUSBAND: No, I don't mean that.
WIFE: What do you want me to do?
HUSBAND: I don't want her here at mealtimes.

B. 1. ____JOYCE: I'm having a rough time. Things are really going wrong at work, at home . . .
PHIL: Oh, come on now, stop being so melodramatic! You always make everything in your life sound like a soap opera!

2. ____JOYCE: I'm having a rough time. Things are really going wrong at work, at home . . .
PHIL: Oh come on now, stop being so melodramatic! You always make everything in your life sound like a soap opera!

JOYCE: (*hurt*) Are you saying that I exaggerate everything?

PHIL: No, I don't mean that. I just think that you take everything too seriously.

C. 1. ____HUSBAND: (*frustrated*) You are always late and I am sick and tired of it.

WIFE: I guess that means that you want me to change something, right?

HUSBAND: Yes! I want you to be on time.

WIFE: It would help me to know exactly what it is that you are complaining about. What could I do to be "on time"?

HUSBAND: That's simple. You could be on time whenever we have to go somewhere together. Like last Saturday, when we went to the party, you were late, as usual.

WIFE: That helps a lot to have an example to talk about; I want to be sure that I understand your point of view on this. I was ready by 8:00, and we got to the party by 8:30. The party didn't start until 8:00, but you consider that late, right?

HUSBAND: Yes. Because I wanted to be there early.

WIFE: I didn't know that. What can we do to keep this from happening again?

JOYCE: (*hurt*) OK, forget it. I won't tell you about it. If I'm so melodramatic and exaggerate everything, I won't burden you with listening to me! (*walks off*)

2. ____HUSBAND: (*frustrated*) You are always late and I am sick and tired of it.

WIFE: I am not always late. You are just exaggerating.

HUSBAND: No, I'm not. I should know how often I sit around, waiting for you. That's how I spend a lot of my time.

WIFE: That's not so.

HUSBAND: (*loudly and angrily*) How can you stand there and deny it? Just face the facts. You are never ready!

WIFE: Here we go again. You're picking on me again, and I get sick and tired of that! To hear you talk, you'd think that you were perfect! You must never do anything wrong. I'm the only one who makes mistakes.

HUSBAND: That's true. You are the only one who makes mistakes. Compared to you, I am perfect.

WIFE: That's a really nice thing to say! I can't take this. I hate it when we argue like this. Why do you have to be so mean? (*starts to cry*)

HUSBAND: Shut up. I can't stand cry babies, and I don't want to hear it. I'm going downstairs to read — and leave me alone!

SUMMARY

Providing relevant, precise, and accurate information involves the following principles:

Providing Relevant, Descriptive, and Precise Information 249

1. Tell the other person the important parts of what you are thinking. Do not assume that others can guess what is in your head. Be sure to explain what happened, what you think or feel, how you are affected, and how this relates to the other person. If you expect a response, be sure to tell your listener what response you want. For example, if you want to tell your spouse that you are in a bad mood but that it has nothing to do with him or her, be sure to say, "I had a rough day at work and am in a terrible mood, so my grouchiness has nothing to do with you. Rather than leaving me alone, I'd like you to sit here with me and keep me company while I work on these bills."

   Sometimes, it is helpful to explain why you are saying something. For example, "This is just an idea that I'm throwing out for discussion. What about revising our filing system, since it's giving all of us some trouble? What do you think of that?"
2. When you tell the other person what you are thinking, be descriptive and, in this way, provide as much information as possible. Explain who, what, when, where, and how. Be specific.
3. Avoid the following.
   a. Blaming, accusations, and interpretations. For examples, do not say, "You try to get all the attention, wherever you are." Instead, say, "At the family gatherings, you do most of the talking, and you don't ask anyone else about what they are doing. I don't like that. I'd like you to draw other people into the conversation."
   b. Vague, subjective, and evaluative terms. For example, do not say, "You are so *wonderful*." Instead, say, "I really like it when you remember my birthday."
   c. Unfavorable comparisons or preaching. For example, do not say, "If you were more like your father, you might be successful." Instead, say, "If you socialized more and joined more clubs, you would get more contacts and bring in more business."
4. Language affects our thinking as well as our listener's interpretation and understanding of what we say. In order to be precise and facilitate accurate understanding, check the accuracy of your thoughts and statements by following these steps:
   a. Ask yourself, Are these really the facts? Is this what I mean? Is this exactly what happened? Is this exaggerated?

b. Check the frequency. (Did it happen "twice in a month" instead of "always" or "never"?)
c. Check the strength or degree of the words. (Is it "disappointing" instead of "awful" or "terrible"? Was it "boring" instead of "miserable" or "the worst way to spend an afternoon"?)
d. If you find any inaccuracies or exaggerations, revise your thoughts and statements. Describe what happened factually.
5. Check out how you came across to others, especially in the following situations.
   a. Whenever it is important to be understood as accurately as possible.
   b. Whenever you are emotional or intensely involved.
   c. Whenever another person seems to have misunderstood you or your intentions.
      For example: "What did it seem that I said?" "Does that make sense?" "Does my suggestion seem reasonable to you?"
6. When you are involved in a conversation where the other person is exaggerating, blaming, interpreting, or using vague terms, do the following.
   a. If s/he omits relevant information, ask for it. For example, "I'm not clear . . . you've been complaining bitterly about your job. Is there something that you want me to do?"
   b. If the other person is judging, accusing, evaluating, or making unfavorable comparisons, do not become defensive. Check your impressions, explain that you do not understand, and ask for specific information. Encourage the other person to be descriptive by asking questions that begin with who, what, where, when, and how. For example, "You just called me obnoxious. I don't understand — what did I do?"
   c. If the other person exaggerates, ask him or her to specify when, what, or how. For example:
      WIFE: You never think of me.
      HUSBAND: When was the last time that I didn't think of you?

REVIEW

The following section provides an opportunity for you to apply the skills and principles discussed in this chapter.

I. Below are conversations that do not follow the rules of being de-

Providing Relevant, Descriptive, and Precise Information 251

scriptive. Underline the words or phrases that are blaming, vague, evaluative, and those that make comparisons or interpretations. The first is done for you.

A. BOSS: You did not behave in a <u>mature</u> manner. I would have expected more from you.
B. HUSBAND: I wish that you were less sloppy and disorganized. I don't know how you ever find anything.
C. FRIEND: I know why you did that. You're ignoring me just because you got that promotion, and now you think that I'm not good enough for you.
D. NEIGHBOR: You shouldn't be taking this so hard. If you had some stamina, you'd be able to grit your teeth and come through.
E. BOSS: Miss Jones, the outfits that you wear to work are simply too seductive.
F. CO-WORKER: I'm sick of you. You try to control everything around here. You just want all the attention and all the credit for everything.
G. MOTHER: Why can't you fix your hair so that you can be as pretty as the other girls in your class?

II. The column on the left contains nondescriptive statements. The column on the right contains statements that are descriptive and avoid judgments, accusations, interpretations, evaluations, and comparisons. Match the nondescriptive statement with the more descriptive one.

Nondescriptive	Descriptive
A. BOSS: You did not behave in a mature manner. I expected more from you.	1. When I'm talking, I'd like you to look at me. Otherwise, I begin to feel that you're not interested in what I'm saying. Last night, when we were out to dinner, you stared at everything else in the restaurant but me.
B. FRIEND: I know why you did that. You're ignoring us just because you had that promotion at work and think that we're not good enough for you.	
C. WIFE: Why can't you be warm and act interested in me, as if I meant something to you. It's as if I don't mean a thing to you. You don't care about me at all.	2. I realize that you have your own way of handling things. But I wish that you'd organize your recipes or else take them off the shelf so that I don't have to see that big pile.

D. HUSBAND: I wish that you were less sloppy and disorganized. I don't know how you ever find anything.

E. BOSS: Miss Jones, the outfits you wear to work are simply too seductive.

F. HUSBAND: Why can't you think as clearly and rationally as I do?

G. CO-WORKER: I'm sick of you. You try to control everything around here. You just want all the attention and credit for everything.

H. MOTHER: Why can't you fix your hair so that you can be as pretty as the other girls in your class?

I. FRIEND: Thanks for being such a wonderful friend.

3. We usually do something together every Saturday, and you haven't called us in three weeks. I'm hurt and puzzled.

4. I don't like how you handled that situation. I'd prefer it if you held back your anger — although it's justified — and let Bill hang himself.

5. In front of the boss, you talk about our joint projects in the first person — 'I did this and I did that.' I want you to be clear with him that we're working on this together.

6. I really appreciated your offering us your car and then coming over in this cold weather to help us get this one started.

7. Miss Jones, I'd prefer it if you wore your skirts a bit longer.

8. Please do not continue to complain about the budget. We overspent this month, but it's not a major problem. We'll make it up next month.

9. I'm just making a suggestion. Have you ever considered parting your hair down the middle or pulling it back with a barrette?

III. The examples below contain a description of a situation and an exaggerated, inaccurate statement of it. Some possible consequences are listed after each exaggerated statement. Circle the most likely consequences and then rewrite the statement more accurately.

A. Situation: Mary's husband is thirty pounds overweight. He has started to diet twice but has not done it successfully. Around the house, he wears blue jeans and old shirts which Mary does not like. Mary would like him to lose weight and dress differently.
Exaggerated thought: My husband makes me sick. He's a big fat slob, and he never even tries to diet. What makes it worse, he

Providing Relevant, Descriptive, and Precise Information 253

dresses like a slob, too. He is disgusting. I deserve better than him. He'd better shape up or I'll leave him!
1. Consequences: If Mary thinks this way about her husband, how is she likely to feel and react? (Circle those that you think are likely.)
   a. She may keep the situation in perspective and remember her husband's good qualities as well.
   b. She will be satisfied with her marriage.
   c. She will be frustrated and angry at her husband.
   d. She may pity herself for having to put up with him.
2. Mary tells this to her husband and nags him. For example,
   MARY: Why don't you go on a diet and dress differently?
   HUSBAND: I've tried to diet. I just can't diet and work, too. I'll lose weight this summer when I'm more active.
   MARY: (*frustrated*) That's what you always say! That's what you said three years ago, and you're still the same fat slob . . . maybe ever fatter. I can't stand fat men, and I swore I'd never have a slob for a husband.
   If you were the husband, how would you feel and react? Circle the likely reactions.
   a. Be happy.
   b. Be hurt and angry.
   c. Not pay any attention.
   d. Be defensive and counterattack; call her names.
   e. Tell her you love her.
   f. Get upset, eat even more, and blame her for making you eat more.
3. Look at the description of the situation again and rewrite a more accurate thought for Mary.
   Revised thought:

B. Situation: Mrs. Collins prefers that her married son come for Sunday dinner and maintain close ties with her and her husband. Her son's wife, Lisa, is polite but is not talkative at these family get-togethers. Lisa often turns down invitations to come over. Usually, she and John come to the Collins' home only one Sunday a month. Lisa invites her in-laws over for dinner a few times a year.

Exaggerated thought: This is awful! That Lisa just doesn't like family things. She never comes over and never invites us to their place. She's a cold person. And she's persuaded John to be the same way. She has no appreciation or understanding of other people, and she doesn't even realize how much she's hurting me by keeping my son away from me. She's selfish and mean in a lot of ways, and she seems to get worse instead of better. In a few years, she will probably keep John away from here altogether!

1. Consequences: If Mrs. Collins thinks this way about her daughter-in-law, how is Mrs. Collins likely to feel and act? Circle those that you think are most likely.
   a. She will be frustrated and angry at Lisa.
   b. She will continue to exaggerate Lisa's faults and shortcomings.
   c. She will continue to try to understand Lisa and keep the communication open between them.
   d. She will keep the situation in perspective.
   e. She will pity herself for having to put up with this situation.
   f. She will be satisfied with her daughter-in-law and with her son's marriage in general.

2. Sometimes Mrs. Collins nags at her son about Lisa. She doesn't seem to get anywhere with this, so one day in frustration she blows up at Lisa. The following conversation takes place:
   MRS. COLLINS: All I ask is one small thing — that you come over for Sunday dinner — and you can't even bother to do that. You are one of the most selfish, coldest people I know — you have no consideration for my feelings or anyone else's.
   LISA: That's not so. It's just that I like to spend my free time at home. Besides, I'm trying to diet, so I don't like coming to these dinners where there's so much food.
   MRS. COLLINS: Well, that's too bad if you're dieting. This is John's family, and you have to make some sacrifices. You're so wrapped up in yourself that you don't care about anyone. I don't know why, of all the girls he went with, John had to marry you!

If you were Lisa, how would you feel and react? Circle the likely reactions.

Providing Relevant, Descriptive, and Precise Information   255

   a. Be happy.
   b. Try to be understanding and loving.
   c. Stop phoning and don't go to dinner any more.
   d. Ignore her.
   e. Go to dinner more often just to please her.
   f. Be hurt and angry.
   g. Be defensive and counterattack.
3. Look at the description of the situation again. Using the skill of checking accuracy of facts, frequency, and degree, revise Mrs. Collins' exaggerated statement to a more accurate one. Write it in the space below.

Revised thought:

IV. Below are conversations. At certain points, two responses are suggested. Check the more effective one.
A. Situation: A husband and wife have some time alone before dinner. The wife wants to tell her husband that she doesn't like it when he corrects her in public. The night before, they had been out with some other couples, and he corrected what she said three times during the evening. It is not a big deal, but she does want him to know about it and ask him not to do it.
   1. WIFE: There's something I'd like to mention.
      a. ____"It's no big deal but I want you to know that I don't like it when you correct me in public."
      b. ____"Don't correct me in public."
   2. HUSBAND: When have I ever corrected you?
      a. ____WIFE: You always correct me.
      b. ____WIFE: Well, you did last night when we were out to dinner.
   3. HUSBAND: Stop picking on me! You always find something to complain about!
      a. ____WIFE: Me complain! You're the one who is never pleased with anything!
      b. ____WIFE: Did I sound complaining? I didn't mean to pick on you. But I did want you to know how I felt.

B. Situation: An employee is having a discussion with the boss.
EMPLOYEE: I really think that we need more emphasis on morale around here. I'm not pleased or satisfied and I know plenty of others who aren't either.

1. BOSS: You don't come to work for pleasure!

   a. ___EMPLOYEE: Well, morale is important. If morale is bad, production is bad. You should know that.

   b. ___EMPLOYEE: Did I sound like I was blaming you? That's not what I meant.

2. BOSS: It sounds to me that you're saying that you and everyone else are dissatisfied. And I should do something about it!

   a. ___EMPLOYEE: Things are not all bad around here. As a matter of fact, most things are good — and I certainly appreciate the efforts you've made to get us all the latest equipment.

   b. ___EMPLOYEE: Well, I feel miserable and dissatisfied. So things must be pretty bad. Something has to change pretty soon.

3. BOSS: What's your beef?

   a. ___EMPLOYEE: The atmosphere around here is awful. You never tell anyone what you want them to do or what you expect. And that's not the way for a boss to behave.

   b. ___EMPLOYEE: Many times I don't know what you want or what you expect. I'd like you to tell me explicitly what you want in terms of my performance — what I'm doing right or wrong.

V. Below is a number of conversations. Pairs of statements are presented. In each case, check the statement that asks for more information or the one that is more descriptive or complete.

A. MOTHER: I wish you'd be a more considerate son.

   1. a. ___SON: Why can't you be a more understanding mother?

   b. ___SON: I don't understand. What is it that you want me to do?

   2. a. ___MOTHER: You're lucky to have had me for a mother. The least that you can do is to show some appreciation. Your brother has no trouble in being considerate. Why can't you be like him?

   b. ___MOTHER: I'd like you to come up for dinner on Sundays or call us. You and Jean don't seem interested in us.

Providing Relevant, Descriptive, and Precise Information 257

3. a. ____SON: We are interested in you, but we often find Sunday is our only day to relax.

b. ____SON: You always did pick on me, and Ed always was your favorite. Besides, you two are exactly alike—hard headed and selfish.

B. HUSBAND: There you go again, dropping crumbs all over the floor. Can't you pay attention to what you're doing? I get sick and tired of you being so sloppy!

1. a. ____WIFE: I've had it. I don't like being called sloppy. I do the best I can, and I don't worry about a few crumbs here and there. If you want to worry, fine. But leave me alone.

b. ____WIFE: You are too much for me. I'm sick and tired of your constant complaining. You must really be neurotic.

2. a. ____HUSBAND: But do you have to go around making a mess all the time? You must do that deliberately just to upset me.

b. ____HUSBAND: I don't worry. I just like things neat and clean. That's just my preference.

3. a.____WIFE: You must pick on me deliberately. You take out all your frustrations on me.

b. ____WIFE: You have a right to your preference. But when you criticize me, I get very upset and frustrated.

4. a. ____HUSBAND: I didn't mean for you to feel upset. I just wanted you to keep the floor clean.

b. ____HUSBAND: Well, I'm frustrated. I don't know of any other wife who's as sloppy as you are.

C. JEAN: If you're going to be upset over something that I said, then I think that there's something wrong with you. You'd better get yourself straightened out, so that you're normal like the rest of us.

1. a. ____BOB: Normal? If your idea of normal is to insult me, just as you did, you're all wrong. You're not normal—you're obnoxious.

b. ____BOB: Now that you called me abnormal, I feel angry and hurt. I don't feel much like talking.

2. a. ____JEAN: I'm not obnoxious, but I am stupid for having put up with you this long.

b. ____JEAN: I didn't mean to hurt you. I just don't understand why you are so upset with me.

CHAPTER SIX

Communication as Interaction

THIS CHAPTER IS BUILT ON the concept of communication as an interaction between you and the other person, with each of you eliciting responses from the other. It focuses on how to increase satisfaction in a relationship that is important to you, and explains how and when to apply some of the skills presented in earlier chapters.

SKILL 1: RELATIONSHIPS: BASIC ELEMENTS AND DECISIONS TO BE MADE

There are some things that distinguish satisfying relationships from those that are frustrating or unsatisfying. In satisfying relationships, both people feel valued and respected by each other. You feel noticed and important; you feel responded to in ways that you want. Everyone wants to be liked and valued, especially by the people who are important to them.

Furthermore, in good relationships, each person feels accepted by the other. Strengths and assets are acknowledged; experiences are accepted; differing opinions, weaknesses, and characteristics are tolerated and do not threaten the relationship. The other person's liking of you does not depend upon your "being perfect" or "measuring up" to a set of standards. This leads to relaxation, security, and comfort in the relationship. None of us likes to sense that people we value are judging us continually and changing their opinion of us, depending on what we do.

There is a feeling of being understood. You feel that the other person is making an effort to see your point of view, to comprehend your experiences, and to find out a little of what it is like to be in your place. This diminishes a sense of aloneness, validates your experiences, and feels comfortable and satisfying. The relationship is a continuing process of caring and trying to understand, and it has an atmosphere of trust and openness. Both people feel free to exchange experiences, feelings, and ideas. You sense that the other person cares and is not intending to hurt, betray, control, or use you. The other speaks honestly and does not lie. Promises and commitments are kept and honored; statements and compliments are genuine. In these relationships, words are followed up by actions. Statements of involvement and caring are accompanied by demonstrations of the same. Both people can risk telling about themselves. This creates an opportunity for closeness, and the people involved feel free to be honest. They do not have to play a role, put up a facade, or be on guard.

There is a sense that the relationship is important to both people. Problems are seen as temporary, and difficulties can be worked out. Both are willing to spend time and energy to work out frustrations and solve problems. You feel secure in knowing that the other person is willing to work at the relationship, and there is a general feeling that the relationship matters to both of you.

In contrast, there are relationships in which the people involved feel ignored, insignificant, and unappreciated; each feels criticized and disapproved of by the other. You sense that you have to play a role or behave in certain ways in order for the other person to approve of you. In these relationships, you cannot trust the other person with your feelings, experiences, or opinions because what you say may be used against you. Your experiences may be ignored, denied, or contradicted. There may be too many instances of criticism, too many hurt feelings and broken commitments. Too many lies, intentional or otherwise, or too many false compliments have destroyed credibility and trust. When this atmosphere prevails, you feel manipulated, disregarded, betrayed, or controlled. You are likely to feel misunderstood and frustrated. All of us have experienced some relationships like this with acquaintances, co-workers, neighbors, with persons in authority positions, or with people in competition with us. Some of these distrusting, uncomfortable relationships must be maintained for practical reasons, but most of us prefer that our close, important relationships be of the satisfying, comfortable type.

A relationship is a continuing process of getting to know another person and getting to know yourself as well. This process of understanding yourself and the other person is accomplished by means of communication: the words, actions and responses exchanged between the two of you. This communication keeps the relationship alive and, for each person, shapes a picture of the relationship. The picture can range from, "This person cares about me. I feel good when I am with this person," to, "This person does not care about me. When I am with this person I feel uncomfortable and bad. I cannot trust him." This picture reflects the atmosphere created in the relationship. It is the sum total of the communication: the responses and failures to respond, the expressions and actions, the statements and silences, and the similarity between words and actions. In a satisfying relationship, you demonstrate and enhance what you say by your actions; your behavior parallels your words and reflects caring and involvement.

Statements and actions contribute in some way to the total picture of a relationship. The examples below show how specific communications help to create the atmosphere between two people.

Creates an Uncomfortable, Dissatisfying Atmosphere	*Creates a Comfortable, Satisfying Atmosphere*
Negative expression of value. ("You really are a pest.")	Direct expression of value. ("Your friendship really means a lot to me.")
Failure to mention what the other person did that you appreciate.	Mentioning what you notice. ("Thank you for taking out the trash.")
Failure to show interest in the other person's view of the relationship. WIFE: We don't talk as we used to. HUSBAND: Of course we do.	Showing interest in the relationship. WIFE: We don't talk as we used to. HUSBAND: I hadn't noticed. What do you mean?
Unwillingness to work on problems in the relationship. LOVER: This is something that we need to talk out. I'm not comfortable with our living together like this. LOVER: You should've thought about that earlier. (*walks away*)	Willingness to work on problems. LOVER: This is something we need to talk out. I'm not comfortable with our living together like this. LOVER: I'm too upset to talk right now. I'll talk about it later with you. Right now I want to be alone.

Not seeking out the other person's opinions. ("I called the travel agent today. We'll be leaving April 1.")	Seeking the opinion of the other. ("I have to give the travel agent a date for our vacation. How is April 1 for you?")
Showing no affection, holding back.	Showing affection.
Being unresponsive, making no effort at involvement, no expression of interest in the other person.	Being responsive, involved, showing interest in the other person. ("I'm glad that you had a productive day and that you feel good. What did you do?")
Criticizing and complaining.	Making self-esteem-generating statements. ("I really like how you handle the kids.")
Making empty threats. ("You do that one more time and I'll leave you for good. I'm not going to put up with you.")	Stating a preference. ("I don't like it when you drink too much. Please don't do that again.")
Expressing a preference by blaming. ("As usual, you left this place in a total mess. Why are you such a slob?")	Expressing a preference without blaming. ("I don't like it when you leave the newspapers lying all around. Please don't do that.")
Refusal to be supportive. ("What do you mean you want some sympathy? I get sick and tired of your wanting support from me. You're the weakest, most childish person I know, and when you're like that I really can't stand you.")	Willingness to be supportive. ("I care about you and I want to see you happy. What can I do to help? How can I show you that I care?")
Being inconsistent, phony, telling lies. ("I know I said you looked good in that blue dress, but I was lying. You look awful in it. Wear that brown outfit.")	Being consistent and truthful. ("I've said all along that I don't like that blue dress. You have other outfits that I think are more becoming to you.")

The types of communication in the examples on the left create an uncomfortable, unpleasant atmosphere in relationships. The persons involved probably will not feel important, liked, valued, or accepted by each other. They will find it difficult to trust, rely on, and believe each other.

In contrast, the communication on the right establishes and maintains an atmosphere of trust and liking. You feel important and valued; you are free to relax and confide in the other person; you are secure in knowing that the relationship is important and that difficulties are momentary and can be worked out.

All relationships involve decisions, some more obvious than others. The first decision that you make about a relationship with spouse, friend, neighbor, boss, or co-worker concerns the significance of that person and that relationship to you. Even after you have decided that a person and a relationship are important to you, there are other choices to be made, sometimes on a day-to-day basis. To help you become more aware of these decisions, this section outlines three important steps.

1. Deciding how much you will invest in the relationship—how willing you are to listen, understand, and be involved.
2. Expressing your decision to the other person.
3. Checking with others about their view of the relationship.

Skill 1a: Deciding How Much You Will Invest

In any relationship, it is helpful to ask yourself some of these questions.

General Questions for All Relationships

1. What sort of relationship is this? Friend, partner, lover, confidante, parent, supervisor?
2. Is it equal or unequal? Supportive? Dependent or independent?
3. Does this relationship really matter to me?
4. What do I want from this relationship?
5. Am I willing to work at maintaining and improving this relationship? Or do I expect to establish it, only to later take this person for granted?
6. Am I willing to try to see the world from the other person's perspective?
7. Am I willing to let this person see things differently than I do?
8. What do I want from this person and this relationship?
9. Am I willing to compromise?

Questions for Important, Close Relationships

1. How willing am I to be involved in this relationship? When

problems occur, am I willing to spend time working them out? Or do I not want to be bothered?
2. Am I willing to be supportive and involved in times of trouble?
3. Am I willing to listen to this person and try to understand his or her experiences? Or am I unwilling to hear anyone's experiences but my own?
4. Do I want to be understood?
5. Am I willing to demonstrate that this relationship matters to me?
6. Am I willing to translate my words into actions? Am I willing to show that I care and am involved? (Or, do I just want to say nice things, make promises and commitments and not follow through?)

Questions for Superficial, Less Important Relationships
1. What do I want from this relationship? (For example, keep my job, get along, avoid trouble)
2. Do I trust this person? Is he or she trying to manipulate or control me? Am I trying to manipulate or control him or her?
3. Is there something I must do in this relationship in order to protect myself?
4. What are the limits of this relationship?

These decisions are not permanent. There are times when, because of other pressures or involvements, your investment in a relationship changes. Commitment and willingness to understand may shift depending upon the situation or other events in your life. For example, when you have had a bad day at work and your boss wants a report done by morning, you probably will be less willing to understand your spouse's experiences. For this reason, you may ask yourself some of these questions and review these decisions and commitments on a daily basis.

Skill 1b: Expressing Your Decisions to the Other Person

After you ask yourself these questions and decide on your investment in the relationship, it sometimes is helpful to let the other person know your decision and your purpose in the relationship. This skill involves expressing your commitment to the relationship and the decisions that you have made. It can be particularly helpful at a difficult time in a relationship to tell the other person how important the relationship is to you, how willing you are to listen, and what your limits are. Use this skill in an established, close relationship whenever the two of you are expressing different viewpoints, exploring sensitive topics, expressing complaints or limits, or working on a problem in the relationship. Long statements about your involvement and commitment are unnecessary and often seem insincere and protesting. Simple and uncomplicated statements usually work best. For example, "I don't want to argue about this. It is really important to me that we understand each other's view of the situation. So, please try to listen and understand my views and I'll try to understand yours."

Most frequently, people do not express the importance or the limits of a relationship to the other person. Instead, they assume that the other person knows the significance that they attribute to the relationship and what they want from it. This is a mistake. If you do not tell others your views, they cannot be expected to know.

This skill of telling the other person about your decisions and investment in the relationship works for the following reasons.

1. It recognizes the other person in the relationship and acknowledges his or her importance.
2. It gives the other person information about your view of the relationship. This provides a context for the statement or the interaction that follows.
3. When two people have some knowledge of each other's views and expectations, there is less chance of eventual disappointment, betrayal, or discrepant expectations. This increases the possibility of clear communication, understanding, and a satisfying relationship.

The examples below help to point out the differences between statements that do not tell the other person the limits, views, and importance of the relationship and those that do.

Does Not Express Decisions about the Relationship	*Expresses Decisions about the Relationship*
WIFE: I want to tell you what happened at work.	WIFE: I want to tell you what happened at work.
HUSBAND: I don't want to hear about what happened at work.	HUSBAND: I want you to know that I care about you very much. But, I do have a hard time listening to your complaints about your job. It's not that I don't care—I get upset when you tell me the frustrations you have.
WIFE: You really don't care about me, do you?	

FRIEND: If you keep acting so angrily toward me, what do you expect me to do? I'm going to be angry right back.

FRIEND: Look, our friendship is important to me and I want to work out this disagreement that we had. But these are my limits. I can't keep trying to work this out if you won't. If you continue to act so angrily toward me, I'll stop trying.

BOSS: Now tell me your complaints and we'll see what we can do.
EMPLOYEE: (*thinks that boss is insincere and does not want to hear his complaints or will do nothing about them*) There's nothing to do anything about.

BOSS: I really want to try to understand your complaints and what's going on out there. I want to help. Perhaps there's something I can do to make things better.

BOSS: This is my policy on this.
EMPLOYEE: Wait a minute! You're not out there working as a salesman as I am. You shouldn't be dictating the policy so blindly.
BOSS: (*angrily*) I've been here for twenty-five years and I know what should be going on!

BOSS: It is important to me that you understand my policy on this and my reasons. I will tell you what I expect you to do on the job.
EMPLOYEE: OK. What if I disagree?
BOSS: I have already made up my mind and I do not want to hear your suggestions.

In the examples on the left, the speakers do not express their expectations, views, or involvement in the relationship. The listeners hear only the statements and are unaware of the perspective on the relationship. In sensitive situations, the lack of some statement about perspective is more likely to elicit hurt, anger, and defensive reactions. This shuts off communication and promotes confusion and misunderstanding in the relationship.

In contrast, the examples on the right clearly express a perspective on the relationship and a desire to interact with the other person. (For example, "I want you to know how I feel.") As a result, the other person is more likely to feel acknowledged and, at the same time, has a better idea of how the speakers see the relationship. This provides a clear context for the statement or interaction that follows. It promotes exploration of ideas and is likely to lead to clearer communication and better understanding. The chances for a mutually satisfying relationship are increased.

Remember: You first must decide honestly on your purpose in communicating. If you are giving an order or a command, say so. If you do not care to understand the the other people's viewpoints and do not care whether they understand yours, say that.

Practice

This section provides practice in making decisions about relationships and expressing them to another person.

I. Some relationships and situations are described below. In each case, ask yourself the questions that are listed and make a decision about the relationship.

Write a statement that will convey these decisions to the other person.

A. Situation: From time to time a husband complains that his wife does not pay attention to him — she is too involved with the church, her club, and the children. One night the wife is sewing Halloween costumes for the children. The husband comes home, says that he has had a bad day, and asks her to go out to dinner.

WIFE: I can't . . . I have to finish these . . .

HUSBAND: What's more important? Me or Halloween?

WIFE: You are, but I must get these done . . . we don't have to go out to eat to relax, do we?

HUSBAND: That's how much you know! I want to go out! I want you to pay some attention to me!

WIFE: The kids will be upset if these aren't finished. . . .

HUSBAND: Are you married to me or to the kids?

At this point, it would be helpful for the wife to stop and consider these questions.

1. Am I willing to be involved in this relationship?
2. Am I willing to work at maintaining and improving it?
3. Am I willing to try to see the world from my husband's perspective?
4. Am I willing to show by actions that I care and am involved?

Assume that the wife answered yes to the above questions. Write a statement that would reflect these decisions to her husband.

WIFE:

B. Situation: Two co-workers have been good friends, both on the job and off, for several years. Fred received a promotion and began to supervise some of John's work. One day Fred, particularly pressured by the new job, strongly criticized John for the way John handled a customer. An argument developed. Fred continued to criticize and put John down in front of secretaries and other workers. John was offended by this. After a week, he still felt angry and had not spoken to Fred. The following encounter takes place:

FRED: What's wrong with you, John? You're walking around with a chip on your shoulder!
JOHN: I'm still angry.
FRED: Oh, come on. There's nothing to be angry about. We're still friends . . . let's work this out once and for all.

John stops to consider these questions:

1. Am I willing to work out problems in this relationship?
2. Am I willing to work at maintaining this relationship?
3. Am I willing to try to see Fred's point of view?
4. Do I trust Fred?

John decides that he is angry and upset, that he does not trust Fred, and that, at the moment, he is not willing to see Fred's point of view or to work out the relationship. Perhaps, at a later time, he can change this but not now. Write a statement expressing John's decision.
JOHN:

II. Below are pairs of conversations. One conversation expresses a perspective on the relationship; the other does not. Place a check to the left of the one that expresses perspective or a decision about the relationship.

A. 1. ____WIFE: I want us to have a good time this weekend. I don't want to quarrel over small things. How can we work this out?
HUSBAND: I don't want to quarrel either.

2. ____WIFE: Now let's sit down and get this settled once and for all!
HUSBAND: Forget it! You never let anything get settled once and for all!

B. 1. ____FRIEND: Look, I can't handle your marriage problems. You need to see a psychologist or a marriage counselor!

2. ____FRIEND: Look, you are my closest friend and I care very much about you. But I just don't know how to handle your marriage problems. I think it would be best for you to see a psychologist or a marriage counselor. And you know you have my support all the way.

Skill 1c: Checking with Others about Their View of the Relationship

As stated before, we only have an idea of what other people intend and what they are trying to say or do. For this reason, within a relationship, it is sometimes helpful to check with the other person about his or her willingness to listen, to understand, or to work out a problem. This can be accomplished by expressing your view of the relationship and asking the other person about his or her view. Simple statements and questions usually work best. For example, "This relationship is important to me and I want to settle this. How willing are you to work on this?" "I think that we may see things differently. Are you willing to hear my point of view?" "This is important to me. Are you willing to listen?"

Nonverbal cues, of course, are always important. Asking someone their views with a pleasant, interested expression and tone of voice is far different and more effective than accompanying your question with negative nonverbal cues.

By using this "check-out" skill, you give others the opportunity to make a more honest decision about the relationship, to clarify their motives or purpose, and to express these decisions to you. As with the previous skill, this is to be used in established, ongoing relationships when the persons involved are exploring sensitive topics, expressing complaints or limits, or working out problems.

Instead of doing this, however, people often assume that the other person's view of the relationship is the same as their own view. Without checking, they assume to know the other person's willingness to listen and to understand. When you do not check these issues with the other person in a relationship, there is little exchange of information about how important the relationship is to each of you, how involved you are, and what you expect from each other.

This skill of checking with others about their views of relationships works for the following reasons:

1. It gives other people the opportunity to make a decision about how they see the relationship, how willing they are to be involved, and what their limits are. This skill does not guarantee that others will be honest with you, but it does increase the likelihood of this occurring.
2. It increases the awareness of relationship decisions and also increases the chances for an exchange of views about the relationship. The more information in this exchange, the better understanding each person will have of the other's expectations and views of the relationship. Again, this skill does not guarantee that the other persons will respond and discuss the issue of the relationship, but it increases the chances of this occurring. (If it does not happen, your options are (1) to tell the other person how important the issue is to you and ask to set aside some time to work on it and (2) if he or she still refuses, to make a choice about the relative importance of the issue and the relationship. This special case is discussed further in the last section of this chapter.)
3. When each person has some understanding of the other's expectations and views, there is less chance for eventual disappointment and betrayal. The possibility of a mutually satisfying relationship is increased.

The examples below help illustrate the difference between not checking on the other person's view of the relationship and doing so:

Does Not Check Other's View of Relationship or Willingness to Listen

STAN: I'm really having a tough time at work.
BILL: What's wrong?
STAN: It's really been tough with a new boss.
BILL: (*cutting him short*) Well, that's how it goes . . . you have to learn how to roll with the punches. How about playing tennis this weekend?
STAN: Well, I guess so . . . see you.

Checks Other's View of Relationship and Willingness to Listen

STAN: I've been having a tough time at work and I'd really like to talk about it with you. Would you be willing to take the time?
BILL: Sure. Except tonight my daughter's in a play and I have to be home early for dinner. But I want to hear about it. Can you meet me for lunch tomorrow?

Discussion: In the example on the left, Bill, in a rush to see his daughter's play, cuts Stan short, perhaps without realizing it. Distracted and not asked about the relationship, or his willingness to listen, he becomes superficial and does not acknowledge his friend's desire to talk. Stan leaves feeling dissatisfied and somewhat hurt. In contrast, in the example on the right, asking Bill if he is willing to listen elicits the response that he wants to hear about Stan's problems but at another time. Bill expresses his interest in his friend while also stating his limits.

Does Not Check Other's View of Relationship or Willingness to Listen	*Checks Other's View of Relationship and Willingness to Listen*
HUSBAND: Look, I've had it. Let's cut out this arguing.	HUSBAND: Look, I want us to get along and I don't want to fight. Do you want to fight, or are you willing to stop arguing over this and come to some compromise?
WIFE: Cut it out? You're the one who started it. First you start something and then you tell me to stop it! (*walks off, slams door*)	WIFE: Well . . . I don't want to argue over this, either. But I don't see a way to compromise. What do you suggest?

Discussion: In the example on the left the statement, "Let's cut out the arguing," sounds like a command. The wife is not asked how she feels about the relationship and the situation at hand. As a result, she reacts defensively and the interaction ends unpleasantly. In contrast, in the example on the right, the husband states his view of the relationship and checks with the wife about her intention. As a result, she gives a more honest view of the situation and the relationship.

Does Not Check Other's View of Relationship or Willingness to Listen	*Checks Other's View of Relationship and Willingness to Listen*
JANE: I realize that in five years of being friends, this is the first big disagreement we've had. But I didn't mean what I said. So forget it, OK?	JANE: I realize that in five years of being friends, this is the first big disagreement we've had. Our friendship means a lot to me and I want to straighten this out. But what about you? Are your feelings hurt? Or do you think we can repair the damage and upset and try to be friends again?
ELLEN: You can't just make it go away like that, Jane. No, I can't just forget it. Why didn't you think of that before you started the argument?	

JANE: What about you? You said some pretty hurtful things back, too.
ELLEN: Maybe I did — but only because I was hurt.
JANE: Well, forget it. I don't have time to worry about overly sensitive people.

ELLEN: My feelings are pretty hurt. I can't really say right now if the damage can be repaired or not. I wish it could . . . because our friendship was very important to me, too. It will just take time.

Discussion: In the example on the left, Jane doesn't ask for or acknowledge Ellen's view of the relationship. As a result, there is a sequence of blaming and counterblaming statements, and the end result is unclear and unpleasant for both. In contrast, in the example on the right, Ellen is encouraged to consider her feelings and to present her view of the relationship.

Does Not Check Other's View of Relationship or Willingness to Listen

Checks Other's View of Relationship and Willingness to Listen

WIFE: I'm disgusted and fed up with this whole situation! I've had it! I'm changing the way I live around here! I'm not cooking anymore!
HUSBAND: As usual, you never think of me. Go right ahead. Don't cook! Then I'll stop living here!

WIFE: I'm disgusted and fed up with this whole situation! I've had it! I'm changing the way I live around here! I'm not cooking anymore!
HUSBAND: I live here and I also have some reactions and ideas. Are you willing to listen to them or do you already have your mind made up about what you want to do?
WIFE: No, I don't want to hear anything right now. It has nothing to do with you — I just don't want to cook.

HUSBAND: I'm too angry to talk.
WIFE: Well, I'm upset! I'm going to finish telling you what I think!
HUSBAND: No, you're not. (*walks away*)

HUSBAND: I'm too angry to talk.
WIFE: Do you want to hear my view of the situation?
HUSBAND: No, right now I just want to be angry. I'll discuss it when I'm not angry and upset.

Discussion: In both examples on the left, the spouses do not check with each other about the relationship. In the first example, the husband assumes that the wife does not want to hear this point of view ("You never think of me."). But then, in order to defend himself, he threatens her ("Then I'll stop living here!"). In the second example, the wife assumes that her husband will listen to what she is trying to say and he responds by walking away. Both situations are unpleasant. It is important to note that frequent quarrels and unpleasant situations like this create uncomfortable, frustrating relationships.

In contrast, in the examples on the right, the spouses check out the other's view of the relationship and willingness to listen. In the first example, this gives the wife the opportunity to tell her husband that her decision to stop cooking has nothing to do with him. Similarly, in the second example, the husband clarifies that he wants to remain angry, for the moment. In both examples, checking with the other person elicits some decision making and a statement about the relationship. This increases the spouses' knowledge of each other's expectations and increases the chances for effective communication and mutual satisfaction.

In general, in the examples on the left, both people are annoyed, uncomfortable, and less likely to listen. Instead of exploring each other's ideas and views of the relationship, they assume to know the other's expectations and intentions. Misunderstanding and disappointment are increased.

In contrast, in the examples on the right, the speakers encourage the other people to consider and express their feelings about the relationship. In this way, the listeners are given the opportunity to determine their willingness to be involved, to listen, to understand and to compromise. As a result, each person has a better idea of "where the other is coming from" at this moment in the relationship. The chances for understanding and mutual satisfaction are increased.

Practice

This section provides an opportunity to practice the skill of checking the others' decisions about relationships.

I. Below are pairs of statements. One statement checks the other person's decisions about the relationship; the other does not. Place a check to the left of the one that does.

A. 1. ____EMPLOYEE: I have some complaints and hard feelings about how raises are given around here. Do you want to hear them?

2. ____EMPLOYEE: I have some complaints and hard feelings about how raises are given around here. Everyone gets a raise, whether he or she works hard or not. I think that's bad business and it's bad for morale.

B. Situation: A husband and wife are having a mild disagreement about family finances.

1. ___WIFE: I don't suppose you care to hear my ideas about how to save money. You'll think they're silly.

2. ___WIFE: I have some ideas about how to save money. Do you want to listen?

C. 1. ___FRIEND: Look, ever since our disagreement, you haven't been the same. You've acted hurt and angry and won't speak. But I've had it. Whenever I try to smooth things over, you still act angry and offended. So, forget it. I'm just not going to bother!

2. ___FRIEND: Look, ever since our disagreement, you haven't been the same. You've acted hurt and angry and won't speak. I'd like to straighten this out because I want our friendship to remain as it was. Do you want to settle this?

D. 1. ___WIFE: You don't usually tell me about what you do at work, what upsets you, what you enjoy or don't enjoy. I'd like it if you did. Do you trust me enough to tell me about your feelings?

2. ___WIFE: You don't tell me what you do at work, what you like or don't like, what upsets you. Sometimes I think I'm married to a stranger. What's wrong with you, anyway?

II. In each of the examples below, write a statement that checks the other person's view of the relationship.

A. Situation: You and a co-worker get along most of the time. Recently the work load has increased and you have had a disagreement as to how to divide the work. Either you will have to work it out between you or take it to the boss. You prefer to work it out without involving the boss.

Write a statement expressing your preference and asking him if he is willing to work things out.
YOU:

B. Situation: You and your spouse have different priorities when it comes to money. You like to save money; your spouse does not. At the moment, your spouse wants to spend a lot of money for new furniture and an expensive stereo outfit. You object and a quarrel has resulted. You don't want to fight over this, but you do want to resolve some of these problems concerning finances.

Write a statement that expresses your views and checks your spouse's willingness to work on this problem.
YOU:

SKILL 2: IMPACT

In a relationship, words and actions do not exist in a vacuum. What you say or do affects the other person. The effect or impact that you have can be positive, negative, or neutral; it can be encouraging, hurtful, supportive, or destructive. The other person reacts to your words, actions, and impact, and that reaction, in turn, has an effect upon you and upon what you say and do. Many times, people do not have the impact that they intend. For example, you intend to be complimentary or pleasant, but the other person reacts as if criticized. Surprised by this unexpected response, a common reaction would be to behave defensively and, in this way, compound the misunderstanding. Failing to judge impact accounts for many arguments and misunderstandings between people. For this reason, it is important to become aware of your impact on others and their impact on you. (You can do this by building upon and refining the skill of considering consequences, which you learned in the first chapter.)

This section will help you to become familiar with the concept of "impact." It presents the following skills.
1. Checking your impact.
2. Recognizing and acknowledging the impact that you have on the other person; when the impact you have is not what you intended—restating your intention.
3. Anticipating your impact.
4. Telling another person of his or her impact on you.

Note: The order of these skills is based on ease of learning and does not represent the sequence in which you would use them.

Skill 2a: Checking Out Your Impact

Checking your impact involves asking other people to tell you how you came across and what their thoughts, reactions, opinions, and impressions were. For example, "When I said I didn't want to visit your parents, what did you think? Were you upset?" "Did I sound critical when I said that?" "I've been making a special effort to be considerate. Do you notice a change?" "You're so quiet. Did I say something to hurt your feelings?"

People often fail to do this. Instead, they assume that they were understood and that their words and actions had the effect that they intended. As a result, they do not know the impact that they had nor are they aware of the other person's reactions. The chances for mutual understanding between the two people are dramatically decreased.

This skill of checking your impact and asking others for their reactions works for the following reasons.

1. It acknowledges and takes responsibility for your words and actions and the effect that you had.
2. It encourages others to express their reactions to what you said or did. This also gives you information about your impact and thus increases your self-awareness.

The following examples help to point out the difference between not checking your impact and doing so.

Does Not Check Impact

HUSBAND: I can't even enjoy this dinner! Nothing tastes good.
WIFE: Thanks a lot! Remind me to say nice things like that to you!
HUSBAND: What's with you? You're being awfully sensitive.

Checks Impact

HUSBAND: I can't even enjoy this dinner! Nothing tastes good.
WIFE: Thanks a lot! Remind me to say nice things like that to you!
HUSBAND: Wait a minute. Did I say something that sounded critical?
WIFE: Not critical—nasty.
HUSBAND: Did it sound like I was blaming you because I wasn't enjoying dinner?
WIFE: Yes.
HUSBAND: That's not what I meant to say. I was just complaining about this cold I have. It has nothing to do with your cooking.

FRAN: I hope you don't think I'm being narrowminded when I tell you not to date Greg. I'm just a good friend of yours and I don't want you mixed up with him.

FRAN: When I told you not to date Greg, did I sound more like a mother than a friend?
JUDY: No . . . not really.

	FRAN: Well, I came on pretty strong. How did you feel when I gave you that lecture about Greg last night? JUDY: Very angry. In fact, it made me even more determined to continue dating him. You just think that I don't have good judgment on my own. FRAN: That's not so. You have a good head, but I just don't want you hurt.
HUSBAND: My friends from Texas will be in town next weekend, so I'll ask them to stay with us. That will be fun. WIFE: It will not be fun and they are not staying here. I have to make up a test for my class, and I need time to work. HUSBAND: You're being awfully stubborn. The least you could do is be nice to my friends! WIFE: I am not here to play hostess! I am also a teacher, and I have things to do! You like my salary just fine, but you don't want to acknowledge that I have a job. Find yourself another hostess! Take your friends to your sister's. She has nothing to do but clean house, cook meals, and get fat!	HUSBAND: My friends from Texas will be in town next weekend, and I'd like them to stay with us. What do you think about that? WIFE: I don't want any guests next weekend. I have to make up a test for my class, and it will take time. I don't want the added work of houseguests. Can you understand that? HUSBAND: Yes. I'd prefer they stay here, though. What if I did all the work? Does that seem reasonable? WIFE: It may be reasonable, but I just would rather not have guests to worry about.

In the examples on the left, the speakers do not ask about their impact nor do they encourage their listeners to express reactions. As a result, confusion and misunderstandings multiply. Whenever people are not asked for their reactions, the chances for defensiveness, resistance, withdrawal, and resentment are increased. This is one of the surest ways to shut off communication and to promote dissatisfaction and upset.

In contrast, in the examples on the right, the listeners feel acknowledged and encouraged to express their reactions, ideas, and feelings.

When this occurs, communication is kept open. Exploration of one another's ideas is increased and an atmosphere of understanding prevails. The chances for clear communication and some degree of mutual satisfaction are increased.

Practice

This section provides practice in checking out your impact.

I. Below are pairs of conversations. One of the conversations notices and checks out impacts; the other does not. Place a check to the left of the statement that checks out impact. Underline the portion of the statement that checks out impact. The first one is done for you.

A. 1. ____Boss: Why haven't you come up with any new ideas lately? You're usually on to several things.
EMPLOYEE: I don't know.
Boss: Well, get with it . . . where's all your usual enthusiasm?

2. ✓____Boss: Why haven't you come up with any new ideas lately? You're usually on to several things.
EMPLOYEE: I don't know.
Boss: (*notices employee is quiet*) <u>Say, did that sound critical</u>?
EMPLOYEE: Yes.
Boss: Well, I didn't mean that. I just wanted to encourage you and let you know that I appreciate your enthusiasm.

B. 1. ____SUSAN: That was really a good presentation you gave at the board of directors meeting. I was impressed.
DON: Oh, come on . . .
SUSAN: What do you mean? Did that seem insincere?
DON: Well . . . a little. I guess I don't see you as one who is easily impressed.
SUSAN: I thought you did a good job.

2. ____SUSAN: That was really a good presentation you gave at the board of directors meeting. I was impressed.
DON: Oh, come on . . .
SUSAN: (*teasingly*) What's the matter? Can't you take a compliment?
DON: I guess not. (*walks off; feels she is phony and insincere*)

C. 1. ____HUSBAND: I think it would be worthwhile to build a two-car garage. It will help with the resale value of the house.
WIFE: Well . . .
HUSBAND: I'm not trying to force it on you.

2. ____HUSBAND: I think it would be worthwhile to build a two-car garage. It will help with the resale value of the house.
WIFE: Well . . .
HUSBAND: I'm not trying to force it on you. Does it make sense, or does it seem I'm being extravagant?

WIFE: Yes, you are. You're always coming up with more ways to spend more money.

WIFE: You're not being extravagant. But I'd like to be a bit more cautious and think about this for a few days before we decide.

II. Situations are described below. In each case, write a statement that checks out your impact.

A. Situation: You and a friend have had a disagreement. As far as you are concerned, the quarrel is over and there are no hard feelings. Your friend, however, still seems distant and careful around you. You remember that, in a moment of anger, you had said, "You're certainly no friend of mine" and several other harsh statements. You wonder if your friend is still reacting to these statements.

Write a statement to ask your friend how you came across. Perhaps you might ask what you could do to show that you want to rebuild the friendship.
YOU:

B. Situation: Your spouse sometimes surprises you by doing some of your chores. You thank him or her but wonder if your appreciation really shows.

Write a statement to find out if your spouse understands how thoughtful this seems to you and how appreciative you are.
YOU:

Skill 2b: Recognizing, Acknowledging, and Being Responsible for Your Impact

In the previous section, you learned how to check with others about your impact. This skill builds upon that principle and also includes accepting the other person's reaction and clarifying your intentions.

Follow these steps.

1. Use the previous skill of asking others about their reactions and how you came across. For example, "Did I seem angry?" "How

do you feel about what I just said?" "You're frowning. Was what I said unclear?"

2. When the other person tells you the effect that you had, accept it as valid, even if it is not what you intended. For example, if a friend says that he or she feels offended, you might say, "I can see how you might think I was being critical of you" instead of "How ridiculous of you to feel offended because of what I said. I didn't say anything critical at all; you must be oversensitive."

Caution: Use step 2 only with people whom you trust. Some people might use your statement as a way to disown responsibility for their feelings. (For example, "It's all your fault! You're the one who never realizes how you come across!") With these people, omit step 2. Accept their reactions silently and proceed to step 3.

3. If the other person's reaction was not what you intended, explain that. Then, restate your intentions and explain the effect that you wanted to have. For example, "I didn't intend to hurt your feelings or sound critical. I meant what I said as a suggestion."

Use this skill whenever you are confused or surprised by the reactions of someone. Let this be a cue that you probably had an impact you did not intend. Instead of this, people usually do one of two things.

1. They fail to ask about their impact unless the other person spontaneously volunteers it; they assume that they had the impact that they wanted to have.
2. They do not accept that reaction that the other person expresses. They criticize or blame the listener for having such a reaction. ("How silly for you to get angry. There was absolutely nothing to get angry about.")

When you do not check your impact and assume that you had the effect you intended, you add confusion and misunderstanding to the relationship. For example, you might assume that a friend took your statement as a suggestion, when, in fact, he or she felt hurt and angry. You think that your suggestion was well-received, but your friend, meanwhile, is hurt, angry, upset, and is hiding that behind a facade of cool politeness.

The consequences of not accepting the other person's reaction are detrimental to relationships. When you do this, the other person feels that his or her experiences have been denied or contradicted and this usually leads to feelings of frustration and resentment. If you deny the experience of another and then try to correct the impact that you had, he or she will be too distracted by your original denial to hear what you have to say. This increases the chances for unpleasantness and misunderstanding and can contribute to an atmosphere of distrust and dissatisfaction in the relationship.

On the other hand, recognizing and acknowledging your impact works for the following reasons.

1. It tells others that their reactions are acceptable and valid. This decreases the chances for defensiveness and misunderstanding.
2. It keeps communication open and is more likely to lead to exploration of ideas. If your impact was not what you intended, you will have a better chance of clarifying the situation. In general, the chances for some degree of resolution and mutual understanding are increased.

The examples below demonstrate the difference between not recognizing and acknowledging your impact and doing so.

Not Recognizing and Acknowledging Your Impact

HUSBAND: Why can't you ever keep this house organized? Your sewing room is a mess, the family room is a disaster, and this kitchen is awful! When are you going to start being neater? What's the matter with you?
WIFE: Stop picking on me and lecturing me! You just don't appreciate how hard it is to keep things clean with three kids!
HUSBAND: Stop blaming it on the kids. You're the one who's the slob!
WIFE: (*starts crying*) Thanks a lot!
HUSBAND: Stop being a crybaby and get to work cleaning this place. Our guests will be here by five.
WIFE: I'm too upset now to do any-

Recognizing and Acknowledging Your Impact

HUSBAND: Why can't you ever keep this house organized? Your sewing room is a mess, the family room is a disaster, and this kitchen is awful! When are you going to start being neater? What's the matter with you?
WIFE: Stop picking on me and lecturing me! You just don't appreciate how hard it is to keep things clean with three kids!
HUSBAND: I guess I could've sounded unappreciative. I didn't mean to . . . I just . . .
WIFE: You sounded more than unappreciative! You sounded pretty nasty and critical and I'm upset and hurt.

thing! You clean it up yourself . . .
HUSBAND: How silly for you to be upset! All I did was try to point out what you were doing wrong so that you'll try to improve a little. If you had any sense, you'd appreciate these helpful comments I make. Besides, you'd better get going. I'm sure you don't want the Smiths to see the house looking like this.

BOB: (*trying to be helpful*) Look, it's just not good for you to be moping around like this. I know a divorce isn't easy, but you're carrying on too much. Every time I see you, you moan and complain for two or three hours and you never smile. You sit around and do nothing. You're feeling sorry for yourself.

MARK: (*feels hurt and criticized and more depressed; says nothing; leaves soon afterward, feeling rejected*)

HUSBAND: I'm sorry. I didn't want to upset you. What I wanted to do was encourage you to get organized and get going. I know how hard it is with the kids. Will it help if I take the kids out so that you have some peace and quiet?
WIFE: Yes.

BOB: (*trying to be helpful*) Look, it's just not good for you to be moping around like this. I know a divorce isn't easy, but you're carrying on too much. Every time I see you, you moan and complain for two or three hours and you never smile. You sit around and do nothing. You're feeling sorry for yourself. (*notices that Mark has grown more quiet and is staring down at the floor*) You haven't said a word. Did I say something to offend you?
MARK: I feel hurt—like you're criticizing me for being down in the dumps. So now, I'm even losing my friends.
BOB: You're not losing me. I can understand how you might think I was being critical. I didn't want to hurt your feelings. I want to help. Is there something I can do?

BOSS: You're doing an excellent job, Tom.
EMPLOYEE: Now look. Two days ago, in a moment of anger, you said that you had never meant any of the positive things that you had said about my work. You said that they were all lies—to keep my morale up and my production high. So, I'm not falling for any more of your phony compliments.

BOSS: You're doing an excellent job, Tom.
EMPLOYEE: Now look. Two days ago, in a moment of anger, you said that you had never meant any of the positive things that you had said about my work. You said that they were all lies—to keep my morale up and my production high. So, I'm not falling for any more of your phony compliments.

BOSS: Now, Tom . . . don't be so sensitive. I was just in a bad mood the other day—I didn't mean what I said. Come on, you know me better than that . . .
EMPLOYEE: Yes, I know enough to realize that you don't mean 90 percent of the things you say. I'll never believe one more of your compliments. Just tell me what you want done and nothing else. I won't listen to any more of your phony encouraging statements.
BOSS: You're being silly. You're making a big deal out of nothing.

BOSS: I realized later that I should not have said that. I was just very angry and that was my way of getting rid of it.
EMPLOYEE: I still don't know if I believe you.
BOSS: OK, I accept that. I'll see if I can rebuild your trust in me.

In the examples on the left, the husband, the boss, and Bob do not recognize their impact. The other person's reactions are ignored or denied. When this happens, the wife, the employee, and Mark feel frustrated, annoyed, and misunderstood. Since it is particularly frustrating to have one's reaction contradicted or denied, people usually respond by withdrawing from the situation and relationship or by attacking the other person. Both responses increase confusion and misunderstanding and contribute to dissatisfaction in the relationship.

In contrast, in the examples on the right, impact is recognized and acknowledged. The wife, the employee, and Mark feel acknowledged and validated; their feelings and reactions are accepted and understood. As a result, there is a better chance of clarifying intentions and the likelihood of achieving some degree of understanding is increased.

Practice

This section provides an opportunity to practice the skill of recognizing, acknowledging and being responsible for your impact.

I. Below are pairs of conversations. One conversation in the pair acknowledges impact; the other does not. Place a check to the left of the one that acknowledges impact.

A. 1. ___WIFE: You're late.
HUSBAND: Yes, I'm sorry. Have you been keeping dinner warm?
WIFE: I just finished it ten minutes ago, so it's not too bad . . . just inconvenient.

2. ___WIFE: You're late.
HUSBAND: Oh, don't start that . . . I don't need any nagging.
WIFE: I'm not nagging, just telling the truth.

HUSBAND: I know. I'm sorry. I didn't mean to inconvenience you.

B. 1. ___FRIEND A: I felt slighted when you didn't invite me to your party.
FRIEND B: That's silly. That was a party to pay back all our dinner obligations.
FRIEND A: I still felt left out. It would've been different if you had explained it to me . . .
FRIEND B: Oh, come on. You're not that thin-skinned, are you? I can't remember to tell you everything!

HUSBAND: Just be quiet and let's eat.
WIFE: (*is silent but remains annoyed throughout dinner*)

2. ___FRIEND A: I felt slighted when you didn't invite me to your party.
FRIEND B: I guess I can understand that. I didn't mean for you to be slighted. That was a party to pay back all our dinner obligations.
FRIEND A: I still felt left out. It would've been different if you had explained it to me . . .
FRIEND B: I didn't intend for you to feel left out.

Skill 2c: Anticipating Your Impact

The impact you have on another person can be very strong. When the other person has an intense reaction that you did not intend (e.g., he or she feels betrayed, becomes upset, resistant, hurt, or angry), you cannot expect to resolve the misunderstanding quickly. People need time to recover from their reactions. Only then can they listen to your explanations of what you meant to say or do. Of course, there is no guarantee that he or she will accept your second explanation. Because of the misunderstanding that this promotes, it is helpful to learn to anticipate the effect or impact you may have.

In relationships, there are some areas in which, based on previous experiences, you can predict the other person's reactions. You are familiar with some of the other person's sensitive areas. For example, you know that a certain friend becomes upset and defensive if you talk about religion. Or, with your spouse, it may be acceptable to complain about his sister but criticizing his mother starts an argument. On other issues, you may not know the other person's limits. If you have not discussed finances with your fiance, this is an unexplored area between the two of you and you do not know how he or she will react to what you say or do.

This skill is to be used in a relationship whenever your words may have a strong impact — namely, when you are discussing an unexplored area or issue, when you are discussing a topic that is important to you or to the other person, or when you are discussing an issue about which either of you are sensitive. By using this skill at these times, you may be able to avoid having an impact that you do not want.

This skill of anticipating your impact involves looking ahead to the consequences of what you say or do.

1. Judge how the other person may react. Ask yourself.
   a. What do I want to say or do?
   b. What effect would this action or statement have on someone? (Would he or she be likely to feel good, flattered, rebuked, hurt, upset, angry, etc.?)
   c. In terms of what I know about this particular person, how will he or she react? (Is he or she self-critical, easily hurt, thick-skinned, tolerant, easygoing, etc.?)
   d. In the past, when I have done something similar, how has he or she reacted (pouted, laughed, thought it was nothing, didn't speak for two days, etc.)?

2. Decide what the other person's reactions may mean to the relationship on a short-term and long-term basis. For example, in a moment of anger, you tell your friend that you can't stand him or her and that you have lied all along and said nice things when you didn't really mean them. The other person is likely to feel betrayed and upset; trust in you and in the relationship is likely to be markedly diminished and may never recover. On the other hand, if you complain about your in-laws to your spouse, he or she is annoyed for a few moments but forgets it quickly.

   In terms of what you want to say or do, ask yourself:
   a. What short-term effects will this have?
   b. What long-term effects will this have?

3. Decide if you want these short-term and long-term effects. Ask yourself:
   a. Is this situation or issue so important that I want to risk the relationship?
   b. What is most important: the issue, the situation, my feelings, the relationship?
   c. Am I willing to risk the short- and long-term effects of this?

4. If you decide that you do not want to risk the short- or long-term consequences, reconsider your intentions. Change them if necessary.

Here is an example of how you might use this skill: Your wife is sensitive about her appearance. She returns from the hair stylist with a new haircut. It is short, and you prefer it long. She asks if you like it. You do not, but you are hesitant to tell her that. You do not want her to think that you find her unattractive, and you do not want her to feel hurt or criticized.

Using this skill, follow these steps.

1. What I want to say or do: I'd like to avoid the whole issue and tell her that the haircut is fine and that I like it.
   Probable reaction: Her reaction will be good. She will be happy.
2. Short-term effect: She will be happy.
   Long-term effect: She may get her hair cut short and may think that I like it when I do not. If, someday, I tell her that I do not like her hair that way, she will feel hurt and will wonder why I have lied to her all along.
3. Do I want these short-term and long-term effects? I do not want to take this long-term risk. I would rather tell her the truth.
4. If not, what effects do you want? I want her to know that I prefer long hair. This is important to me, but, on the other hand, I do not want her to feel hurt. I want her to know that I find her attractive, no matter how she wears her hair.

   After thinking this through, you decide to say, "You look attractive either way, but I prefer your hair long."

Using this skill of anticipating impact takes time and thought. If you are upset, it is probably best to delay speaking or acting until you have a chance to think through these steps. In fact, strong emotion can be a cue to you to stop the interaction and take time to use this skill.

Frequently, people do not anticipate their impact. They say or do the first thing that comes to mind, even when they are angry or upset. They do not stop to consider the effect that they may have upon the other person and upon the relationship. For example, a wife knows that her husband is sensitive about his salary. Without considering the consequences, she says, "When are you going to start earning more money? We can't get along on what you make!" He becomes upset and his feelings of comfort, trust, and acceptance in the relationship are diminished. He is bothered enough so that he will not hear or accept his wife's attempts to smooth things over and restate her intentions.

The situation may pass, but it could be come a "sore spot" in the relationship.

In contrast, the skill of anticipating your impact has the following advantages.

1. It takes the other person into account. By considering sensitive areas and possible reactions, you show more concern about the relationship.
2. It increases your self-awareness and diminishes the likelihood of having an impact contrary to your intentions, or detrimental to the relationship. This lessens the chances for misunderstanding and confusion and makes it more likely that you will achieve your purpose.

The following examples demonstrate the difference between not anticipating your impact and doing so.

Situation: Husband usually becomes upset whenever his wife criticizes his family.

Not Anticipating Impact

HUSBAND: My parents would like us to be there for dinner on Mother's Day.
WIFE: I refuse to go. Today at your parents it was awful as usual. Your mother talked the entire time, stuffed us all with food, and went through all the gossip of the last three months. I can't stand her — every time I'm there I get a splitting headache and I'm bored to tears.
HUBAND: If you knew how to make conversation, maybe you wouldn't be bored.
WIFE: I know how to make conversation just fine. But I don't have a chance with your family. They're so involved with local gossip and senseless chatter — I've never heard people who could babble so much and say so little.

Anticipating Impact

HUSBAND: My parents would like us to be there for dinner on Mother's Day.
WIFE: I don't want to go. I wouldn't mind if we went for dinner and left immediately, but we usually stay there the entire afternoon, and I don't enjoy myself there. Would you be willing to go alone?
HUSBAND: I'd rather you came. You could come for dinner and then have some excuse to leave. I'll stay for a few hours more.
WIFE: OK, I'll try that.

HUSBAND: They can't hold a candle to you! That's what you've been doing for the last ten minutes!
WIFE: That's not so!

Discussion: In the example on the left, the wife voices her complaints about her husband's family. He becomes upset and defensive and criticizes her. She, in turn, becomes more upset and reacts even more strongly. The situation ends in a quarrel. In contrast, on the right, the wife anticipates the impact that her criticism would have and decides to state her preference in descriptive, nonevaluative terms ("I don't enjoy myself there"). The situation ends on an agreeable note with both spouses working toward a solution.

Situation: A husband is quite reserved and hesitant to show affection. He and his wife have discussed this repeatedly, and he has resolved to try acting more demonstrative. On several occasions, he has been more affectionate.

Not Anticipating Impact
WIFE: I'm glad you've started being more affectionate. It's about time!
HUSBAND: Thanks a lot . . . if that's all the response I get, why should I bother?

Anticipating Impact
WIFE: You've been very affectionate lately, and I appreciate it very much. You've really made an effort to change.
HUSBAND: I didn't realize that it was that noticeable. The fact that you noticed really makes me feel good.

Discussion: In the example on the left, the wife expresses her reactions but does not anticipate the impact that her negative comment will have on her husband. He feels unappreciated and, as a result, may decide to go back to being reserved and unaffectionate. In contrast, on the right, the wife realizes the impact that a negative statement may have and chooses, instead, to tell her husband what she has noticed in a positive way.

In general, when discussing sensitive issues, failure to anticipate your impact is likely to lead to misunderstanding, confusion, and conflicts. In contrast, anticipating your impact increases the chances of achieving your purpose. The likelihood of being sidetracked by an effect that you did not intend is diminished. By anticipating the impact that you may have, you are taking the other person and the relationship into account, and the chances for effective communication and mutual satisfaction are increased.

Practice

The following section gives you the opportunity to practice the skill of anticipating your impact.

I. This section provides practice in judging the reactions of the other person and deciding what effects these reactions may have on the relationship. Read the descriptions of the situations. Then answer the questions that follow.

A. Situation: You and your spouse do not have children. You want a family, but your spouse is unsure. Whenever you mention having children, you spouse gets upset, defensive, and seems to feel criticized or pressured into having a family.

   You feel the need for some discussion and resolution to this issue. You feel frustrated and want to say: "I want a child, and you still don't know if you do or not. Why can't we just take the risk and start a family, just like everyone else? Why do you have to be different?"

   1. With what you know about your spouse's reactions, how is he or she likely to react? Circle the likely reactions.
      a. Feel criticized.
      b. Feel calm.
      c. Feel flattered.
      d. Feel "bad" or "different" for not wanting children.
      e. Feel pressured to agree with you.
   2. How is he or she likely to behave?
      a. Sit down and calmly discuss this with you.
      b. Agree to have a child but with much resentment and anger.
      c. React defensively and attack you.
      d. Work on a resolution of the issue with you.
      e. Become upset or angry.
      f. Refuse to discuss it.
   3. What long-term consequences might this have?
      a. None.

b. There will be no resolution of the issue because your spouse is too upset to discuss it.
c. Spouse will be angry or upset.
d. This issue becomes a "sore spot" in the relationship.
e. There will be a resolution of the issue.
f. You have a child; your spouse resents being forced into this decision.

4. You decide that you do not want these short-term and long-term consequences. What you want most is a resolution of the issue so that the two of you can make plans. You do not want to force your spouse to agree with you.

What can you say that would bring about a calm discussion and some way to resolve the issue?
   a. "What's your hang-up about kids?"
   b. "Maybe you should go to a shrink and find out why you don't want a family."
   c. "Are you ever going to decide about having a family?"
   d. "I'd like to now where we stand in terms of starting a family. I'd like to know your thinking and to tell you mine, so that we can come to some decision or compromise."

B. Situation: A close friend has been having trouble with his children. Two of them have gotten into trouble at school, and he is very upset. In fact, he is so upset that he is not doing well at work.

For a long time you have wanted to tell him how he and his wife should handle their children, and now you really want to tell him to stop pampering them. In the past, you avoided the issue or said complimentary things about the children.

He has been a good friend to you, and you definitely want to maintain this relationship. You don't know what to do and are quite frustrated with the situation. You want things to go well for him but he continues to be upset. You feel like saying, "You'd better shape up. You're really making a mess of things—you have to stop pampering those kids. I've never told you any of this because I didn't want to make you mad or hurt your feelings. I've kept silent, but I can't stand to see you make a fool of yourself like this. If you don't do something soon, you'll all end up in a psychiatrist's office! And I don't want any part of it."

1. Based on your past experience with your friend and on what you

know of people's reactions in general, how will he probably feel? Circle the likely reactions.
   a. Attacked
   b. Evaluated or criticized
   c. Calm
   d. Defensive
   e. Less upset
   f. Lied to, betrayed
   g. Angry
   h. More upset
2. How is he likely to respond?
   a. To say, "I'm so glad that you spoke up."
   b. To say, "You don't understand."
   c. To say, "Thank you for what you said."
   d. To ask, "Why did you wait until now to say this?" and feel that you had lied to him.
   e. Laugh and think you're kidding.
   f. To say, "I'm not making a fool of myself!"
   g. To say, "I agree with everything you said, and take your advice.
   h. Understand that you really want to help him.
   i. Attack you — "You're the one who had better go to a shrink."
3. What long-term consequences might this have?
   a. Your friend will face the issue and be eternally grateful to you.
   b. He may feel criticized and angry but gets over it quickly and the relationship continues as before.
   c. The relationship will be seriously damaged; he no longer trusts you.
4. If your purposes are to be helpful to your friend, to point out the consequences of his present mood and actions, and to maintain the friendship, what might be a more effective statement to make? Circle the two best answers.
   a. "I know you're upset, but it will work out somehow."
   b. "You're my friend."
   c. "I do see that this is affecting you on the job and upsetting you in general, so I would like to see you resolve this."
   d. "I want to do something to help and I don't want you to be upset. Your friendship is very important to me and I don't

want to risk losing it by giving you advice that you don't want to hear.

II. After each situation below are some possible reactions. One anticipates impact; the other does not. Check the one that anticipates effects.

A. Situation: Your spouse is sentimental about special occasions such as birthdays, anniversaries, and so on. When you have forgotten one of these special days in the past, he or she is disappointed.

1. ____You are tired of choosing gifts and decide to stop catering to your spouse's desires for thoughtfulness and say, "I am tired of remembering special days. You're too sentimental."

2. ____You would like to stop feeling obligated to buy gifts on special occasions and tell your spouse, "I know that you like to remember special days and I like to please you. But I'd prefer to do it spontaneously and not feel obligated. What would you think of that?"

B. Situation: You have noticed that your boss reacts positively to arguments and confrontations. If you sound compromising and reasonable, she or he usually reacts as if you are weak. If you are angry and argumentative, she or he seems to think that you are bright and a "go-getter." An argument occurs between you and a co-worker. Your boss calls you in to find out what happened.

1. ____You speak reasonably and say, "I can understand Pete's point . . . it was just a mix-up."

2. ____You sound angry and say, "I try to be fair, but I will not tolerate Pete's behavior. I'd like you to do something to straighten him out."

C. Situation: The husband is on a diet. The wife has just baked a cherry pie and is encouraging him to have some. She says, "Just one slice won't hurt you."

1. ____HUSBAND: Yes, it will. I don't like it when you try to get me to go against my diet. I'd like some support from you to help me stick to the diet, not break it.

2. ____HUSBAND: You make me mad when you do that. Just because you're overweight doesn't mean that I have to stay overweight.

3. ____HUSBAND: Oh . . . OK. (*doesn't like the way she sabotages his diet but says nothing and feels frustrated; saves it to use against her in an argument*)

III. Below are listed conversations where people deny or contradict their impact. Cross out the statements that do deny or contradict and, in the right-hand column, write a statement that acknowledges impact or restates intention.

A. Situation: Married son and wife receive a kitchen table and chairs as a gift from his parents. They like it but are too busy to call and thank his parents for the gift until ten days later.

Rewrite:

1. MOTHER: You never called and never called, so we worried that they hadn't delivered it. Then, I started thinking that maybe you didn't like it. So I didn't know what to think . . . I was worried.
2. SON: How silly! There was nothing to worry about! We're just too busy to call.
3. MOTHER: I didn't know if we had offended you or Susan by choosing furniture . . . or if we didn't know your tastes or what.
4. SON: Don't be so sensitive! We can't be calling you all the time just because you're a worrywart!

B. Situation: Nancy and Jean had a disagreement with a co-worker, Tom. Jean thought that Tom was out of line in what he had said and done. She went to the boss to complain. When she returned to the office, she told Nancy what she had done. Nancy became upset.

Rewrite:

1. NANCY: You went to see the boss without me? How dare you do that!
2. JEAN: Why are you upset? I was sticking up for you, too.

3. NANCY: That's just it. This is my battle, too. In fact, Tom was worse to me than to you. And you just went over my head and stole my thunder. You made it into your battle and I'm really upset and angry with you.
4. JEAN: You are being stupid. Tom is the one who attacked you and I came to your defense. So all I did was go to the boss. If you're going to be that irrational, I'm not going to bother talking with you. You can pout all by yourself.

Skill 2d: Telling Others about Their Impact on You

In order for others to become aware of their impact on you, it is necessary for you to describe your reactions to what they have said or done. This skill involves the following steps.

1. Decide if your reaction is something that the other person should know about. If the relationship or the issue matters to you, it is probably important to let the other person know how you feel. If you remain silent, the other person cannot be expected to read your mind.
2. Express your reaction in a responsible fashion. For example, "I want . . . ," "I don't like it when . . . ," "I feel hurt/angry/sad when . . . ," or "I like it when . . . ," instead of, "You make me mad/sick/hurt/sad/happy, etc."
3. Use descriptive, nonevaluative terms. For example, "When you don't remember my birthday, I am disappointed" instead of "You must be awfully insensitive and inconsiderate to forget my birthday."
4. Follow the guidelines discussed earlier—namely, check the consequences of your statements and anticipate your impact. Remember that appropriateness is important, too. Choose the right time and place and be certain that your comment is appropriate

to the relationship. For example, it is more appropriate to tell your spouse privately why you are angry. It is not a good idea to express angry reactions in front of others.

This skill is to be used in close, ongoing relationships when you can trust the other person with your feelings. Use it when it is important for the other person to know how you feel or what you think. If the situation or issue matters to you, it is better to tell the other person your reactions — positive or negative — instead of keeping him or her uninformed. For example, if a wife enjoys hearing about her husband's day at work, she should tell him, "I like it when you tell me about your work. I feel that you value my opinion and want me to know what you are doing." Similarly, if a husband really dislikes pork chops, it would be wise to tell his wife. Otherwise, she will assume that he likes them and will continue to prepare them on a weekly basis. Meanwhile, as he eats them, his resentment builds, and one day, in the middle of an argument about something else, he shouts, "I've eaten those awful pork chops every week for ten years, and I've hated them all the time! That's how little you know about me!"

In relationships in which the other person cannot be trusted, use this skill to describe your limits. For example, you might say to a co-worker, "I do not like it when you tell me off in front of the secretaries. I will not tolerate that." Do not use this skill to disclose personal feelings of hurt, upset, or vulnerability to people whom you do not trust. For example, do not tell a competitive co-worker that you were hurt when he or she told you off, nor is it wise to tell some bosses that you felt upset or angry about something that they did. In these situations, your reactions may be seen as signs of weakness or as something that can be used against you. In general, follow the guidelines on appropriateness and check the possible consequences of your statements and actions. In each instance, decide if your words or actions are appropriate to the particular relationship. If the other person uses information to control, manipulate, or hurt you, use this skill to express your limits but do not disclose personal information.

Instead of expressing their reactions, people often assume that they do not need to explain their feelings. They think that the other person knows how they feel. This is a common occurrence, especially between spouses and friends. They fail to express positive feelings and then are surprised when the other person is unaware of them. When negative feelings are involved, they remain silent, assuming that the other person knows of their upset. "Saving" negative feelings only increases their intensity and builds up resentments.

People who do not express reactions eventually get to the point where they "blow up" and unload their bitter, hurt, and angry feelings. This shocks the person who is hearing these reactions for the first time. He or she probably will feel unjustly attacked, uninformed, and betrayed and will wonder why you did not speak sooner and may lose trust in you. In general, failing to express positive reactions and "saving up" negative ones contributes to misunderstandings and discomfort in relationships.

Another way that people handle their reactions is to tell the other person about his or her impact in evaluative, nonresponsible ways, usually by blaming or criticizing the other person. For example, "You were so obnoxious at the party that you made me ashamed to be with you" and "You change your mind so much that you are driving me crazy." As a result, the other person becomes defensive and is unable to listen and to understand.

Since people cannot guess what is going on in your head, it is important to tell them your thinking and reactions in ways that they can hear and understand. It is equally important to tell them your thinking and reactions soon after you are aware of them. If you delay a long time in expressing your reactions, the other person is usually surprised, cannot understand the intensity of your reaction, and may begin to doubt your credibility. If your reactions are described in critical, blaming ways, the other person will become defensive and will be less likely to listen and to understand.

This skill of telling the other person about your reactions responsibly and descriptively works for the following reasons.

1. It provides important information to the other person about your reactions and about his or her impact.
2. When your reactions are expressed responsibly and descriptively, it decreases the chances of eliciting defensiveness in the other person and increases the chances of being understood.
3. It provides important information in the relationship and increases your self-awareness as well as the other person's knowledge of you. It lets the other person know about your reactions, preferences, or limits. In this way, the chances for mutual understanding and a satisfying relationship are increased.

The examples below help to show the difference between telling others about their impact and failing to do so.

Not Expressing Your Reactions

WIFE: (*says nothing, pouts, does not speak*)
HUSBAND: What's wrong?
WIFE: If you can't guess, I won't tell you. I guess you just don't understand me.

SUPERVISOR: (*mentions nothing negative but writes a negative evaluation and lowers the employee's performance rating; negative feelings follow between supervisor and employee*)

FRANK: (*says nothing for several months, then one day goes to pick up Bill. Bill is late and Frank explodes*) That's it. You've gotten later and later these past several months, and I've had it! Find yourself another ride to work and, while you're at it, find yourself another friend.

HUSBAND: (*does not mention what he likes; wonders why his wife does not say the things he likes to hear; feels unappreciated; broods about it and holds it against his wife*)

Expressing Your Reactions

WIFE: I was disappointed when you didn't remember Valentine's Day. I would have liked it if you had bought me flowers or something.
HUSBAND: I never realized that Valentine's Day meant that much to you.

SUPERVISOR: I don't like it when you question my judgment in front of the others. The next time that you do that, I will put it in your evaluation and lower your performance rating.

FRANK: When I come to pick you up in the morning and you are late, I get angry and resentful.
BILL: I didn't realize that. I'll try to be on time.

HUSBAND: I like it when you notice all the odd jobs I've done around the house. Then I feel appreciated.

In the examples on the left, the wife, the supervisor, Frank, and the husband are playing a game that only hurts themselves, the other person, and the relationship. In all four cases, they expect the other person to read their minds, guess their reactions, and act accordingly. This creates confusion and misunderstanding and decreases the chances of resolving issues and achieving some degree of mutual satisfaction in the relationship.

In contrast, in the examples on the right, the speakers told the other person their thoughts and reactions. This contributes to greater knowledge about themselves and about the other person. This exchange of information increases the chances for clear communication and understanding in the relationship.

The examples below show the difference between expressing your reaction in an evaluative, irresponsible manner and doing so descriptively and responsibly.

Expressing Reactions in an Evaluative, Irresponsible Way

HUSBAND: You really make me angry when you criticize me in front of people. If you're going to be that rude and impolite, I'm going to be rude and impolite to you.
WIFE: I was not rude and impolite.
HUSBAND: Don't tell me that. If you don't think you're rude and impolite, you are even more stupid than I thought.
WIFE: You're the one who wins the prize for being stupid. (*walks away*)

SUSAN: You really upset me when you disagreed with me at the board meeting. If that's how disloyal and unreliable you are . . . you're really some friend.
LINDA: No, just a minute. You're not silly enough to think I have to agree with you all the time. I do have my own ideas. You're pretty immature about this.
SUSAN: All last week you agreed with me — then, at the meeting, you were entirely different. What a hypocrite you are! You disgust me. I hope that you'll never again be on the same board with me.
LINDA: (*angrily*) That's fine with me.

Expressing Reactions in a Descriptive, Responsible Way

HUSBAND: I don't like it when you criticize me in front of people. I get really angry at that.
WIFE: When did I criticize you?
HUSBAND: When you kept telling everyone that I have two left thumbs and can't fix a thing around the house.

SUSAN: When you supported John at the board meeting and disagreed with me, I felt very betrayed and very angry.
LINDA: Well, I agreed with John and not with you.
SUSAN: Last week, I thought that you agreed with me. At the meeting, you seemed to have changed your mind.
LINDA: I meant to tell you that I had coffee with John and we talked, and his idea made sense to me.
SUSAN: I don't like surprises like that. Next time, tell me when you've changed your mind.

In the examples on the left, the husband and Susan express their reactions by criticizing the other person. Both the wife and Linda become quite defensive and respond with accusations and blaming statements. This results in a series of attacks and counterattacks; confusion and misunderstanding are created, and the relationship is threatened.

In contrast, on the right, the husband and Susan express their reactions in a way that is easier for the other person to hear and understand. Information is exchanged and the chances for understanding and mutual satisfaction in the relationship are increased.

Practice

This section provides the opportunity to practice the skill of expressing reactions descriptively and responsibly.

I. Three situations are described below. After each description are possible responses. One of the responses describes impact and reactions; the other does not or else does so in evaluative, blaming terms. Place a check to the left of the one that expresses reactions descriptively and responsibly.

A. Situation: A husband says to his wife, "I invited the boss over for dinner tonight. I hope you don't mind this short notice."

1. ____WIFE: Oh no. (*feels resentful and annoyed but doesn't express it even after the guest is gone; saves these resentments up and then explodes*)

2. ____WIFE: (*after guest leaves*) That was really inconsiderate of you. You never have the decency to tell me about guests ahead of time.

3. ____WIFE: (*is polite but after the guest is gone says*) I didn't like what happened tonight. I feel unappreciated and imposed upon. From now on, if you want to have someone over for dinner, tell me ahead of time.

B. Situation: Ted, a friend of Ann's, says to Ann, "Someone asked me to describe you. I said that you were the skinny one in the office."

1. ____ANN: Oh, really?

2. ____ANN: Maybe you're trying to be funny, Ted, but I don't appreciate being called skinny. That really turns me off.

3. ____ANN: Well, that was a stupid thing to say. But what can I expect from you?

C. Situation: An employee tells his boss, "I'm pretty frustrated with these new rules you started."

1. ___Boss: Frustrated? That shows you're not flexible—you'd better change that.

2. ___Boss: I can accept your reaction, but that's not what I intended to have happen. I wanted these new rules to make things smoother. It would help if you could explain to me what exactly is frustrating.

II. The following examples do not express reactions or else they do so in a blaming, evaluative way. Write a descriptive, responsible statement in the third column.

Situation	Does Not Express Reaction or Does So Evaluatively	Expresses Reaction Descriptively
A. Your boss transfers you to a new division but does not tell you until just before the change.	You say nothing because you figure that there's no use telling him that you do not like the way he handled it.	
B. A friend makes critical remarks in a teasing fashion. You do not like this.	YOU: Only someone who is immature or insincere would tease like that.	
C. You are working on the budget. Your spouse offers to help, and you like this.	You say nothing because you figure that your spouse knows how you feel.	

SKILL 3: DECISIONS TO BE MADE WHEN CONFLICT OCCURS

Conflicts occur even in close and satisfying relationships. When this happens, there are further decisions to be made. This section outlines the following skills to help you resolve disagreements.

1. Deciding the importance of a particular situation or issue.
2. Finding common ground.

Skill 3a: Deciding the Importance of a Particular Situation or Issue

When conflict occurs in a relationship that you consider important, it may be helpful to ask yourself these questions.

1. How important is this issue or situation to me?
2. How important is this issue or situation to the other person?
3. Am I willing to give in on this? Or, do I feel so strongly about it that I refuse to give in?
4. Am I willing to work on ways to resolve this issue or to solve this problem? Or, do I want things to be *my way* or not at all?
5. Do I want to change the situation? Am I willing to work at that?
7. What if the other person is hurt, angry, upset, or annoyed by what I say or do? Am I willing to risk that in this case?
8. What if the relationship is threatened by what I say or do? Am I willing to risk that? What is most important to me at this moment — my feelings and reactions or my relationship with the other person?
9. If the relationship is most important to me, what action would be in the best interest of maintaining it? Am I willing to do that?
10. Am I willing to hear the other person's views? Or, am I not ready for that?
11. Am I willing to acknowledge his or her reactions? Or, do I think that mine are the only valid ones?
12. Is a compromise possible?
13. Will I work on and agree to a compromise?

If, for example, you do not care much about an issue (e.g., whether or not you go to the movies or out to dinner), you may decide to give in to the other person's preference. If the issue is relatively unimportant to both of you (e.g., you vote Republican and your spouse votes Democrat), you may agree to disagree and each maintains his or her own opinions.

The situation is different when there is disagreement on an issue that is important to one or both persons (e.g., the wife wants to return to work; the husband thinks that she should stay home). In a case like this, it may be a good idea to ask yourself the questions listed above. These questions will help you to clarify your thinking and determine the consequences of your actions. If you decide that the issue is important enough to risk the relationship or the other person's upset, anger, or resentment, then you assert your view with full knowledge of possible consequences in the relationship. If, on the other hand, you decide that the relationship (e.g., with spouse, family, or close friend) is more important than the particular issue, the two of you still must develop some resolution to the problem. Otherwise, by avoiding a problem or neglecting to solve a problem, one of the following is likely to occur.

1. The one person who raised the issue or most wants it settled (e.g., the wife who wants to return to work) may start frequent arguments. This may be elicited by frustration or resentment and may be an attempt to get the problem settled.
2. The person who raised the issue remains frustrated or upset and raises the issue repeatedly. The other person reacts by withdrawing from the relationship, becoming more steadfast in his or her view, telling the "nagger" to be quiet (which infuriates the "nagger"), or giving in but only with a great deal of bitterness and resentment. Any of these reactions are detrimental to the relationship.
3. The person who raised the issue threatens to take action even if the other disagrees (for example, "I'll just go back to work whether you like it or not!").
4. The person who raised the issue continues to be frustrated but is silent and, instead, builds up feelings of anger and resentment. The issue or problem thus becomes a sore spot in the relationship. It is brought up directly or indirectly during subsequent disagreements or quarrels (for example, "You never would agree to my going back to work"). The person who did not raise the issue (for example, the husband who wants the wife to stay home) may anticipate the issue as a threat and may think, "She may go back to work, anyway" or "I wonder when she'll bring this up again. We can't go for two weeks without her saying that she wants to go back to work!" This reaction leads to negative expectations and to a gradual undermining of trust in the relationship.

A resolution can be accomplished by a small step such as setting aside time to discuss the issue. For example:

HUSBAND: You forgot to turn off the stereo again! You are worse than a little kid! If you don't remember to turn it off, you can't use it!
WIFE: I don't like it when you talk down to me like that. I feel like a little kid!
HUSBAND: Well, you act like one.
WIFE: I do not. I get very upset when you criticize me.

HUSBAND: Be quiet, will you?
WIFE: No, I will not. This issue is important to me. You are frequently very critical of me and I don't like it.
HUSBAND: I'm going to watch TV.
WIFE: (*angrily*) I want to settle this!
HUSBAND: OK, OK . . . I can see it's important to you. I'm tired right now. But we'll talk first thing in the morning.

When a disagreement or problem arises and you want to maintain the relationship, it is necessary to find common ground where the two of you can agree. This skill is described in detail below.

Skill 3b: When Problems or Disagreements Arise: Finding Common Ground

Resolving an issue or problem by finding common ground involves these steps.

1. Summarize your view and the other person's view. Accept his or her point of view, even if you see things differently. For example, say, "This doesn't seem that important to me, but I can see that it's important to you. So we'll do something to work it out." Or, "Having someone home with the children is important to me, but it's not much of an issue for you."

    This acknowledges your differing opinions and lets others know that it is understandable and acceptable to have a different opinion than you do. Do not criticize others for their views; do not deny or contradict their experience by saying that there is no problem or that the issue is not important. For example, do not say, "How silly to get worked up about this! This is something very minor." "You keep talking about this problem. There *is* no problem, except you." "You say this is no big deal. But it is — you're just too stupid to see it."

2. Acknowledge that there is a problem to be discussed and resolved. Define the issue. For example, "OK, we disagree on this. I want to stay here and you want to move. I realize that this is important to you. So, this is an issue that we will have to work on."

3. Express the idea that the solution is not black or white — in other words, it does not have to be one way or the other.

4. Offer options and alternate solutions, negotiating with one another to arrive at a solution or method of solution that is agreeable to both of you. There is no set pattern for solving problems: you and the other person can come up with various solutions, depending upon each of you and upon the particular issue. Here are some options to consider.
    a. Set a time to work on the problem. For example, "This is a problem for us and I don't see a way to resolve it right now. We'll probably have to work on it for awhile. Let's set aside an hour Friday night to discuss it. Next week, we'll set aside time Tuesday and Friday, and we'll do that until we have a solution." Or, "I'm too angry to talk right now. Let's talk tomorrow when I get home from work."
    b. Set up a trial period. For example, "OK, you want to go back to teaching. I would like to see how it works out. How would you feel about teaching this school year? Then we'll see what happens: how you get along, how the kids get along, how I feel about helping with the chores. I'd like to be able to negotiate again next year."
    c. Go along with one person's view for a specified amount of time; then follow the other's view for an equal period. For example, "You want to eat with your parents on Sunday and I want to be with my parents. Let's alternate. One week at yours and the next at my parents. What do you think of that?"
    d. Each person comes part way and a compromise is achieved. For example, "I want to take dancing lessons and you don't. You want me to help you with projects around the house and I don't like to do that. How about this? If you come to dancing lessons once a week, I'll help you on a project once a week."
5. Check to be sure that the other person agrees with the proposed solution. For example, "Is this agreeable to you?"

Here is an example that demonstrates all five of these steps:

WIFE: You want a new car, and I want to save money for a new house. Both ideas are reasonable. Can we set up a priority system so that we each can be satisfied? For example, can we take our monthly savings and split them? We could put half toward a car and half toward a house. What do you think of that?

HUSBAND: We'll never get a car that way. What about two-thirds toward a car and one-third toward a house?
WIFE: Well, that would be OK for the rest of this year. But next year, the house gets priority.
HUSBAND: I agree. This year the car gets two-thirds of the savings, and next year the house gets two-thirds. Is that OK with you?
WIFE: Yes.

Frequently, people do not try to find common ground. Instead, they avoid problems, hoping that they will resolve themselves. Or, they try to settle the issue by making threats, criticizing others, or trying to persuade them that their own preference is better, smarter, and more just. It is common for one person to criticize the other or accuse him or her of "bad" motives. For example:

WIFE: You want a car, and I want a house. It's foolish to want a car. We don't need a new car — ours is only two years old!
HUSBAND: Well, that shows how much you don't know. A car depreciates in two years. Besides, we don't need a house. I'm content just where I am.
WIFE: You're content because you don't take pride in a nice home. You never think of how important a house is to me! You're just immature and selfish enough to want a car!

Criticism and name calling like this is not effective. The other person feels attacked and obliged to defend his or her position even more strongly. Backing down becomes increasingly difficult, and each person becomes more firmly entrenched in his or her own position. Unless one person is forced to concede, a stalemate may ensue, a series of quarrels may develop, or the issue may become a "sore spot" in the relationship. Even if one person concedes, he or she is likely to feel manipulated, beaten, or resentful. None of this leads to comfort and satisfaction in a relationship.

In contrast, by using this skill of finding common ground, the relationship is enhanced. This skill has the following advantages.

1. Each person feels that his or her preferences, desires, and views are acknowledged and accepted.
2. Problems are seen as manageable, and solutions are possible.
3. Several options may be offered and negotiated, and the opportunity for understanding between the two people is increased.

4. A sense of "we can work things out" is established. This increases the atmosphere of trust in each other and in the relationship.
5. The action of "finding common ground" demonstrates a commitment to the relationship and a willingness to work out solutions. It contributes to a feeling of involvement and caring in the relationship.

The following examples demonstrate the differences between not finding common ground and doing so.

Does Not Find Common Ground

HUSBAND: I don't care if you can't find a job in Denver. The job I like is there and that's final!
WIFE: That certainly doesn't take me into account!
HUSBAND: Well, that's the way it is. We go where I have a job. If not, that's tough. If you don't like that, maybe we should not be married. As I see it, there's nothing more to be discussed.
WIFE: (*says nothing, is intimidated by his threat, and goes along with move to Denver, feeling resentful about this for years*)

Finds Common Ground

HUSBAND: I like the job in Denver.
WIFE: I can't find a job there. The job I like best is the one I was offered in Atlanta.
HUSBAND: I can see your point of view. I know you want a job that you enjoy and I want the same thing for myself. How can we work this out?
WIFE: Would you be willing to get a job where I want for a year? After all, you haven't even looked in Atlanta.
HUSBAND: Well, I'll try Atlanta. If I find something decent there, we'll go for two or three years. After that, we'll go where I want to go for another two or three years. Fair?
WIFE: OK. But what if you don't find a job in Atlanta?
HUSBAND: We'll go to St. Louis where we both have job offers that are OK but not great. How's that?
WIFE: I guess that's fair.

BOSS: No, that's final. No more secretarial help. You don't need a secretary.
EMPLOYEE: Yes, I do. I can't get all the paper work done without a secretary!
BOSS: That's too bad. You'll just have to do it on your own.

BOSS: No. I'm not willing to hire any more secretarial help.
EMPLOYEE: It would make a big difference. What can I do to convince you?
BOSS: If your efficiency would be increased by a secretary, then I might consider it.

EMPLOYEE: I'm not going to do it. (*leaves, slams door; both are angry and frustrated with each other and with the situation*)

EMPLOYEE: OK, I would like a secretary on a trial basis. If the work I turn out per month increases, then I get a permanent secretary.
BOSS: OK, only if your reports are increased by 20 percent each month.
EMPLOYEE: It's a deal.

In the examples on the left, the people do not understand each other and, in fact, they feel somewhat misunderstood themselves. This might be acceptable if these persons were never to encounter each other again. However, when relationships are of a continuing nature, misunderstandings, frustration, and resentments continue and affect the relationship. The examples above are applicable to all relationships of a continuing nature, e.g., spouse, family members, friends, boss, co-workers. In any relationship of this type, when people fail to compromise or to look for common ground, lines are drawn more tightly. One person cannot be reached by the other person and, in turn, does not reach out. This usually leads to feelings of misunderstanding and isolation. Situations and issues are exaggerated and they become black or white, lose or win, live or die. When people do not find some common ground, they miss out on options and possibilities. As a result, this failure leads to stale, frozen relationships.

In contrast, as in the examples on the right, finding common ground keeps a relationship open. It acknowledges each person's right to his or her thinking and preferences. It demonstrates that this relationship is important to both people and that something *can* be worked out if each person tries. Options are widened; communication remains open. The relationship remains flexible, vital and growing. Seeking common ground adds strength and stimulation to the relationship, and the chances for understanding and satisfaction are increased.

Practice

This section provides the opportunity to practice the skill of finding common ground.

I. Below are pairs of statements. One of the statements accepts the other person's point of view and acknowledges that there is an issue to settle; the other does not.

Place a check to the left of the statement that sets the stage for finding common ground.

A. 1. ____"Watching television is not something I prefer to do, but I know you like it. I'd like us to do things together, and that's important to me. This is an issue that we have to settle."

2. ____"I want us to do things together and you never listen. Why can't you understand that I like to do things with you? Why do you have to watch so much television?"

B. 1. ____"There is no problem that I can see. You're just making this into a problem!"

2. ____"This is not an issue for me, but it sounds like it's important to you. Is there something that we have to work out?"

C. 1. ____"This is really important and, if you were the least bit sensitive, you would realize that. But not you — you don't see the other person's side."

2. ____"This is not important to you, but it means a lot to me. We will have to do something about it so that both of us are satisfied."

II. Below are pairs of conversations. One of each pair finds common ground; the other does not. Place a check to the left of the one that resolves the issue.

A. Situation: Both husband and wife have full-time jobs. The wife has been doing all of the cooking, dishwashing, and housecleaning. Recently, she received a promotion. Her job is harder, and she is more tired when she comes home.

1. ____WIFE: I don't want to continue doing all the housework. I want some help.
HUSBAND: My cooking is awful, I miss spots on the dishes, and I don't know how to clean.
WIFE: This is a problem that we have to solve.
HUSBAND: There's nothing to solve. Just do what you've always done.
WIFE: No, I want things to change.
HUSBAND: Well, I don't. I like them just as they are.
WIFE: Would you be willing to wash the dishes and vacuum? That would be a good beginning.

2. ____WIFE: I don't want to continue doing all the housework. I want some help.
HUSBAND: I don't like to do housework.
WIFE: We have to work out some solution. Would you be willing to do the dishes and the vacuuming?
HUSBAND: I would rather not. I'd rather we hire someone to do the housework and buy a dishwasher.
WIFE: Will you help with the cooking?
HUSBAND: No, I'd rather eat out. On nights that you're too tired to cook, we can go out or buy fried chicken.

HUSBAND: Now, why are you getting so worked up over this?
WIFE: I get so frustrated with you! (*walks off*)

WIFE: Well . . . what if we try that for a month and see how it works?
HUSBAND: OK. I'll look for a dishwasher tomorrow and you check out people who clean. Is that agreeable?
WIFE: Fine.

B. Situation: Two co-workers are involved in a project together.

1. ____CO-WORKER A: I am not satisfied with the amount of time we're putting in. You seem very busy with other things. I'd like to work on this four hours a week.
CO-WORKER B: I can't possibly spend that much time. It's out of the question.
CO-WORKER A: We have a deadline on this of September 1. We won't get it finished.
CO-WORKER B: You heard wrong. It can't be September 1. If it is, you'll just have to do most of the work yourself or we'll have to get an extension.
CO-WORKER A: I can't do it alone. I'd be willing to stay after work if you would."
CO-WORKER B: No way. I have a family at home, you know.
CO-WORKER A: (*angrily*) So do I.
CO-WORKER B: I have to go. I have an appointment.
CO-WORKER A: (*frustrated*) I'm going to speak with the boss.

2. ____CO-WORKER A: I am not satisfied with the amount of time we're putting in. You seem very busy with other things. I'd like to work on this four hours a week.
CO-WORKER B: I can't possibly spend that much time. It's out of the question.
CO-WORKER A: This is a problem. What can we do to work this out?
CO-WORKER B: I'm not as flexible as you are in my schedule. The only way that I can find some time is if we'd work during lunch hours.
CO-WORKER A: OK. I don't like the idea, but I'll do it until we get this done. Let's meet Monday through Thursday for lunch. Is that OK with you?
CO-WORKER B: Fine.

SUMMARY

This chapter focuses on communication as an interaction with another person. It outlines the elements of satisfying relationships and stresses how communication affects these elements. It also outlines the decisions to be made in your interactions with people.

1. Within a given relationship, you must:
   a. Decide how much you are willing to invest in the relationship.
   b. Determine how willing you are to listen, understand, and be involved.
   c. Review these decisions and commitments on a daily basis, depending on other pressures and involvements.
2. When you are discussing sensitive topics, working out a conflict, or setting limits with someone who is important to you, it is helpful to express your view of the relationship and your commitment to it. For example, "Look, our friendship is important to me and I want to work out this disagreement that we had." This provides a context for your words and actions and reminds both of you of the relationship.
3. Do not assume that the other person's view of the relationship is the same as yours. Check this or her willingness to listen, understand, and be involved. For example, "This is important to me. Are you willing to listen and try to understand?"
4. Recognizing the effects of your words and actions is very important, especially in relationships that you consider important. Learn to notice other people's reactions to what you say and do. If you are unclear about the impact that you had, check with the other person. For example, "You seem quiet. Did I offend you?" "I don't know what you think of my suggestion. What is your reaction?"
5. When others tell you their reactions to what you have said or done, accept them as valid. Do not criticize or deny their experiences. When you have an impact that you did not intend, explain that this was not your intention. Then clarify what you meant to do. For example, "I didn't mean to sound critical. What I wanted to do was encourage you."
6. Learn to anticipate the impact of your words and actions. Whenever you are discussing an important or sensitive issue, learn to judge how the other person may react. Decide what these reactions may mean to the relationship on a short- and long-term basis. Decide if these fit in with your purpose. If not, reconsider your intentions.
7. In relationships that are important to you, it is necessary to tell others about their impact on you. Describe your reactions in spe-

cific and nonevaluative terms. For example, "When you are late, I feel angry and resentful." "I like it when you notice the work I've done."
8. When conflict or problems occur in a relationship that you consider important, you must decide on the relative significance of the issue at hand. What is more important to you—the issue or the relationship?
9. Once you have made this decision, the two of you must arrive at some resolution. In important relationships, it is helpful to find common ground. Follow these steps:
    a. Summarize your view and the other person's view. Accept his or her point of view, even if you see it very differently. For example, "This doesn't seem important to me, but I can see that it's important to you. So we'll do something to work it out."
    b. Acknowledge that there is a problem to be discussed and resolved. Define the issue.
    c. Express the idea that the solution is not black or white.
    d. Offer options and alternate solutions, negotiating with each other to arrive at a solution or method of solution that is agreeable to both of you. Consider the following options.
        - Set a time to work on the problem.
        - Set up a trial period.
        - Go along with one person's view for a specified amount of time; then follow the other's view for an equal period.
        - Each person comes part way, and a compromise is achieved.
    e. Check to be sure that the other person agrees with the proposed solution.

Following these guidelines should increase the chances of resolving conflicts and settling issues in relationships that are important to you.

REVIEW

This section gives you an opportunity to practice the skills presented in this chapter.

Decisions about Relationships and Issues

This section reviews the skills of deciding about relationships and issues, expressing your decisions to others, and asking others about their views.

I. The examples below describe situations. Follow the steps outlined.

A. Situation: Your sister often calls you at 7:00 A.M. to chat for ten minutes. You are getting ready for work at that time. You like talking with her, but you want her to call at a more convenient hour. It is Friday, 7:05 A.M., the phone rings, and it's your sister.

- Make a decision about the relationship.
- Do you want to maintain it?
- Are you willing to risk the relationship over this issue?

If you decide that the issue is important but you do not want to risk the relationship, what should you say?

1. ___YOU: (*angrily*) Look, why do you always call at 7:00A.M.? Don't you know I'm getting ready for work then?
2. ___YOU: Sharon, I enjoy talking to you and I'm glad that you phone — but not at 7:00 A.M. I'm busy getting ready for work, so please call at a different time.
3. ___YOU: I've had it. Don't call me at 7:00 A.M. anymore. That is really inconsiderate of you.

B. Situation: Dan had pneumonia and has been absent from work for awhile. When he returns, his boss begins teasing him, saying, "We know — you really weren't sick. You were loafing." Dan ignores this, but it continues on a daily basis. At the end of his first week back, Dan asks for an extension of time on a particularly lengthy report that he is writing. His boss replies, "Just this once, Dan. Don't try to keep playing for sympathy just because you were sick. You're not going to get away with this."

Dan thinks to himself, "I've had it. I've reached my limit. I will not stand for anymore of this teasing and these implications." Dan must make a decision about the issue and about the relationship.

- Is this issue important enough for me to mention?
- Am I willing to risk the relationship?
- Since this person is in a position of power over me, is there something that I must do to protect myself?

Dan thinks that the issue is important enough to mention. However, he does not want to lose his job. What should he say? Check the one that you think is most effective.

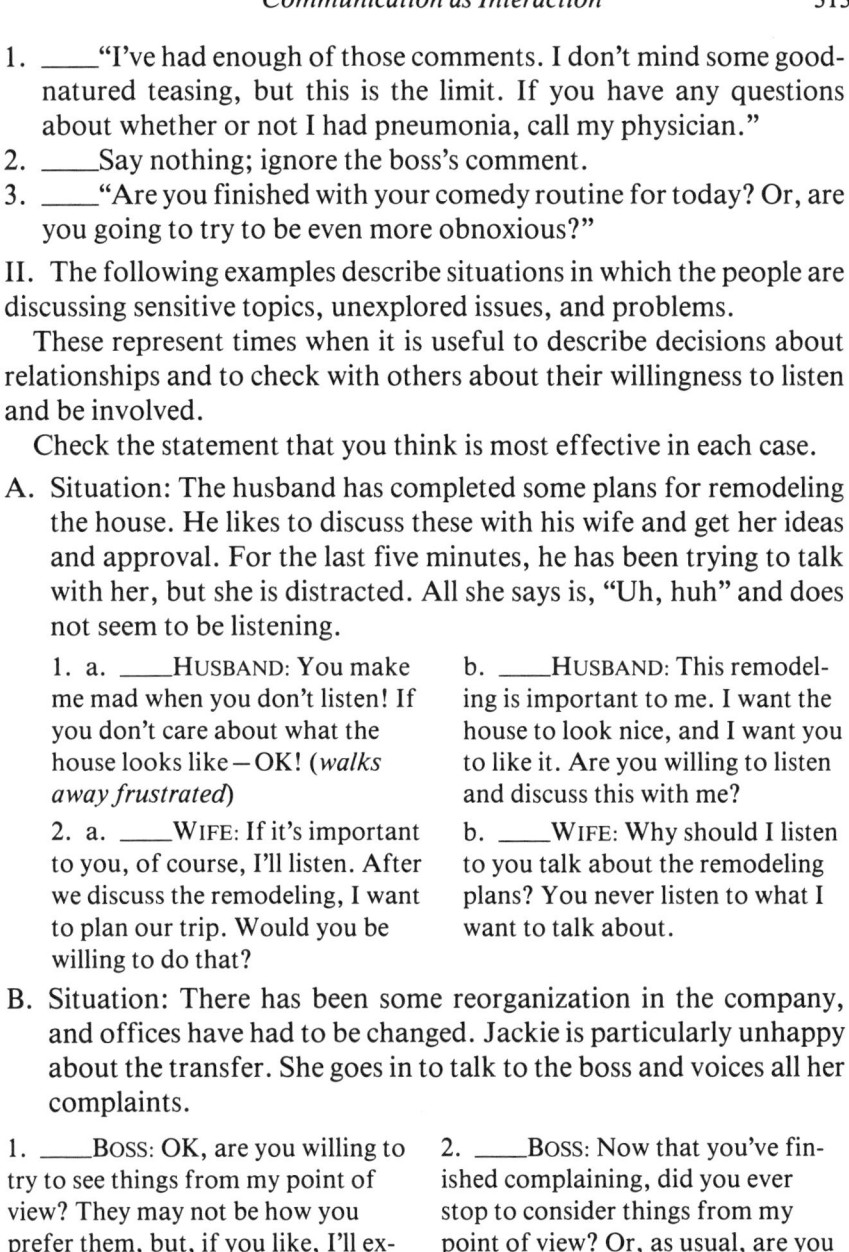

1. ____"I've had enough of those comments. I don't mind some good-natured teasing, but this is the limit. If you have any questions about whether or not I had pneumonia, call my physician."
2. ____Say nothing; ignore the boss's comment.
3. ____"Are you finished with your comedy routine for today? Or, are you going to try to be even more obnoxious?"

II. The following examples describe situations in which the people are discussing sensitive topics, unexplored issues, and problems.

These represent times when it is useful to describe decisions about relationships and to check with others about their willingness to listen and be involved.

Check the statement that you think is most effective in each case.

A. Situation: The husband has completed some plans for remodeling the house. He likes to discuss these with his wife and get her ideas and approval. For the last five minutes, he has been trying to talk with her, but she is distracted. All she says is, "Uh, huh" and does not seem to be listening.

1. a. ____HUSBAND: You make me mad when you don't listen! If you don't care about what the house looks like—OK! (*walks away frustrated*)

b. ____HUSBAND: This remodeling is important to me. I want the house to look nice, and I want you to like it. Are you willing to listen and discuss this with me?

2. a. ____WIFE: If it's important to you, of course, I'll listen. After we discuss the remodeling, I want to plan our trip. Would you be willing to do that?

b. ____WIFE: Why should I listen to you talk about the remodeling plans? You never listen to what I want to talk about.

B. Situation: There has been some reorganization in the company, and offices have had to be changed. Jackie is particularly unhappy about the transfer. She goes in to talk to the boss and voices all her complaints.

1. ____BOSS: OK, are you willing to try to see things from my point of view? They may not be how you prefer them, but, if you like, I'll explain how and why these transfers were made.

2. ____BOSS: Now that you've finished complaining, did you ever stop to consider things from my point of view? Or, as usual, are you too involved in your own problems?

314   A WAY WITH WORDS

C. Situation: A neighbor repeatedly borrows tools from you and forgets to return them. He just came over and asked to borrow one of your drills. You are hesitant to lend it to him.

1. ___YOU: No, I'm sick and tired of lending you things and not getting them back. When you're not so irresponsible, let me know.

2. ___YOU: Ted, you're a good friend, and I like you. I wouldn't risk our friendship over something silly like a drill. But I really get frustrated when you borrow things and don't return them. I'll give you this on the condition that I have it back by the weekend.

D. Situation: Husband and wife need to decide where to spend the Christmas holidays. Usually, this is a sensitive subject because the wife likes to go to Michigan to be with her family and the husband does not like to drive that far. The husband began the discussion, and it seems about to develop into an argument.

1. ___WIFE: I don't want to quarrel over this. Let's sit down and try to work out a solution. Obviously, you're much more important to me than where we spend Christmas.

2. ___WIFE: Why can't you see my point of view? I want to see my parents. It's just a small thing and there's no reason to quarrel.

Impact

This section gives you the opportunity to practice the skills of checking your impact, acknowledging and anticipating your impact, and telling others how they came across to you.

The section below describes various situations. After each situation are several suggested responses. Check the one that you consider to be most effective.

A. Situation: Your friend Carol was thirty pounds overweight and has been dieting successfully for the last month. She said that she has lost twenty pounds. Without thinking, you remark, "That much? I didn't realize it." She responds defensively, "Yes, do you think I'd lie?"

1. ___Tease her. ("Sure, you always lie.")

2. ___Tell her not to be so defensive.
   3. ___Acknowledge your impact and restate your intention. ("Of course, I don't think you'd lie. I just didn't realize that you had lost that much so soon.")
   4. ___Give her advice. ("Take it off more slowly. Otherwise, it won't stay off.")
B. Situation: You are having coffee with a friend, and she is telling you about a frustrating experience that she had at a school board meeting. You are in a jovial mood and keep joking with her. The more serious that she gets, the more you joke with her and say, "Come on, loosen up. Don't take life so seriously." Suddenly, she seems in a hurry to leave and says, "I must get back." You are surprised because she had said that she wanted to have a long coffee break. What should you do?
   1. ___Tease and joke with her more. ("Hey, slow down.")
   2. ___Argue with her. ("You don't need to go back so soon.")
   3. ___Check your impact. ("Why are you leaving so soon? Did I say something that bothered you?")
   4. ___Criticize her. ("There's something wrong with you if you can't take things less seriously.")
C. Situation: You and your spouse were raised in two different religions. Your family was not strict, and you no longer attend church. Your spouse, on the other hand, is religious and would like you to go to church. Whenever you discuss religion, he or she becomes very upset. Somehow, your not going to church seems a personal affront to him or her. Just now, he or she has brought up the subject of going to church.

SPOUSE: You really should come to church, you know. You don't set a good example for the kids this way.
YOU: Look, I don't want to go to church.
SPOUSE: You know how much it means to me, and yet you continue to stay away. I don't understand you. Why couldn't you go, just once in awhile?

What would be best for you to do?
   1. ___Threaten and act angry. ("If you don't stop harping on this, I'm going to walk out of here.")

2. ____ Express your preference. ("This has nothing to do with you. I just don't want to go to church.")
3. ____Give in. ("OK, OK, I'll go . . .")
4. ____Ignore your impact. ("I think people who are religious are stupid!")

D. Situation: Your mother-in-law is visiting. She has very conservative views on everything: she vehemently opposes abortion, alcohol, women's rights, marijuana, and transcendental meditation; she espouses capital punishment, prayer, and Republicans. The news is on, and the feature story is about a woman with four young children who went to medical school and is now a practicing physician. Your mother-in-law says, "That is ridiculous. She should be home, raising those children instead of taking a job away from a man. I'm sure that she never could do as good a job as a man, anyway. You'd never find me going to a female physician."

You and your spouse are quite open-minded and are very much in favor of women holding equal jobs for equal pay. What would be best for you to do?

1. ____Tell her off. ("You are so old-fashioned and close-minded that there's no use talking to you.")
2. ____Anticipate your impact. (If we disagree, she gets angry and argues. There's not point in trying to change her mind, so I'll say nothing.)
3. ____Argue with her. ("There are plenty of female physicians who are better than male physicians.")

Finding Common Ground

In the situation below, follow the steps for finding common ground. Check the statement that seems to work toward a resolution of the problem.

Situation: A man has just bought a new sailboat and is eager to take it out on the lake. Meanwhile, his wife had been planning to do some painting and wallpapering.

HUSBAND: Well, I'm all set to take the boat out tomorrow.
WIFE: Not tomorrow!
HUSBAND: What do you mean, "not tomorrow"?

WIFE: I have a day off, and we planned to get that painting and wallpapering done in the bathroom.
HUSBAND: That can wait.
WIFE: We don't have another weekend off together for a month. Besides, you promised we'd do it this weekend.
HUSBAND: That was before I bought a boat!
WIFE: So?
HUSBAND: A month isn't very long.
WIFE: Yes, it is. Besides, your sister and her husband will be here in two weeks, and I wanted the bathroom to look nice for them.
HUSBAND: Who cares? We don't have to be fancy for them.
WIFE: I don't want to be fancy, just decent.
HUSBAND: Well, you figure it out. I'm going sailing.

At this point, the conversation and interaction is heading for trouble. Let's suppose that the wife remembers some communication skills and says, "Wait a minute. We're in this together and you're more important to me than a bathroom or wallpaper. How can we work this out?" This sets the stage for finding some common ground. The pairs below are possible responses. Check the one in each pair that would be more effective.

A. 1. ____HUSBAND: There's nothing to work out. I'm going sailing.

2. ____HUSBAND: What do we need to work out?

B. 1. ____WIFE: There's sailing versus wallpapering, and fixing the bathroom must come first. Otherwise, you're going back on your promise. Besides, if you want your sister to think we're slobs, go right ahead!

2. ____WIFE: You want to sail, and I want to wallpaper. Sailing is important to you and fixing the bathroom is important to me. What do you suggest?

C. 1. ____HUSBAND: OK. We have to figure out how to get in both sailing and wallpapering or some kind of compromise.

2. ____HUSBAND: Are you going to deprive me of what little relaxation I have by sailing? All you want me to do is work, work, work.

D. 1. ____WIFE: I don't want to deprive you of anything or me of anything. What if you went sailing tomorrow morning and helped me wallpaper in the afternoon?

2. ____WIFE: It's not as if I enjoy wallpapering. It's just something that we have to do. Something's got to go. You'll have plenty of time for sailing next month.

E. 1. ____HUSBAND: I am going to sail as much as I want. And then if I have time for wallpapering, I'll do it – and then again maybe I won't. If you hadn't been so pushy, I might've done it. Now I won't.

2. ____HUSBAND: I'd like to take the sailboat out just one day, and then I'd be satisfied. What if I go out tomorrow and then spend the next several days painting and wallpapering. Would you help after work?

F. 1. ____WIFE: I'm only doing this for your own good. You'll be sorry when your sister comes and you're ashamed of your house. Then you'll blame me . . . and I don't want to hear it. But, go right ahead – go out on your boat and let your house look like a mess.

2. ____WIFE: I think it's reasonable for you to sail tomorrow and then we will both work hard on Sunday and during the week until we're done. How's that?

G. 1. ____HUSBAND: There's no way to solve this. I'm leaving. (*walks away*)

2. ____HUSBAND: Fine with me.

Conversations

This section gives you the opportunity to apply the skills in this chapter in everyday situations and conversations. Read the situation below and choose the most effective answer.

A. Situation: It is your father-in-law's birthday on Sunday. Your spouse wants to visit his or her family, go for dinner, and buy a gift. You have some bitter feelings. For the past three years, your in-laws have not remembered your birthday with a card, phone call, visit, or gift. You are angry enough that you are willing to risk the relationship with your in-laws. Your spouse understands your point of view and disapproves of his or her parents' rudeness. Your mother-in-law calls and says, "You'll both be up for dinner on Sunday, won't you?" Now is your time to speak. What do you say? Check your answer.

1. a. ____YOU: Why should I come up? You no more care about me than I care about you. Let's stop being phony!

b. ____YOU: I will not be there, but your son (or daughter) will come.

MOTHER-IN-LAW: We want both of you there. Why aren't you coming?

2. a. ____YOU: I'm not coming because I don't have to put up with people like you. There is no excuse for how you have treated me and now I'm going to be that way, too.

b. ____YOU: I don't feel very welcome there. Perhaps that's not what you intend, but I prefer not to intrude on your family gatherings.

B. Situation: You and your spouse are talking and he or she expresses some discontent, "Why can't you be sexier and more romantic?" What do you say?

1. a. ____YOU: That sounds pretty serious to me. Are you dissatisfied with our relationship that much?

b. ____YOU: I can't be sexy and romantic unless someone turns me on, and I sure don't get turned on around here.

SPOUSE: I can't help it if I don't turn you on. I don't know what's happened. I feel like you don't care about me.

2. a. ____YOU: I don't care! What about you?

b. ____YOU: What makes you think I don't care?

SPOUSE: You never act like you're glad to see me . . . you don't act like I'm special.

3. a. ____YOU: That's a bunch of baloney.

b. ____YOU: I'd like to show you that you're special. But would you also let me know I'm special?

SPOUSE: I don't know . . . I'm ready to give up. Maybe marriage is meant to be miserable.

4. a. ____YOU: You are special to me and I probably don't know how to show it in ways that you like. And maybe you don't know how to let me know that I'm special to you. But we can work on this.

b. ____YOU: Great . . . give up . . . you're about as encouraging as a wet blanket. If you expect me to be romantic, you're going to have to do something other than whine and complain. Do you realize that when things go wrong, you whine? You're nothing but a baby.

SPOUSE: You are very important to me, and I don't know what to do to show that.

5. a. ___YOU: That's your problem. You're smart enough to know what to do to please me. If you can't figure it out, that's your tough luck.

b. ___YOU: We're both in the same dilemma. We'll have to work on this together to find a solution. The important thing is that we do it together. You're not in this alone, and neither am I.

A FINAL COMMENT

There is a lot of information in this book, and it may be helpful for you to go back and read portions of it again. The more that you review and practice these principles, the easier and more natural they will become. You become effective at communication and relationships in the same way that you master anything else — by experience and practice. So, continue to develop your skills with people by using what you have learned.

The principles in this book are very important, but they alone will not suffice. The key is to use these principles with a sincere interest in others and an honest effort to understand their point of view. With this attitude and the skills that you have learned, chances are that you will enjoy people more, and they, in turn, will enjoy interacting with you.

APPENDIX A

Answers to Practice Exercises

CHAPTER 1

Skill 1a
A. 3
B. 4

Skill 1b
  I. The following should be circled: A, C, F, H
II. A. 1
    B. 1
III. A. 2
    B. 3-a

Skill 1c
  I. The following should be matched:
    A. 6
    B. 4
    C. 5
    D. 7
 II. A. 2
    B. 2
III. A. 4
    B. 2
    C. 2

Skill 2
  I. A. 1
     B. 2
     C. 2
     D. 2
     E. 1
 II. 1. Something like: "John called me a stuffed shirt. Do I come across like that? Do I seem overbearing to you?"
     2. Something like: "I'm discouraged that I haven't lost those five pounds. It would help if you'd reassure me and tell me I look OK."
III. A. I'd like your advice on this. There's a used car I want to buy, but I'd like your opinion.
     B. I'd like you to know my expectations of new employees. I want you, most of all, to be here promptly at nine. I expect you to be well groomed, courteous, and ready to work. And, whatever procedures you don't understand, be sure to ask.
     C. I'm starting on a new project, and I would appreciate your cooperation.

Skill 3a
  I. A. 1
     B. 2
     C. 2
     D. 2
     E. 1
 II. The following should be matched:
     A. 2
     B. 3
     C. 1
III. A. 2
     B. 2

Skill 3b
  I. A. 1
     B. 1
     C. 2
     D. 1
     E. 1
     F. 2
     G. 1

Appendix A 323

II. A. Something like: "I prefer that you do not contradict what I say to the kids. It is important to me that we agree on rules for them."
    B. Something like: "I'd really like to live somewhere else."

Skill 3c

I. The following should be crossed out: A, E, F
The following should be circled: B, C, D

II. A. 1
    B. 2
    C. 1
    D. 2

Skill 4a

I. A1. No
   A2. Yes
   A3. Pleasant, non-challenging tone of voice. Nonverbal cues should be positive, not accusatory.
   B1. No
   B2. Yes
   B3. Yes
   B4. Positive, not accusatory.

II. A. 3
    B. 2
    C. 1

III. A. Something like: "It's important to me that we go over our budget. Whenever I bring this up, you ignore me or change the subject. Are you not interested?"
    B. Something like: "You have interrupted me three times in the last five minutes, and I'm getting frustrated. Were you aware of interrupting me?"

IV. A. "Would you rather talk about vacation plans tomorrow?"
    B. "Are you trying to say that I'm not working up to my potential?"

Skill 4b

I. The following should be checked: A, C, E, F

II. A. 2
    B. 1

Skill 4c
  I. A1.a
     A2.b
     B1.a
     B2.a
     C1.b
     C2.a
     C3.b
     C4.b

 II. A1.d
     A2.c, e, g
     B1.f
     B2.b

Chapter Review

Considering Consequences
  I. A1. asked for help
     A2. he or she will help with the chores
     A3. Yes
     A4. Yes

     B1. respected; asked to explain his thinking; aware that you're upset
     B2. try to find out why you're upset; explain his thinking
     B3. Yes
     B4. Yes

 II. A. 2
     B. 1
     C. 1
     D. 3
     E. 2

Decide on Your Purpose
A. Most effective is: 3. Let him know that you appreciate the thoughtful gesture.

Appendix A 325

B. Most effective are:
   1. Express your preference.
   5. Get some sympathy and reassurance.
   8. Arrange for some solitude.

Expressing Intentions

I. A. 2
   B. 1
   C. 1
   D. 2
   E. 1
II. A. 6
   B. 3
   C. 4
   D. 1
   E. 7
   F. 5
   G. 2
III. A. "This is just a suggestion. When you have a sore throat, maybe you shouldn't smoke."
   B. "I want to make a request. Will you please water the flowers? I'll mow the lawn."

Expressing Ideas and Preferences Directly

A. 2
B. 1
C. 1
D. 2
E. 1
F. 2
G. 1

Checking Your Impressions of Others

I. A, B
II. The following should be checked:
A. 3
B. 1
C. 1, 2
D. 2
E. 3, 4
F. 1

The following should be marked as dishonest questions (Q):
A. 2
B. 3
C. 4
D. 1
E. 1
F. 2

Application of Skills
  I. A. criticized or put down
     B. frustrated, angry, hurt, criticized, or put down
     C. frustrated, angry, misunderstood, criticized, put down
     D. encouraged, willing to talk
     E. Frustrated, misunderstood
 II. (This is to be read — no answers).
III. A. (Already done for you)
     B. Put brackets around: HUSBAND: Why can't you be like Bill's wife? Why can't you do anything on your own? How can you expect me to still find you interesting and attractive?
        Underline: WIFE: I did these things because I thought that's what you wanted. I had kids because I thought you wanted them. I wanted to please you. HUSBAND: I don't want a wife who . . . is boring. I want you to lose weight . . . and pay attention to me, not the kids. I'd also like it if you did something independent.
        Put brackets around: WIFE: How can I be independent when you have the car, the money, the status? What is it? Are you having an affair with Bill's wife?
        Underline: HUSBAND: I don't want this mess. I don't want us to be upset with each other. I want us to get along. I just want you to stop this housewife-mother routine you're in.
     C. Underline: WIFE: I want to decide on some new ways of doing things around the house. I won't want to do all the working and cleaning. I want to hire someone to clean and go out to eat a lot. HUSBAND: I don't like to go out to eat. I like your cooking. WIFE: I'm in no mood to cook when I get home.
        Put brackets around: HUSBAND: You're taking your job too seriously. You work too hard! For your own good, I think you should not take your job so seriously. It's good for you to cook and forget about work.

Underline: HUSBAND: I don't like to eat out. WIFE: I don't see any other way.

Put brackets around: HUSBAND: Why can't you cook like you always have? Maybe, if you got better organized or cooked on weekends or left work at five o'clock instead of six. WIFE: You certainly are self-centered. All you're thinking of is you, not me! HUSBAND: If you really cared about me, you'd like to cook for me. Are you going to do it (the yard work) for the next several years? You just ruined my whole evening by bringing this up.

Underline: WIFE: I'm going ahead with my plans.

Put brackets around: HUSBAND: Do you want me to get over my ulcer or not? WIFE: Do you want me to collapse from overwork? HUSBAND: If you were better organized and less tense about everything . . . You're just a nervous wreck about this job. I can't be happy when you're not happy.

Underline WIFE: I will be happy when I hire someone to cook and clean.

Put brackets around: HUSBAND: Maybe you're the kind of woman who never should've gotten married. WIFE: There are other men . . . who don't want to be babied. Your whole problem is that your mother spoiled you rotten and you expect the world to revolve around you. You'd better straighten your thinking out. HUSBAND: You're driving me crazy. I'm going to need a psychiatrist and it's all because of you.

CHAPTER 2

Skill 2

Figure 2.23 - happiness
Figure 2.24 - skepticism
Figure 2.25 - anger
Figure 2.26 - disgust
Figure 2.27 - affection
Figure 2.28 - self-confidence

Skill 4

I. A. 1
   B. 1

II. A. 1-c
    2-b
    3-a
   B. 1-b
    2-a
   C. 1-c
    2-a

Skill 5
 I. A. 1
   B. 1
II. A. 1
   B. 2

Chapter Review

Matching Nonverbal Cues to Purpose

A. 2   F. 1
B. 1   G. 2
C. 1   H. 2
D. 2   I. 1
E. 1   J. 2

Interpreting Nonverbal Cues

A. 1
B. 3
C. 2
D. 3
E. 1

Checking Out Impressions and Asking for Clarification

A. 2
B. 1
C. 3

Choosing a Purpose and the Most Effective Means of Accomplishing It
The following should be matched:

A. 1-c   B. 1-a
   2-b   2-c
   3-a   3-b

Applying Knowledge of Nonverbal Cues to Conversation
A. lack of interest
B. 2
C. Circle the following: interested, questioning tone of voice
   Cross out all others.
D. 3

CHAPTER 3

Skill 2
   I. A. 3
      B. 1
      C. 2
  II. A. 1
      B. 1
      C. 1
 III. A. 1. Negative
         2. No
         3. "I like your new dress."
      B. 1. Negative
         2. No
         3. To gauge her speech to the audience, probably by acknowledging the traditional roles.
         4. She should contact the person who invited her to speak and ask her opinion of the audience and what would elicit their interest and response.
      C. "I heard you're taking a new job. Any particular reason?"

Skill 3
   I. A. 1-b
      A. 2-c
      B. 2
  II. A. 2
      B. 1
 III. A. 1. after 5:00 P.M.
         2. She could ask, "When is the best time for me to phone?"
      B. 1. When she is not busy fixing dinner.
         2. He could say, "I want you to hear about this business deal, and I need your full attention. When could you listen?"

Skill 4
   A. 2
   B. 1

Review
   I. The following should be matched:
      A - 4 - d
      B - 6 - a
      C - 2 - f
      D - 3 - e
      E - 5 - b
      F - 1 - c

   II. A. 1. No   B. 1. Yes   C. 1. Yes   D. 1. Yes
          2. No   2. No   2. No   2. No
          3. No   3. No   3. No   3. No
          4. No   4. No   4. Yes   4. No

   III. A. 4
        B. 4

   IV. The following should be checked: C, G, H, J.
       The others should be marked out as inappropriate.

CHAPTER 4

Skill 2
   I. A. The following should be checked: 2, 3, 6
      B. 1, 2, 5, 8, 9
   II. A. 2
       B. 1
       C. 1
   III. A. 2
        B. 1
        C. 2

Skill 3
   I. The following should be matched:
      A. 3
      B. 1
      C. 4
      D. 2

II. A. 2
   B. 1
   C. 2
III. A. Is it interesting?
    B. Are you dissatisfied with your present job?
    C. What have you been doing?

Skill 4

I. The following should be matched:
   A. 3
   B. 1
   C. 2
II. A. 2
    B. 1

Skill 5

I. A. 1. Underline "I realize that other people don't feel the same way."
   B. 2. Underline "That doesn't mean that you have to feel the same way I do!"
   C. 2. Underline "We're each a little bit right and a little bit wrong."
   D. 1. Underline "That's not to say that you should say the same thing I do. What do you think would help you to relax?"
II. A. "I can understand why you're bitter and angry about your heart attack. As you know, my brother had one, and he says he feels lucky to be alive. But not everyone has that same reaction."
    B. Say nothing about your likes or dislikes. Ask your friend what he or she enjoys (or doesn't enjoy) about the community. If he or she asks your opinion, say "I would prefer a larger town, but that's just me."

Skill 6

I. A. 2
   B. 1
   C. 2
II. A. 2. Exaggerating.
    B. 1. Acknowledging something that is not a significant part of the person's values or self-image.
    C. 3. Minimizing.
    D. 4. Acknowledging something which is inaccurate or inconsistent with the person's self-image.

Summary

Paying Attention to Others
   I. A. 3
      B. 1
  II. A. 2
      B. 1
      C. 2

Showing Interest in Others
A. "What did you like about it?" or Where is it located?" or "What kind of house is it?"
B. "What are your feelings about that?"
C. "How has work been? Have those problems been worked out?"
D. "Tell me about London."
E. "What are you working on?"

Being Courteous: Avoiding Presumptions
A. Call first or drop over and say, "If you're free and feel like eating out, we'll treat you. Are you in the mood to go out?"
B. Telephone friend and say, "After I invited you here tonight my sister-in-law came over with their four small children. They're from out of town, so they will be staying for a few hours more. You're welcome to come over, but I didn't know how you'd feel about an evening with four small kids running around. I can change my invitation to Thursday, if you prefer."
C. Say, "I was looking at dishwashers. I think we can afford one, if we forego our usual Christmas and birthday gifts to one another. I'd really like a dishwasher, but I don't know how you feel about it. What do you think?"

Giving the Other Person the Right to Think Differently
A. "I know that you like that color scheme, but I don't. We each have our own preferences. Maybe you could use that in your study. But, since we both use the den, can we work out a compromise?"
B. "I'm sure you enjoy oysters. I would rather not taste them."

Inaccurate, Incomplete Acknowledgments
A. 2
B. 1
C. 2

Appendix A 333

General Review and Practice

Acknowledging the Presence, Absence, or Actions of Others
 I. A. 2   C. 1
    B. 1   D. 1
 II. A. "John, your reports are usually very good—brief and well-organized. Last week, you turned in a couple that were not up to your usual standard. What happened?"
    B. "Hi. My day wasn't too good. I'd like to be quiet and collect my thoughts for a few minutes. Then I'll come in and tell you about it."
 III. The following should be circled: A, B, C, F, J, K, P, Q
    The following should be crossed out: D, E, G, H, I, L, M, N, O, R

Acknowledging Appearance and Other Nonverbal Cues
 IV. A. & B. Already done for you.
    C. "Your hair is beautiful, long like that."
    D. "That's a nice jacket. The color is not my favorite but it looks nice."
    E. "That's a pretty ring. Is it a gift for a special occasion?"
    F. "Is something wrong?"

Acknowledging the Statements of Others
 I. A. 2
    B. 2
    C. 3
    D. 2
 II. A. "That's great, How did you decide to go there?"
    B. "That's good news. I know you've been wanting to start a family. When is the baby due?"

Acknowledging the Experiences of Others
A. 2
B. 1
C. 2

Acknowledging the Self-Perceptions and Intentions of Others
A. 2
B. 1
C. 1
D. 2

General Application of Skills and Principles
A. 1. "What is it about them that you dislike?"
   2. "I can understand that. I would like to see them. Would you mind if I went over and spent the day with them?"
B. "What kind of work do you do?" (followed by another question or two about her job)
C. "We've never learned to enjoy it, but that's just us."

CHAPTER 5

Skill 1
   I. A. 2
      B. 1
      C. 2
      D. 1
      E. 2
   II. A. 2
       B. 3
       C. 1

Skill 2
   I. A. 2
      B. 1
      C. 1
      D. 2
   II. The following should be circled: B, E, G, H, K, L, M, P, Q, S, U, V
   III. A. Already done for you.
        B. "I notice that you get colds easily and seem to be tired a lot. Maybe you need more rest or vitamins or something. Have you been to a physician?"
        C. "I started to tell you what happened, and you started reading the paper. I don't like it when you don't pay attention to me."

Skill 2b
   I. A. 2. Underline: more initiative, good impression.
      B. 1. Underline: no good, unglued, childish, impulsive.
   II. The following should be circled: D, F, G, H, I, J, M, O, P, Q, T, U
   III. The following should be underlined:
        A. (MARK) in our meetings; you don't speak; unless the chairman specifically asks you a question; to speak up more often; whenever you talk, the point is usually right on target.

Appendix A 335

    B. (HUSBAND) On week nights after supper, you're usually working on some project; sewing, baking, or playing the piano; sit with me and watch television; about once a week.
IV. A. "I'd really like to get away this weekend and spend a few nights in the city. I feel like shopping and eating out."
    B. "Even while you're in college, your father and I prefer that you earn your spending money. We do not want you to depend on us for all your expenses."

Skill 2c
I. A. 2
   B. 1
   C. 2

II. The following should be underlined:
   A. (HUSBAND) a better cook and hostess; as well as you should; my mother never did that; a lot more imagination than you
      (WIFE) boring; as hard-headed and obnoxious as your mother is; as opinionated; homebody as your sister is; you're a long way from what I wanted in a husband; understanding, supportive; as understanding as a husband should be; encouraging
   B. (SON) Why aren't you generous like Carl's parents?
      (FATHER) Carl is a lot more appreciative and grateful than you are; done a lot more for you kids than other parents; congenial and polite; why can't you be as mature as he is; get along better with people and be more successful, like you should be

III. 1. Already done for you.
    2. "Sometimes, when guests come over, you don't greet them at the door or you don't act interested in the conversation. My boss is coming over for dinner tonight, and this is very important to me. I'd like you to talk with him and seem interested. Make him feel welcome."
    3. "I like it when you remember special days like my birthday, Valentine's Day, our anniversary. You don't have to give me anything big — just a card or something small. But that really means a lot to me and shows me that you care."

Skill 3
I. A - 3 - d
   B - 1 - c
   C - 4 - b
   D - 2 - a

II. A. 1
   B. 1
   C. 2
   D. 2
   E. 1
III. A. "I know you don't feel well, but I'm trying to hang this picture and I need some help. Could you come over here and see if this is straight?"
   B. "I am uncomfortable because you supervise my work so closely. Do you think I'm doing something wrong? I feel like you are looking over my shoulder most of the time."

Skill 4

I The following should be underlined:
   A. "Wait a minute, did it seem that I was including you in what I was fed up with?"
   B. "What did I do to give you that impression?"
II. A. 2
   B. 3
   C. 1

Skill 5

A. 2. Underline: Do you mean that . . . ?
B. 1. Underline: Are you saying that I exaggerate everything?
C. 1. Underline: I guess that means that you want me to change something, right; What could I do to be on time; But you consider that late, right; What can we do to keep this from happening again.

Review

I. Underline the following:
   A. mature
   B. sloppy, disorganized
   C. I know why you did that; not good enough
   D. shouldn't; if you had some stamina
   E. seductive
   F. you try to control everything around here; you just want all the attention and all the credit for everything.
   G. as pretty as the other girls in your class
II. The following should be matched:
   A. 4   D. 2   G. 5
   B. 3   E. 7   H. 9
   C. 1   F. 8   I. 6

III. A. 1. c, d
2. b, d, f
3. "My husband is overweight, and I prefer that he lose weight. I know that he has dieted before, and gets discouraged, but perhaps this time I could help by encouraging him."
B. 1. a, b, e
2. c, f, g
3. "I would really like to see my son and his wife more often. I do see them once a month, and I'm glad for that. But I call and invite them over every week, and they usually say no. I guess they have their own lives, and that keeps them pretty busy. I can't expect to see them every week."

IV. A1. a
A2. b
A3. b
B1. b
B2. a
B3. b

V. A1. b
A2. b
A3. a
B1. a
B2. b
B3. b
B4. a
C1. b
C2. b

CHAPTER 6

Skill 1b

I. A. "You're more important to me than the kids. I'll finish this sewing later. Let's go out to dinner."
B. "I am still angry and upset. Right now, I'm still not objective about what happened. Maybe, later I can be, but not right now."

II. A. 1
B. 2

Skill 1c

I. A. 1   C. 2
B. 2   D. 1

II. A. "We don't agree on how to share the workload. I'd rather that we work this out between us and not have to take it to the boss. Are you willing to try to work this out?"
B. "We have been quarreling about money. I know we have some different views on how to spend our money. Neither one of us is right and neither one of us is wrong, but we need to resolve this. Are you willing to try to work on a compromise?"

Skill 2a
I. A. 2
B. 1
C. 2
II. A. "I wonder if I came across as pretty harsh the other day. Our friendship is important to me, and I'd like to resolve this quarrel. Is there something I can do or say to rebuild our relationship?"
B. "You often surprise me by doing some of my chores. I thank you but do I really show how much I appreciate what you do?"

Skill 2b
A. 1
B. 2

Skill 2c
I. A1. a, d, e
A2. b, c, e, f
A3. b, c, d, f
A4. d
B1. a, b, d, f, g, h
B2. b, d, f, i
B3. c
B4. c, d
II. A. 2
B. 2
C. 1
III. A. Cross out 2 and 4.
For 2, substitute something like: "We meant to call and tell you how much we liked it. We just got busy and put it off. I'm sorry if we worried you."
For 4, substitute: "I can understand that. But we like it just fine."

B. Cross out 2 and 4.
For 4, substitute:
"I didn't realize that would upset you."
"I understand now. I'm sorry I wouldn't have done that if I had known."

Skill 2d
I. A. 3
   B. 2
   C. 2
II. A. "I accept my transfer, but I want you to know that I didn't like how it was handled. I would have appreciated being informed sooner."
    B. "It seems to me that you're being critical but covering it up with joking and teasing. I don't like that. If you have something to criticize, I'd rather you say it directly."
    C. "I'm really glad that you offered to help with our monthly budget."

Skill 3b
I. A. 1
   B. 2
   C. 2
II. A. 2
    B. 2

Review

Decisions about Relationships and Issues
I. A. 2
   B. 1
II. A1. b
    A2. a
    B. 1
    C. 2
    D. 1

Impact
A. 3
B. 3
C. 2
D. 2

Finding Common Ground
A. 2
B. 2
C. 1
D. 1
E. 2
F. 2
G. 2

Conversations
A1. b
A2. b
B1. a
B2. b
B3. b
B4. a
B5. b